Twelve English Statesmen

PITT

PITT

BY

LORD ROSEBERY

London

MACMILLAN AND CO.

AND NEW YORK

1892

First Edition printed November 1891
Reprinted December 1891, *February* 1892

THIS little book has been written under many disadvantages, but with a sincere desire to ascertain the truth. My chief happiness in completing it would have been to give it to my wife; it can now only be inscribed to her memory.

November 1891.

CONTENTS

CHAPTER I

YOUTH

WILLIAM PITT the younger was born at Hayes in 1759, in the full splendour of his father's famous ministry; in the year that saw Quebec fall before the dying Wolfe; that saw the glorious but inconclusive victory of Minden; that saw Hawke in a November storm crush the French fleet; the year that produced Burns and Wilberforce. None, perhaps, has given us names so honoured and cherished by the human race. Of his parents it is needless to say anything, except in so far as they influenced his career. His father, William Pitt, Earl of Chatham, was the most striking figure and the most dazzling statesman of his time; while, if one may judge of his speeches by their effect, he may be held the greatest orator that England has ever produced. Lady Chatham was the only sister of two remarkable brothers. One, George Grenville, the obstinate minister of an obstinate King, did much to involve us in our most disastrous and unnatural war. The other, Richard Earl Temple, welded his family into a disciplined and formidable force, which lasted as a potent factor in politics for at

B

least two generations; and accomplished its persistent object in the third, by obtaining the luckless dukedom of Buckingham for its chief.

With such parents, the younger Pitt was born a politician; his rare qualities of mind were from his earliest childhood directed and trained for parliamentary work. It did not, indeed, at first appear probable that he would survive to realise the designs of his father, who himself had suffered from the gout before leaving Eton. A feeble constitution hardly promised life, much less vigour; but, fortified by floods of port wine—the prescription of Lord Chatham's favourite physician, Dr. Addington, the father of the Prime Minister—it enabled him to live to be forty-seven, and sustain for near twenty years, almost unaided, the government of the country. From six to fourteen, however, his health was so indifferent that for more than half that period he was unable to apply himself to study; and, when at the latter age he went as an undergraduate to Cambridge, it stands recorded that he was accompanied by a nurse. In the autumn of that year (1773) his disorder reached its crisis; he returned home dangerously ill; but, on his recovery, he seems to have secured a share of health sufficient for the purposes of public life, and troubled only by periodic fits of the gout, then the appanage of statesmanship, which he owed less to his original disease than its original remedy.

But this sickly childhood only makes his undoubted precocity the more extraordinary. Delicate health probably confined him to study, as it had confined his father. We know that he bought Hollwood, because he used to go birdnesting there as a child. Otherwise,

his nursery annals point entirely to learning.   He was,
indeed, one of the rare instances, like John Mill and
Macaulay, of infant prodigy maturing into brilliant manhood.   From his earliest years his parents' letters abound
in allusions to his talents and character.   " Eager Mr.
William," " the Counsellor," " the Philosopher," are their
nicknames for the marvellous child.   In 1766, when he
was seven, his tutor writes : " Lady Hester and Mr. Pitt
continue to astonish as much as ever ; and I see no
possibility of diminishing their ardour either by too much
business or too much relaxation.   When I am alone
reading, Mr. Pitt, if it is anything he may attend to,
constantly places himself by me, when his steady
attention and sage remarks are not only entertaining
but useful, as they frequently throw a light upon the
subject and strongly impress it on my memory."   At
the same age he appears to have displayed the dignity and
self-possession that marked him in after life; and a trifling
anecdote of his stay at Weymouth in that year records
him as having dumbfoundered mature observers by these
qualities.   Another and a later tutor, Bishop Tomline,
says, that " although he was little more than fourteen
years of age when he went to reside at the University,
and had laboured under the disadvantage of frequent ill-
health, the knowledge which he then possessed was very
considerable ; and in particular, his proficiency in the
learned languages was probably greater than ever was
acquired by any other person in such early youth.   In
Latin authors he seldom met with difficulty ; and it
was no uncommon thing for him to read into English
six or seven pages of Thucydides, which he had not
previously seen, without more than two or three mis-

takes, and sometimes without even one. It was by
Lord Chatham's particular desire that Thucydides was
the first Greek book which Mr. Pitt read after he
came to college. The only other wish ever expressed
by his lordship relative to his son's studies was that I
would read Polybius with him." But his latest and
most pregnant study, more important to his career than
the " strange rhapsody of Lycophron," or even Polybius,
was the great work of Adam Smith. He, almost alone
of the statesmen of that day, had mastered and assimilated the *Wealth of Nations,* before entering public life.

A graceful story has been told in which Pitt is made
to declare his indebtedness himself. Dundas asked
Adam Smith to dinner, but the philosopher did not
arrive till all were seated. When he entered the whole
company rose to their feet, and Pitt gaily exclaimed,
" We will stand till you are seated, for we are all your
scholars." The elder Pitt, who seems to have written
many of his letters in a sort of classical nightmare, was,
it may be gathered from this very pedantry, no great
scholar. It was to his training, however, that Pitt owed,
not merely the power to translate at sight, which so
astonished his tutor, but that fluency of majestic diction
and command of correct expression, which afterwards
distinguished him as an orator. His father would make
the boy of an evening read freely into English the
passage which he had construed with his tutor in the
morning. So much did this grow into a habit that, when
in later years an ancient writer was quoted, Pitt always
rendered the sense of the sentence into flowing English, as
if for his own use, before he seemed to enter into it. It was
to these lessons that he always attributed his ready copious-

ness of language.   What was scarcely less valuable,
Lord Chatham, (who, we are told, made a point of
giving daily instruction, and readings from the Bible
to his children), encouraged his son to talk to him
without reserve on every subject ; so that the boy, who
seems to have returned the boundless affection with
which his father regarded him, was in close and constant
communication with one of the first minds of the age.
How strictly political was the bias that his mind thus
obtained, we see from a tragedy, "Laurentino, King of
Chersonese," still extant, composed by William at the age
of thirteen ; in which there is no trace of love, but which
has for its plot a struggle between a faithful minister
and an unscrupulous conspirator about a regency.

The details of the childhood of great men are apt to
be petty and cloying. Hero worship, extended to the
bib and the porringer, is more likely to repel than attract.
But, in the case of Pitt, those details are doubly important ; for they form the key to his career, which without
them would be inexplicable. They alone explain that political precocity and that long parliamentary ascendancy,
which still puzzle posterity. For he went into the House
of Commons as an heir enters his home ; he breathed
in it his native atmosphere,—he had, indeed, breathed no
other ; in the nursery, in the schoolroom, at the university, he lived in its temperature ; it had been, so
to speak, made over to him as a bequest by its un-
questioned master.   Throughout his life, from the
cradle to the grave, he may be said to have known no
wider existence.   The objects and amusements, that
other men seek in a thousand ways, were for him all
concentrated there.   It was his mistress, his stud, his

dice-box, his game-preserve; it was his ambition, his library, his creed. For it, and it alone, had the consummate Chatham trained him from his birth. No young Hannibal was ever more solemnly devoted to his country than Pitt to Parliament. And the austerity of his political consecration lends additional interest to the records of his childhood; for they furnish almost the only gleams of ease and nature that play on his life. He was destined, at one bound, to attain that supreme but isolated position, the first necessity of which is self-control; and, behind the imperious mask of power, he all but concealed the softer emotions of his earlier years. Grief for the loss of his sister and her husband are the only instances of human weakness that break the stern impressiveness of his life, up to that last year when fate pressed pitilessly on the dying man. From the time that he went to Cambridge, as a boy of fourteen with his tutor and his nurse, he seems, with one short interval, to have left youth and gaiety behind.

All this does not amount to much; but it must be remembered that the life of Pitt has yet to be written. That by Richards Green, who wrote under the name of Gifford, need scarcely be mentioned. That by Tomline has been severely judged, more perhaps with reference to what it might have been than to what it is; for there are worse books. But the shores of biographical enterprise are strewn with the wrecks of the private secretaries of that period. There is Tomline; there is Trotter; there is even Stapleton; and there is Bourrienne. The Life by Lord Stanhope remains a standard book; it was written by one born under the shadow of Pitt, and reared in the traditions of hereditary reverence for his name. But it is no disparagement to those delightful volumes to say that there remains a dormant mass of material, that was not then, even if it is now, accessible, which must throw a new light on this period. There are the papers of Grenville, and Harrowby, and Canning; of Liverpool, and Lonsdale, and Mulgrave; more especially the collections of Buckingham and of Tomline, which, it may be presumed, have been rather tapped than drained. The same surmise may be entertained by those who have read what has been published from the archives of Rose and of Malmesbury. There is also the State Paper Office; which, especially in the Foreign Department, seems destined to elucidate much of Pitt's policy. Lord Stanhope gathered and garnered with unwearied sympathy and acuteness. But the materials which he utilised, appear, on examination, to be scanty enough, compared to those, which, it would seem, must necessarily be in existence; even if the papers of George III., which have so mysteriously vanished, should never again see day

Pitt was admitted at Pembroke Hall on the 26th of April 1773, when he was not yet fourteen. By the kindness of the Rev. C. E. Searle, D.D., Master of Pembroke College, it is possible to print here the letter with which Chatham introduced his boy to the authorities. It is addressed to Mr. Joseph Turner, then Senior Tutor of the College and Senior Wrangler in 1767 :—

BURTON PYNSENT,
October 3, 1773.

SIR—Apprehensions of gout, about this Season, forbid my undertaking a journey to Cambridge with my Son. I regret this more particularly, as it deprives me of an occasion of being introduced to your Personal Acquaintance, and that of the Gentlemen of your Society; a loss, I shall much wish to repair, at some other time. Mr. Wilson, whose admirable Instruction and affectionate Care have brought my Son, early, to receive such further advantages, as he cannot fail to find, under your eye, will present Him to you. He is of a tender age, and of a health, not yet firm enough to be indulged, to the full, in the strong desire he has to acquire useful knowledge. An ingenuous mind and docility of temper will, I know, render him conformable to your Discipline, in all points. Too young for the irregularities of a man, I trust, he will not, on the other hand, prove troublesome by the Puerile sallies of a Boy. Such as he is, I am happy to place him at Pembroke; and I need not say, how much of his Parents' Hearts goes along with him.—I am, with great esteem and regard, Sir, your most faithful and most obedient humble Servant,   CHATHAM.

At the University, Pitt led the austere life of a student; never missing hall or chapel or lecture, save when illness hindered. He took his degree, by privilege, at the age of seventeen, but continued to reside at Cambridge for nearly four years afterwards, seeing rather more of his contemporaries, and with habits somewhat less ascetic, than heretofore. He had always allowed himself the relaxation of a trip to London to hear his father speak. " His first speech lasted above an hour, and the second half an hour; surely the two finest speeches that were ever made before, unless by himself," writes the enthusiastic son; and in his nineteenth year it was his fate to support the old statesman to the last scene in the House of Lords. Two months later he was bearing his part as chief mourner in the gorgeous procession that followed

—in the heraldic epithets for once not misapplied—
"the noble and puissant William Pitt, Earl of Chatham,"
to that grave in Westminster Abbey, which, in less than
thirty years, was, in still darker days, to open for
himself.

His father's disregard of money, as complete as his
own, left him with an income of from £250 to £300 a
year; nor was this immediately available. His uncle,
Lord Temple, advanced the sum necessary to purchase
him a set of rooms at Lincoln's Inn. He began to keep
his terms early in 1779; and, although continuing his
residence at Cambridge, to sip with prudence the cup
of London amusements. His share of these mainly consisted in attendance at parliamentary debates; where he
became acquainted with Fox, already a star of the first
magnitude. Nor did he shrink from a visit to the
opera or an occasional rout. He was called to the bar
in June, 1780.

His residence at Cambridge began at this time to
have an object not less solid than study; for he came to
be considered in the light of a possible candidate for the
representation of the University in Parliament. The
eagerness with which he embraced this opportunity,
betokened the mind set steadfastly in this direction by
every influence and predisposition of youth. The dissolution came in September 1780, when he stood for
the University, and was left at the bottom of the
poll. But immediately afterwards, the young Duke
of Rutland, who had been warmly interested in Pitt's
success, applied to Sir James Lowther for a seat for his
friend. Lowther, afterwards Lord Lonsdale, exercised
in the North of England a sway which we can now

hardly measure or imagine. In 1782 he had offered to
build and equip at his own expense a vessel of war with
seventy guns. Boswell and Wilberforce have borne
almost trembling testimony to the splendour of his
court, which exhibited extreme hospitality, tempered by
extreme awe, and which northern politicians haunted
like a northern St. James's One of the chief secrets
indeed of his power lay in his parliamentary influence, the
extent of which was exactly defined in the deferential
nickname of the Premier's Cat-o'-Nine-Tails. To one
of his nine boroughs hé now nominated Pitt; who
accordingly in January 1781 took his seat in the House
of Commons as member for Appleby. Exactly three
years later, he was to enter it as Prime Minister, and hold
that post with unexampled power for eighteen years.

At the time that Pitt stepped into public life, the
administration of Lord North was in its agony. Its thin-
spun life was only preserved by the exertions of the King.
The good-humoured cynicism of the minister had long
ago given way to the most dismal apprehension; he
was more and more determined to retire. But he had
to deal with a stern taskmaster.

The character of George III. is one which it is not
easy to understand, if we take the common and erroneous
view that human nature is consistent and coherent.
The fact is, that congruity is the exception; and that
time and circumstance and opportunity paint with
heedless hands and garish colours on the canvass of a
man's life; so that the result is less frequently a finished
picture than a palette of squeezed tints. George III.,
who "gloried in the name of Briton," who obtained his
initial popularity by being an Englishman born, and

who, indeed, never travelled farther than York, was
the German princelet of his day. No petty elector or
margrave, not the ruler of Hesse, who sold his people
by the thousand as material of war, held more absolutely
the view of property, as applied to his dominions or
subjects.

He saw in the American war, not vanished possibilities in the guidance of a new world, but the expro-
priation of an outlying estate, the loss of which diminished
his consequence. He fought for it, therefore, as doggedly
as a Lord of Ravenswood for his remaining acres. As
to his ministers, he regarded them as the mere weapons
of a warfare waged on behalf of autocracy. So long as
they served him blindly, he lavished caresses on them ;
from the moment that they showed independence, he
discarded them like old coats, and old coats which had
become repulsive to him. It is probable that he never
liked Bute, and that Bute's direct influence over him has
been greatly exaggerated. But, while North was the
complaisant grand vizier, nothing was too good for him.
The Cinque-ports and the Garter, money, terms of en-
dearment, were all freely given. At the time, however,
of Pitt's entry into Parliament, the Minister was flinching under the terrific punishment of the Opposition and
the severity of continual disaster ; it was clear that he
could not long endure ; and the affectionate monarch was
cooling down to freezing point. From the time of his
resignation to his death, Lord North remained a stranger
to George III.

It is doubtful whether the King ever regarded Pitt
otherwise than as an indispensable officer, of whom,
with his "d——d long obstinate face," he stood

painfully in awe. For Pitt, alive and in power, the sole bulwark against Fox and the deluge, he was willing to do anything—to pay his bills or to double the peerage ; but for the dead Pitt's debts he had not a farthing to spare ; and he ungraciously ignored, and even denied, his former promise to contribute £30,000 for that object. At one time he found in Addington the servant that he required; and he wrote to him in terms scarcely less fond, than those which James employed to Villiers, or Maria Theresa to Kaunitz. He adjured the minister to take horse exercise ; he waited patiently with his family at Addington's house till Addington should come ; the favourite was even admitted to share the royal mutton and turnips. No sooner, however, had Addington, appalled by the reduction of his majority to the not inadequate figure of thirty-seven, hurried from the field of battle, than his intimacy with the King ceased also. The Robinsons and the Roses lasted perhaps longer, for they were perennially useful ; nor did Eldon ever give the King the chance, save for a few months, of proving that his affections survived office.

It is strange that any sovereign should display so thorough a contempt for the loyal service he received ; it is stranger still in one whose popularity rested on his English qualities ; on his warm heart, and affectionate disposition. Again, his habits were not less domestic than those of Mr. Perceval; but his home was a hell upon earth. What he cared for in his family relations was to maintain the same power over his children that Frederick William I. exercised over Frederick the Great. As a consequence, they escaped from his roof as soon, and returned to it as rarely, as possible.

This is not a pleasant portrait; but there are better features in it. To his sense of duty, mistaken as we may deem it, he was honestly faithful; he was frugal, and pious, and chaste; though the dulness of his court made virtue itself odious, and his parsimony did not prevent constant and unbounded demands on Parliament for the debts of the Civil List. His talents, like his morals, were not of an attractive kind, but they must not be underrated. He was the ablest political strategist of his day. He had to struggle against men of genius, supported by popular enthusiasm, on the one hand; and an impracticable aristocracy, inured to supreme power, on the other. He had, during his reign, to deal with the elder Pitt and the younger Fox, when they were the idols of the nation; with the haughty alliance of Grenville and Grey; with the intolerable obstinacy of Grenville's father; with the close oligarchy of Whig nobles that had encircled and enchained the throne; and with the turbulent democracy of Wilkes. He defeated or outwitted them all. Pitt impatiently betrayed the truth, after an interview with the King, then just recovering from a fit of insanity. "Never," said the statesman, "has he so baffled me." By a certain persistent astuteness; by the dexterous utilising of political rivalries; by cajoling some men and betraying others; by a resolute adroitness that turned disaster and even disease into instruments of his aim, the King realised his darling object, of converting the dogeship to which he had succeeded, into a real and to some extent a personal monarchy. At any rate, he indefinitely enlarged its boundaries.

It is necessary to dwell on the character of the sovereign, who played so prominent a part before and after our story. Little, however, need here be said of North; for within fourteen months he had ceased to be minister; and, with the exception of his obscure share in the Coalition government, had retired from prominent public life. But his reputation is below his real merits, though it owes something to the majestic eulogy of Gibbon. In the art of gaining affection, and in debating power, he was second only to Fox. He was courageous and resourceful, cool in adversity, of an unruffled temper; he held, moreover, the first place in the State for twelve years, and left office, with all the unlimited opportunities of wealth that were then offered by war loans, even a poorer man than he entered it. His cynical and easy wit, indeed, covered a higher character than many with greater pretensions; and his good nature, facile to a fault, which made him lend himself to reprehensible acts, and to a policy of which at last he clearly saw the folly and the wickedness, is the main reproach that history has to urge against him; though that is heavy enough. He had apparently formed himself on Walpole; with the unlucky difference that, while Walpole had to deal with a Caroline of Anspach, North found his master in George III.

It was of course inevitable that Pitt should attach himself to the Opposition; more especially, as that part of it, which had constituted the personal following of his father, still held together under the leadership of Shelburne. A month after taking his seat he had made his maiden speech (February 26, 1781), and had been hailed by the first men in Parliament, with the ready generosity of genius, as henceforth worthy to rank with them. He spoke on behalf of

Burke's Bill for economical reform, unexpectedly, being
called upon by the House; and his first speech was,
what, perhaps, no other first speech ever was, an effective
reply in debate. Fox and North and Burke vied in
congratulation. "He is not a chip of the old block,"
said the latter; "it is the old block itself." He spoke
again in May on a question of the control of public
expenditure with not less success; and for the third
and last time in the session, on a motion of Fox's for
peace with America. His speeches, therefore, in his
first session were devoted to peace and retrenchment,
and his main effort in the next to parliamentary reform;
the three causes nearest and most congenial to him;
the beacons of his earlier, and the will-o'-the-wisps of his
later career.

We catch glimpses of him now as a lad about town,
leading something of a fashionable life during the season,
though dutifully going the western circuit as soon as
Parliament rose. A club had been formed at Goostree's
of a score of young men who had entered Parliament
together at the election of 1780, an idea, which was
destined to be revived exactly a century afterwards.
Here he supped every night, not, we may be sure, without port wine; here he gambled; until he became sensible of the insidious fascination of the gaming table, and
turned his back on it for ever. The example of Fox
had been perhaps sufficient. We read of Pitt, in 1780, as
going to three parties of an evening; two of them masked
balls, one given by a lady of apparently not unspotted
reputation, and concluding his evening at the Pantheon.
A more remarkable evening was that on which he met
Gibbon. The great man, lord of all he surveyed, was

holding forth, snuff-box in hand, amid deferential acquiescence; when a deep, clear voice was heard impugning his conclusions. All turned round in amazement and saw that it belonged to a tall, thin, awkward youth who had hitherto sate silent. Between Pitt, for it was he, and Gibbon, an animated and brilliant argument arose; in which the junior had so much the best of it that the historian took his hat and retired. Nor would he return. "That young gentleman," he said, "is, I doubt not, extremely ingenious and agreeable, but I must acknowledge that his style of conversation is not exactly what I am accustomed to, so you must positively excuse me."

It is almost a relief after this to find him in 1781 "waging war with increasing success on pheasants and partridges." He did not even disdain the practical jokes of an undergraduate. "We found one morning," says Wilberforce, "the fruits of Pitt's earlier rising in the careful sowing of the garden beds with the fragments of a dress hat in which Ryder had overnight come down from the opera." In truth, no man was less of a prig. He was so loftily placed in early youth that he was compelled to a certain austerity of demeanour in order to maintain respect; and he had indeed something of the lofty shyness of Peel. But, at this unconstrained moment of his life, he was, says one who knew all that was most brilliant in English society for half a century, "the wittiest man I ever knew."

At the end of Pitt's first session, Fox had declared him to be already one of the first men in Parliament. He was to know no flagging in his onward course; his genius was not to want the opportunity for which genius so often pines; the accumulating calamities of his country demanded the best efforts of the noblest ambition. The session had ended on the 18th of July 1781. On the 19th of October Cornwallis surrendered at Yorktown. The news reached London, late in November; and shattered even the imperturbable ease of North. He took it as he would have taken a bullet in his breast. He opened his arms, exclaiming wildly, as he paced up and down the room, "O God, it is all over!" All was indeed over, as regards the Ministry and their policy. British dominion in the revolted colonies, and the administration which had so long asserted it, existed from that moment only in name. The catastrophe was followed by minor disasters : the retreat of Kempenfeldt, the loss of Minorca, and of many of our West Indian possessions : though these were forgotten in the dazzling victory of Rodney. But the long struggle was over; and had ended in the humiliation of Great Britain. It was the lowest point that she had ever touched. "The sun of England's glory," said Pitt, "is set." Twenty years before, it had seemed at its meridian, and in the course of another generation it shone again with renewed lustre ; but now it was totally eclipsed.

Before the end of March, even the King was convinced that he must part with North, and submit to peace and the Whigs. During the fierce contests which raged in Parliament between the surrender of Yorktown and the fall of the Ministry, Pitt bore so conspicuous a part, as to justify the declaration which he made just before the latter event, that he had no idea of forming part of any new administration: "But were my doing so more within my reach, I feel myself bound to declare that I never

C

would accept a subordinate situation." The position
that was offered him by Rockingham, who succeeded
North, was subordinate, but not undignified. The
Vice-Treasurership of Ireland was indeed little more
than a sinecure; but it had been held by Pitt's own
father, and in point of emolument was one of the
prizes of the political world; yet he refused it without
hesitation.

That he was wise, there can be no doubt. He retained his freedom, and used that freedom well. The
new Government had not been formed six weeks, before
Pitt brought forward a motion for parliamentary reform.
It took, indeed, a shape, to which, for constitutional
changes of gravity, objection has sometimes been raised;
for he brought forward no specific plan, but moved "for
the institution of an inquiry composed of such men as
the House should in their wisdom select as the most
proper and the best qualified for investigating this subject, and making a report to the House of the best means
of carrying into execution a moderate and substantial
reform of the representation of the people."

The speech he delivered on this occasion, much ap-
plauded at the time, is worth reading even now and in the
condensed, denuded report that has reached us. It is remarkable for its vigorous declamation against the power
of the Crown, which Fox and Burke could hardly have
exceeded in their speeches on the same subject when
Pitt was minister in 1784. He allowed that, under
the Rockingham Government, "the injurious, corrupt,
and baneful influence of the Crown" had ceased to
exist. But it was the duty of Parliament to provide
for the future, and to take care that this secret and

dark system should never be revived to contaminate the fair and honourable fabric of our Government. At all times, this pernicious influence had been pointed to as the fertile source of all our miseries, and it had been truly said of it that it had grown with our growth and strengthened with our strength. Unhappily, however, for this country it had not decayed with our decay, nor diminished with our decrease. And it had supported North's ministry for a length of years against all the consequences of a mischievous system and a desolated empire.

The irony of political destiny, and the astuteness of George III., could receive no better demonstration than the fact that in less than two years Pitt was defending the prerogative of the monarch against the assaults of North, and of those whom he now described as "a set of men who were the friends of constitutional freedom." Yet in truth the anomaly, as is often the case in politics, was more apparent than real. What he denounced were the crawling race of the Welbore Ellises and the Jack Robinsons, the suspected shadow of Bute and the pervading flavour of Jenkinson, the detailed bribes of Martin, the mingled cajolery and intimidation of Henry Fox. What he defended in 1784 were the rights of the constituencies, betrayed by the formation of the Coalition, against a close and corrupt Parliament, in a struggle where the King had intervened for once as the agent of the people. It was the general election of 1784 that ratified the King's action and cleared Pitt of responsibility : had it turned differently, he might have ranked with Strafford and with Lauderdale.

Pitt, in his first Reform speech, analysed the various

kinds of boroughs, which were either representative shams or, worse still, were open to foreign bidders. Among these purchasers he named the Nabob of Arcot, who "had no less than seven or eight members in this House." Finally, he cited his father, "one of whom every member in the House could speak with more freedom than himself. That person was not apt to indulge vague and chimerical speculations, inconsistent with practice and expediency. He knew that it was the opinion of this person that without recurring to first principles in this respect, and establishing a more solid and equal representation of the people, by which the proper constitutional connection should be revived, this nation, with the best capacities for grandeur and happiness of any on the face of the earth, must be confounded with the mass of those whose liberties were lost in the corruption of the people."

In spite of a speech which was evidently forcible and eloquent, and of the support of Fox "in his very first form," and of Sheridan, then his under secretary, "much above anything he has yet done in the House," the motion was lost by twenty votes. The Government spoke indeed with a divided voice of the subject. The Duke of Richmond, Master-General of the Ordnance and a leading member of the Cabinet, was in favour of annual parliaments and manhood suffrage. Lord John Cavendish was "diffident" of the effect of any such reform, though he voted on this occasion for Pitt. Lord Rockingham gave forth a troubled and ambiguous note, rent as he was between regard for Fox and the dominant influence of Burke, who was vehemently hostile. A few days later, this feeling found overmastering expression when Alderman Sawbridge, Pitt's seconder on this occasion, brought forward a motion for shortening Parliaments, and Burke broke forth in one of his impetuous invectives against Pitt and all who should attempt to touch the sacred fabric of the constitution.

While Pitt in refusing office had retained the positive advantage of independence, he had also gained the negative benefit of not forming part of a Government as divided against itself as its members had formerly been from the Government of Lord North.   Under a stormier star was no administration ever born.   Furious jealousies broke out during the process of formation. Thurlow, North's chancellor, remained in office, to the open mortification of Loughborough, as an abiding source of suspicion and intrigue.   Another legacy of North's, the Lord Advocate Dundas, though less prominent, was not less justly regarded with mistrust as a powerful and unscrupulous politician, whose only connection with the Whigs was the memory of bitter altercation and unsparing conflict; who with a happy instinct sometimes inclined to Shelburne, the proximate Prime Minister, sometimes to the young statesman so soon to follow him and to absorb all the powers of the State.   Shelburne himself formed another element of disturbance.   Not merely did Fox, his colleague in the Secretaryship of State, cherish an hereditary hatred for him, but he had aroused great jealousy by having been at first entrusted with the task of forming the government.   The King dexterously fomented these causes of discord among his enemies, and flatly refused even to see Rockingham; so that all the communications between him and his Prime Minister during the construction of the ad-

ministration were carried on through the ominous
medium of Shelburne, and Shelburne alone. All these
germs of mistrust were quickened when Shelburne
secured peerages and places for his friends from the
King; paid the Chancellor compliments, "which very
much scandalised all good men," as Fox writes; and
intrigued successfully with Dundas. It is, therefore, not
matter for surprise that, within a month of their assuming office, Shelburne and Fox, the two Secretaries of
State, had each their separate plenipotentiary at Paris
negotiating for peace. Such a condition of affairs had
little of comfort or permanency : the Government, ruined
by intrigue and under virtuous but incapable guidance,
could not in any case have continued to exist : the in-
fluenza that carried off Lord Rockingham only acceler-
ated the end of an impossible state of things.

CHAPTER II

THE political atmosphere was charged with electricity, and the breaking of the storm was not delayed. Rockingham died on the 1st of July (1782). That very day the King entrusted the Treasury to Shelburne, who evidently counted on Pitt, and had, it is clear, good reason for doing so. Shelburne received the royal letter on the 2d, and at once communicated the King's mandate to the Cabinet. There was no ambiguity about its reception. The Fox party declared that the nomination of First Minister should rest with the Cabinet; and, to the mortification of the able but impracticable Richmond, recommended Portland for the post. To this pretension the King at once refused to accede. For two days the contest raged. On the third there was a Court. Fox came with the seals in his pocket, and at once took Shelburne aside, asking him if he was to be First Lord of the Treasury. On Shelburne's affirmative reply, Fox merely said, "Then, my lord, I shall resign," went into the closet, and left the seals with the King.

This rupture was a crisis in the lives of Fox and

Pitt, for it marks the commencement of their undying political hostility. Had it not been for Pitt,
Fox must now have triumphed—a fact that neither
statesman could ignore or forget. Of Fox's resignation it may be said that he was right to resign, but
wrong in the manner of his resignation. It was
impossible for him, after what had passed in the Rockingham Cabinet, to remain; he could not have continued
to serve with, much less under, Shelburne. It does not
signify which of the two was to blame for this mutual
mistrust; that it existed is sufficient. It would be too
much to maintain that all the members of a Cabinet should
feel an implicit confidence in each other; humanity—
least of all political humanity—could not stand so severe
a test. But between a Prime Minister in the House of
Lords and the leader of the House of Commons such
a confidence is indispensable. Responsibility rests so
largely with the one, and articulation so greatly with
the other, that unity of sentiment is the one necessary
link that makes a relation, in any case difficult, in any
way possible. The voice of Jacob and the hands of
Esau may effect a successful imposture, but can hardly
constitute a durable administration. But as regards
the effort to impose Portland on the King, the case is
widely different. It was part of the political system
that rendered the narrow selfishness of the close Whig
corporation even more odious to the people than the
tortuous absolutism of the King. To the men of that
day, for whom prerogative was a living force, it was not
less distasteful than to us, for whom an oligarchy is
odious for opposite reasons. For Fox it may be urged
that a dummy Prime Minister offered the only means

of keeping the Government together, for he would not
serve under Shelburne, nor Shelburne under him.   Be
that as it may, the attempt to procure the succession of
a dull, dumb duke to the vapid virtue of Rockingham,
whom George III. had ranked among the meanest
intellects in his household, did not recommend itself
to any large section of the community, and tended
further to alienate from Fox the jealous sympathies
of the people.

It is clear that Shelburne would not have undertaken in July the post from which he had shrunk
in March, had he not relied upon Pitt.   Fox, with
rare sagacity, had foreseen this even at the time when
Pitt was achieving distinction as a parliamentary reformer and denouncer of the influence of the Crown,
and had written of him on the 18th of May : " He
is very civil and obliging, profuse of compliments in
public ; but he has more than once taken a line that
has alarmed me, especially when he dissuaded against
going into any inquiries that might produce heats
and differences.   This seemed so unlike his general
mode of thinking, and so like that of another, that I
confess I disliked it to the greatest degree.   *I am satisfied he will be the man that the old system revived in the
person of Lord S.* (Shelburne) *will attempt to bring forward
for its support.*   I am satisfied that he is incapable of
going into this with his eyes open ; but how he may be
led into it step by step is more than I can answer for.
I feel myself, I own, rather inclined to rely upon his
understanding and integrity for resisting all the tempta-
tions of ambition, and especially *of being first*, which I
know will be industriously thrown in his way, and con-

trasted with that secondary and subordinate situation to which they will insinuate, he must be confined while he continues to act in the general system."

Pitt was not now to be first. But he accepted the great office of Chancellor of the Exchequer, with practically the lead of the House of Commons. His own letters betray no exultation; they speak the indifference not of affectation or satiety, but of long preparation and habitual self-control. "Lord Rockingham's death took place yesterday morning. What the consequences of it will be to the public cannot yet quite be foreseen. With regard to myself, I believe the arrangement may be of a sort in which I *may*, and probably *ought*, to take a part. If I do, I think I need not say you pretty well know the principles on which I shall do it. In this short time nothing is settled, and I only saw what were the strong wishes of *some* who foresaw the event." These sentences are remarkable not merely for their serene simplicity, but also because they show that Pitt the very day after Rockingham's death wrote of his accession to office as a settled affair between himself and those who had foreseen the event. Both parts of the administration, indeed, had long been preparing for it. Fox and Burke on the one side, who were ready with their candidate for the succession; on the other Shelburne and the King, with Pitt as their trump card. Both sides concealed their hands. "Lord Shelburne," wrote the King, on the morning of Rockingham's death, "must see, I am certain, with no small degree of resentment the total ignorance that those who have governed Lord Rockingham cautiously try to keep both me and him in as to the desperate state of that Lord, which certainly is with a view to some arrangement of their own. From the language of Mr. Fitzpatrick it would seem that Lord Shelburne has no chance of being able to coalesce with Mr. Fox; it may not be necessary to remove him at once, but if Lord Shelburne accepts the Head of the Treasury, and is succeeded by Mr. Pitt as Secretary for the Home Department and British Dominions, then it will be seen how far he would submit to it."

While Fox, then, by a resignation which bore too much the appearance of pique, was alienating the sympathies of the public, which by further indiscretion he was within a few months to lose altogether, Pitt, by blameless accession to high office when just twenty-three years of age, was further to attract popular interest and confidence. It is impossible, henceforth, to separate the lives of the two men: and here, where they first come into collision, there is, as George Selwyn said at the time, so much of the contrast of the Idle and Industrious Apprentice between them, that one is irresistibly reminded of Hogarth's famous designs. It is so rare to detect the disciplined youth of Pitt in a slip of judgment. He moves steadily and almost irresistibly onwards, with a cold calmness which seems to govern where perhaps it only skilfully adapts itself to events. On the other hand, Fox, ten years older in age, and fully twelve in political life, who at twenty-three was not less famous, was still, by headstrong impulses and a generous tendency to extremes, committing and recommitting all the errors of his youth. Pitt perhaps was never young, and Fox certainly could never have been old.

So close is the connection of the two lives that it is impossible to sketch the career of Pitt without describ-

ing the character of Fox, if for this reason alone, that
had it not been for that character and its faults Pitt
could certainly not have retained, and possibly could not
have obtained, the premiership. It may be said once
for all that Fox was the most transcendent of all debaters,
the most genial of all associates, the most beloved of all
friends. He was moreover, after Burke, the most
lettered politician in a generation that affected literature. His public career had been one of expansion.
Beginning life as a High Tory, he rebounded briskly
into the ranks of Whiggery and ultimately of Radicalism. This final phase may have been partly due
to his long exclusion from office and to resentment at
the unconstitutional vindictiveness of his sovereign, but
it was mainly owing to the genial kindness and warm
sympathies of his nature :—" large was his bounty and
his soul sincere." His was in truth a large, bountiful,
outspoken soul. Wherever he saw what he believed to
be oppression, he took part with the oppressed—the
American, the Irishman, the Negro : he could not side
with what he thought wrong against what he thought
right, even though they who seemed to him in the right
were the enemies of his country. This extreme abstrac-
tion of principle was perhaps unconsciously aided by
the fact that his country in these contests was often
guided by his political foes. Hence his private correspondence is not always pleasant reading. "An expedition is, after all, gone to France, under General
Doyle, consisting of 4000 British, besides emigrants,
etc. . . . I think nothing can show the complete in-
fatuation of our Government so much as this desperate
expedition, which, *I believe as well as hope*, has not the

smallest chance of success." And of Trafalgar he has
nothing better to say than that, "by its solid as well
as brilliant advantages, it far more than compen-
sates for the temporary succour which it will certainly
afford Pitt in his distress." To complete these painful
extracts, he writes in 1801: "To tell the truth,
I am gone something further in hate to the English
Government than perhaps you and the rest of my friends
are, and certainly further than can with prudence be
avowed. The triumph of the French Government over
the English does in fact afford me a degree of pleasure
which it is very difficult to disguise."

The cosmopolitan character of his liberalism was
thus either above or below humanity, either superhuman
or not human enough. This exaggeration was probably
due to his oratorical temperament. His nature, apt to
extremes, was driven with an excessive reaction to the
most violent negative of what he disapproved. We see
the same excess to a still greater degree in his still
greater master Burke. It is this force of extremes
that makes orators, and for them it is indispensable.
Few supreme parliamentary speeches have perhaps ever
been delivered by orators who have been unable to convince themselves, not merely that they are absolutely in
the right, but that their opponents are absolutely in the
wrong, and the most abandoned of scoundrels to boot
for holding a contrary opinion. No less a force, no feebler
flame than this will sway or incense the mixed tempera-
ments of mankind. The mastering passion of Fox's
mature life was the love of liberty: it is this which made
him take a vigorous, occasionally an intemperate, part
against every man or measure in which he could trace

the taint or tendency to oppression : it is this which sometimes made him write and speak with unworthy bitterness : but it is this which gave him moral power, which has neutralised the errors of his political career, which makes his faults forgotten and his memory sweet.

His fatal defect as a statesman was want of judgment : he was vehement, passionate, carried away by the impulse of the day, without a thought of the morrow, still less of the day after. "The present day," Metternich used to say, "has no value for me except as the eve of to-morrow : it is with to-morrow that my spirit wrestles." This sublime disregard of to-day can have no place in the politics of a parliamentary country, but the disregard of to-morrow is scarcely less dangerous. Fox could, indeed, lay down principles for all time, but, the moment the game was afoot, they ceased to govern his conduct. Had it not been for this, he would have been the most powerful and popular minister that this country has ever known : as it was, he scarcely held office at all. A life of dissipation, hardly paralleled in that dissipated age, did not leave him the coolness or balance which would have made him a match for Pitt : his private life too much influenced his public conduct. At the gaming table he had indeed learned to endure with dauntless bearing the frowns of fortune, whether in politics or at hazard. He had too discovered the charms of that fascinating freemasonry which made the members of Brooks's patiently pay his card debts : but his experience of play had also taught him a low estimate of human nature, a sort of gambling spirit in public affairs.

It is necessary to recall some of Fox's failings and drawbacks, because otherwise it is not possible to understand how, in a country like England, so great a political force did not obtain political supremacy. To comprehend the full prodigy of his parliamentary powers a single example will suffice : it is enough to read Pitt's great speech of the 3d of February 1800, and the reply which Fox delivered the moment that Pitt sate down. The first is a magnificent effort, but the second in dissolvent and pulverising power is superhuman. This is not the place to inquire whether, in these days of verbatim reports and greater pressure on time, Fox would have done so much ; but it is clear that, under every imaginable condition of discussion, he must have been a giant, and that powers which could make an audience forget his coarse features, his unwieldy corpulence, his slovenly appearance, his excessive repetition, and his ungraceful action, would have overcome any obstacles.

Putting his fashionable vices aside, he reminds one of another colossal figure ; another reformer who, though religious rather than political, was not less bold, not less stormy, not less occasionally wrongheaded. To some it may appear a profanation to compare Fox with the German Apostle of light and freedom. But with his passion, his power, his courage, his openness, his flashes of imagination, his sympathetic errors, above all his supreme humanity, Fox was a sort of lax Luther, with the splendid faults and qualities of the great reformer. Whether he would have been a great administrator, we cannot tell ; he had no opportunity and we have no experience : his marvellous abilities were almost always exercised in opposition.

In him, therefore, we have only a portion of the life of a statesman : we judge of him as the limb of a fossil monster or the torso of a Greek god ; and it is difficult, in judging from the part we possess, to place any bounds on our estimate of the possibilities of the whole.

It has been said that his private life was conspicuously disordered. And yet even when it was blamable it was lovable, and it mellowed into an exquisite evening. Whether we see him plunged in Theocritus after a bout at faro which has left him penniless ; or cheerfully watching the bailiffs remove his last stick of furniture ; or drinking with the Jockey of Norfolk ; or choosing wild waistcoats at Paris ; or building with his own hands his little greenhouse at St. Anne's ; or sauntering down its cool glades with a book and a friend ; or prone without either under a tree in the long summer afternoons ; or watching the contests of Newmarket with the rapt frenzy of a boy ; or chatting before the races with Windham on the horses of the ancients and the precise meaning of *argutum caput* ; or corresponding with Gilbert Wakefield about innumerable other niceties of classical reading ; or, when crippled and aged, playing trapball with the children and with more than a child's keenness ; or speechless with generous tears in the House of Commons when quivering under the harsh severance of Burke ; or placid on his deathbed reassuring his wife and his nephew ;—he still exercises over us something of the unbounded fascination which he wielded over his contemporaries. Scarce one of those contemporaries, whose records we know, but mourned his death as a personal loss. He charmed equally the affections of Carlisle and Fitzpatrick, the

meteoric mind of Burke, the pedantic vanity of Parr,
the austere virtue of Horner, and the hedgehog soul of
Rogers.   His nephew, the third Lord Holland, converted his matchless palace at Kensington into a sort of
temple in honour of Fox's memory, where historians
and poets, and authors and statesmen, vied with each
other in burning incense before his shrine. It may
fairly be said that the traditional estimate of Fox owes
something to Holland House.   But without such adven-
titious aids, he stands forth as the negation of cant and
humbug, a character valuable then, invaluable now ;
as an intellectual Titan ; and as the quick and visible
embodiment of every lovable quality in man.

The new splendour of his position did not for a
moment affect the head of the young minister. He
watched with the same cool vigilance the intoxication
of his new chief.   Shelburne could not conceal his joy.
He had dished Fox.   He had retained Richmond and
Conway, Camden, Grafton, and Keppel.   He had secured
the champion who was alone capable of being matched
against Fox.   The negotiation of the peace would rest
with him alone.   He believed that he enjoyed the
complete favour and confidence of the King, and so
would be in reality prime, if not sole, minister.   Thus
infatuated he proceeded to act alone, and to disgust his
colleagues, without securing the King.   The astute
occupant of the throne never trusted Shelburne, but his
reasons for supporting him at this juncture are clear.
In the first place, it enabled him to knock the heads of
the hated Whigs together, and so compass their destruction.   In the next place, the man he most detested was
Fox, and the selection of Shelburne would be sure to

preserve him at any rate for the time from Fox. In
the third place, he had some hopes, real or fanciful,
of Shelburne's assisting him to resist the concession of
American independence, which Fox was determined to
declare. On the very day on which Rockingham died
and Shelburne succeeded him, the King wrote to his new
minister: "I am apprised that Lord Shelburne, though
he has gone great lengths at the expense of his opinion in
giving way as to American independence, if it can effect
peace, would think he received advice in which his
character was not attended to, if he intended to give
up that without the price set on it, which alone could
make this kingdom consent to it. Besides, he must see
that the great success of Lord Rodney's engagement
has again roused the nation so far that the peace which
would have been acquiesced in three months ago would
now be matter of complaint." The first sentence is as
obscure in construction as a speech of Cromwell's, but
the general meaning is clear enough. The suspicion of
contemporary politicians pointed in the same direction,
probably without reason. But Shelburne's habitual
ambiguity, and his resistance to the proposition of Fox
that the independence of America should be recognised
as a preliminary, and not as an accompaniment of negotiation, gave some colour to the hopes of the King.

Parliament adjourned almost immediately after the
new ministers had taken their seats. There was indeed
one animated debate in each House. In the Lords, the
Duke of Richmond announced his reasons for remaining
in office, and Shelburne took advantage of the discussion to make his ministerial statement. Already
there seemed a rift in the lute. Richmond had said

that the influence of the Crown in Parliament was
to be diminished; this was one of the great principles on which the administration was formed.   But
Shelburne announced that he was there to defend the
King's prerogative.   He would not submit to see the
King of England converted into a King of the Mahrattas,
with a peishwah elected by a few great chiefs.   As regards
the independence of America, he had been charged with
changing his opinion.   That was untrue.   It had indeed been ever his opinion that the independence of
America would be a dreadful blow to the greatness of
this country, and that when it should be established
the sun of England might be said to have set.   To
nothing short of necessity, therefore, would he give
way on that head.   As regards the sunset of England
which would follow concession, it was his resolution
so to take advantage of the twilight that the country
might yet see its orb rise again.

The debate in the Commons was already over.   Two
days previously, in a crowded house, Coke of Norfolk,
who was to refuse from Pitt in 1784 that earldom of
Leicester which he was to accept from Melbourne in
1837, called attention to the pension of Barré.   It
cannot be denied that Shelburne's party, though it hardly
numbered a dozen persons, had reason to congratulate
itself on the partiality of its leader.   To Barré had been
given a pension of £3200 a year, and though this enormous sum would not after the payment of taxes and
fees net above £2100, enough remained to be, even in
those days, a fair subject for parliamentary inquiry.
Advantage was also taken of the discussion to allude to
the acquisitions of Shelburne's other main supporter,

Dunning, who in the course of the three months' administration had, through his patron, pocketed a pension, a
peerage, the duchy of Lancaster for life, and a seat in
the Cabinet. Fox made of these grants an opportunity
for praising Lord Rockingham, whose only two jobs
had been for men unfriendly to him in politics. Thence
he diverged into the larger question of his resignation.
He seems already to have been conscious that he had
made a mistake. Four days before, he had written to
Thomas Grenville at Paris: "I feel that my situation in
the country, my power, my popularity, my consequence,
nay, my character, are all risked;" and Temple, a day
earlier, had pointed out to him the invidiousness of resigning on a personal question. In his present speech,
therefore, he placed his resignation on grounds of public
policy—grounds which can hardly be sustained by evidence. But on Conway's challenging him to show in
what respect the principles upon which Rockingham
had accepted office had been disregarded, and expressing
his own adherence to the principle of measures, not
men, Fox rose again, and frankly avowed that one of
his main reasons for withdrawal was the handing over
to Shelburne of the Treasury and its patronage. To
Burke, however, fell the more conspicuous discredit of
debate. His tirade against Shelburne outstripped both
sense and decency. "He was a man that he could by
no means confide in, and he called heaven and earth to
witness, so help him God, that he verily believed the
present Ministry would be fifty times worse than that
of the noble Lord (North) who had lately been reprobated and removed. . . . He meant no offence, but he
would speak an honest mind. If Lord Shelburne was

not a Catiline or a Borgia in morals, it must not be
ascribed to anything but his understanding." Pitt took
but little part in the discussion, and that not as a
minister. He charged Fox roundly with a dislike to
men and not to measures. The uneasiness of Fox was
apparent. Again and again did he rise and explain,
without apparently satisfying himself or his audience.
And so closed the first round between these two great
combatants of the political ring.

The summer and autumn months were spent in
negotiations. Those in Paris were carried on mainly
by Shelburne himself. The retention of Gibraltar
was the one point in dispute which appears to have
been hotly discussed in the Ministry. George III. was
in favour of ceding Gibraltar for some substantial
equivalent, on the ground that no settled peace was
possible while it was withheld from Spain. Grafton
and Shelburne adhered to this view; Richmond,
Keppel, and Pitt were hostile to any cession of the
monumental fortress. Before Parliament met, the disputes had risen so high that negotiation of another kind
was seen to be necessary. Richmond, Grafton, and
Keppel were on the brink of resignation. Camden and
Temple were extremely discontented, and it was evident
that, if the Government was to continue, it must seek
reinforcement from the followers of North or the
followers of Fox. Shelburne appears to have remained
in a sort of fool's paradise to the last. If he had to
conclude an alliance with either chief, it would be with
North; Pitt, on the other hand, who always declined to
associate himself with North, leaned to Fox. But in
truth the negotiations were carried on with little spirit.

Shelburne may well have felt that combination between North and Fox was impossible, and that by their division he might govern. Moreover, he was a little weary of his colleagues, and they were heartily sick of him. No one, indeed, ever trusted him ; no one ever cared to be long associated with him.

The languid overtures of Shelburne were soon obliterated by arrangements of a more practical character. Adam, George North, and Lord John Townshend, under the sinister supervision of Eden and Loughborough, were actively reconciling the two chiefs of Opposition. Already in the previous August Fox had sent civil messages to North. On the 14th of February they met, and the preliminaries of the treaty were agreed upon. In four and twenty hours the Coalition was complete, and within four days a resolution of censure on the Peace had been carried by a majority of 16. Pitt's speech on this occasion was perhaps the least effective of his life ; he had the bad taste to taunt Sheridan with his connection with the stage, and brought on himself the famous retort that the dramatist would be tempted to try an improvement on the Angry Boy in the *Alchemist*. Strangely enough, however, it was the victor in this encounter who seems never to have forgotten or forgiven it.

For some unexplained reason Shelburne did not at once resign, though in a conversation with Dundas on the 12th he had intimated that he considered his ministry as over. On the 21st, the battle was renewed. The allied forces, led by their stalking-horse, the worthy but insipid Cavendish, made another assault. On this occasion Pitt made one of the great speeches of his life. While Fox spoke, the Chancellor of the Exchequer stood holding open with one hand the door behind the Speaker's chair to hear the attack, while he held the basin into which he vomited with the other.   But, when Fox sate down, Pitt at once replied in a speech of nearly three hours.   His defence of the Peace as a work of necessity, though it does not concern this story, was convincing; the cutting sarcasm with which he denounced the Coalition—an unnatural union of which in the public interest he forbade the banns—is classical; and the quotation with which he closed—the *probamque pauperiem sine dote quæro*—is memorable not only for its appositeness, but for the modesty of its omissions: though public opinion supplied the *virtute meâ me involvo*.   Nor did he forget a dignified, yet not extravagant, eulogy of Shelburne. But the opposition again triumphed.   Their majority of 17, when viewed in connection with the calculated strength of parties, does not seem exorbitant.   Eden, no bad judge, had reckoned the forces under North at 120, those under Fox at 90, and those of the Government at 140.   It is clear then that the Coalition must have alienated, or the Peace secured, a considerable number of independent votes.

Shelburne, however, lost no time in resigning, and recommended Pitt to the King as his successor.   Every effort was employed to induce the young barrister to accept the first place.   But he saw that the fruit was not yet ripe.   For a moment he seems to have hesitated.   It was urged on him that the allied forces could not long hold together.   But it was obvious that when once they had so far forgotten the past as to unite at all, there was nothing in public principle that need afterwards dissever them.   To the angry disappointment of the King, who described himself as "one on the edge of a precipice," and as apparently resolved to abdicate rather than submit, he declined the proud post.

This is the first epoch of his career. He had already obtained a first place as an orator; he had held all but the highest office. That, though he was but twenty-three, was now not merely within his grasp, but pressed on him, with authority and with enthusiasm, by Dundas and the King, the most acute political tacticians of their time. With a judgment which can only be described as consummate, and a self-control which few by any experience attain, the young statesman, able, eloquent, and courageous as he was, refused the splendid prize, and prepared to resume his practice at the bar.

In the meantime the monarch was desperate. He caught at any hint that would save him from Fox. He even pressed the Treasury on North, with the condition that North should break with Fox. Gower suggested to him that Pitt's cousin, Mr. Thomas Pitt, might be a capable minister. The King replied that he was ready to apply to Mr. Thomas Pitt or Mr. Thomas Anybody. For five weeks did George III. hunt for a Premier. At last he was compelled to yield. Portland became Prime Minister; Fox and North joint-Secretaries of State. They had pressed Pitt to join them, but in vain. As they kissed hands, a humorous bystander predicted their early fall, for he observed George III. turn back his ears and eyes, just like the horse at Astley's when the tailor was mounting whom it had determined to throw.

Thus was formed the Coalition Ministry of which it is hard to say which was the most complete—the infamy of the proceeding, or the retribution that followed. Fox in 1782 had said of North's government: "From the moment when I shall make any terms with one of them, I will rest satisfied to be called the most infamous of mankind. I would not for an instant think of a coalition with men who in every public and private transaction as ministers have shown themselves void of every principle of honour and honesty. In the hands of such men I would not trust my honour for a minute." He had declared that he could not believe even North's announcement of his own resignation without corroborative evidence. He had urged that North and his colleagues should be brought to trial, and if possible to the scaffold. Later, again, on Shelburne's becoming Prime Minister, he had declared his anticipation that the Government would refrain from no corrupt method of maintaining themselves in power even to the extent of allying themselves with the party of North. Political digestion is tough, but it could not stomach these things. What is also notable, though less remarkable, Fox and North at once assimilated and concluded the very conditions of peace on which they had moved a vote of censure —censure which a cool examination of the articles and of the situation must pronounce factious, and, as coming jointly from the incapable administrator and the fierce opponent of the war, grotesque. Grattan once observed that none had heard Fox at his best who had not heard him before the Coalition. Afterwards, the ability remained, but he felt that he had done something that required defence; the mouth still spoke great things, but the swell of soul was no more.

CHAPTER III

ON 7th May 1783, the anniversary of his previous motion for parliamentary reform, Pitt repeated it. It was supported by one and opposed by the other of the two Secretaries of State, and was rejected by 293 to 149. A month later he introduced a Bill for the Reform of Abuses in the Public Offices. In his speech he produced the famous allegation that North in the last year of his ministry had been credited with the consumption of £1300 for stationery, of which £340 was for whipcord. The Bill passed languidly through the Commons, but was promptly strangled in the Lords, where the Ministry opposed it with vigour ; a proceeding on which the country could not but comment.

In the recess Pitt went abroad for the only time in his life. He was accompanied by his brother-in-law, Eliot, and by Wilberforce. They first established themselves at Rheims, with the view of learning the language, residing for six weeks at the Archbishop's palace. Here Pitt was thrown into close companionship with the prelate's nephew, the young Abbé de Perigord. They were to meet again in 1792, when Talleyrand as a

lay diplomatist was negotiating with Pitt as an auto-
cratic prime minister. Pitt, it is said, did not make
much progress in French, though he proceeded to Paris,
and thence to Versailles. The son of Chatham could not
fail to make a stir in that volatile and curious court; it
is even asserted that he narrowly escaped marriage with
the daughter of Necker who was afterwards to talk
down Europe and write *Corinne*. The queen, indeed,
is said to have considered the young lion awkward and
dull, and so called forth the pun of Chastellux: "C'est
égal: il ne s'en dépitera pas pour ça," but the politicians
came round him "in shoals." Two remarks of his
during that visit have been preserved—one on the
English, the other on the French constitution. Of the
first he said: "The part of our constitution which will
first perish is the prerogative of the king and the
authority of the House of Peers." Of the second he
remarked to a Frenchman, "You have no political
liberty, but as to civil liberty you have more of it than
you suppose." It was here, too, that he paid his famous
tribute, not less generous than true, to Fox. Some one
expressed surprise that a man of so little character
should wield so great an influence. "The remark is
just," replied Pitt, "but then you have not been under
the wand of the magician." He is said also to have astonished Franklin not merely by his talents, but by the anti-
republican character of his sentiments. For the rest, he
seems to have hunted and amused himself. He returned to
England on the 24th of October (1783). Parliament met
on the 11th of November; on the 18th Fox asked for leave
to introduce a Bill for the Better Government of India.
That day month the Government had ceased to exist.

Into the merits of the Bill it is not now necessary to
enter. North, when he saw it, sagaciously described it
as "a good receipt to knock up an administration"; in
its scope and audacity it savoured even more of the elder
than the younger Fox. The objections to its main provision, which handed over the government of India to
irremovable commissioners named for four years, have
been perhaps overstated. But it was clear that it furnished an admirable weapon against an unpopular Coalition which had resisted economical reform, demanded a
great income for a debauched prince, and which now aimed
at securing a monopoly of the vast patronage of India,—
patronage which, genially exercised by Dundas, was soon
to secure Scotland for Pitt. In the House of Commons
the majority for the Bill was over 100; the loftiest
eloquence of Burke was exerted in its favour; and Fox
was, as ever, dauntless and crushing in debate. But
outside Parliament the King schemed, and controversy
raged. There was a storm of caricatures. One of these,
by Sayer, of Fox as an Oriental potentate entering
Leadenhall Street on an elephant, Fox himself admitted
had greatly damaged him. When the Bill arrived at the
House of Lords, the undertakers were ready. The King
had seen Temple, and empowered him to communicate
to all whom it might concern his august disapprobation.
The uneasy whisper circulated, and the joints of the
lords became as water. The peers, who yearned for
lieutenancies or regiments, for stars or strawberry leaves;
the prelates, who sought a larger sphere of usefulness;
the minions of the bedchamber and the janissaries of
the closet; all, temporal or spiritual, whose convictions
were unequal to their appetite, rallied to the royal nod.

Some great nobles, such as Gower and Bridgewater, the one old, the other indifferent to politics, roused themselves to violent exertion on the same side, keeping open tables, and holding hourly conclaves. The result was overwhelming. The triumphant Coalition was paralysed by the rejection of their Bill. They rightly refused to resign, but the King could not sleep until he had resumed the seals. Late at night he sent for them. The messenger found North and Fox gaily seated at supper with their followers. At first he was not believed. "The King would not dare do it," exclaimed Fox. But the under Secretary charged with the message soon convinced them of its authenticity, and the seals were delivered with a light heart. In such dramatic fashion, and the springtide of its youth, fell that famous government, unhonoured and unwept. "England," once said Mr. Disraeli, "does not love coalitions." She certainly did not love this one.

On this occasion there was neither hesitation nor delay; the moment had come, and the man. Within twelve hours of the King's receiving the seals, Pitt had accepted the First Lordship of the Treasury and the Chancellorship of the Exchequer. That afternoon his writ was moved amid universal derision. And so commenced a supreme and unbroken Ministry of seventeen years.

Those who laughed were hardly blamable, for the difficulties were tremendous. Temple, who acted as Secretary of State, resigned in three days, having demanded apparently too considerable a reward for his services. To the young Minister, his first cousin, this was a cruel blow; but Pitt never faltered, though it gave him a

sleepless night ; while Temple retired in sullen magnifi-
cence to Stowe.   On the other hand, the Opposition, already in high and hysterical spirits, were proportionately
elated.   " This boyish prank," writes Elliot, a shrewd
and able Whig, " is already over."   Probably " they (the
embryo Government) mean to gain a few days' time, and
to wear some sort of countenance in order to make a
capitulation, if it can be obtained.   *They have lost all
character*," continues the supporter of the Coalition, " and
are considered as a set of children playing at ministers,
and must be sent back to school ; and in a few days all
will have returned to its usual course."

Pitt's friends seem largely to have shared the views
of his enemies.   Camden, the devoted friend of Chatham,
and Grafton, whom Chatham had made Prime Minister,
both refused office.   For Secretaries of State he had to
fall back on Tommy Townshend, now chiefly remembered by Goldsmith's famous line, who had become
Lord Sydney; and the young Marquis of Carmarthen,
who was upright and well intentioned, but vain and
inadequate.   He secured, indeed, the scowling hypocrisy
of Thurlow and the naval fame of Howe ; but the one
was insidious and the other dumb.   It is always difficult
to understand the principles on which the Cabinets of
the eighteenth century were formed.   Pitt's was a procession of ornamental phantoms.   He himself was the
only Cabinet minister in the House of Commons.   Dundas, lately Lord Advocate and now Treasurer of the Navy,
who was to be his right-hand man from the beginning to
the end of this administration, was outside the Cabinet.
Of the Cabinet ministers, five occupied in solemn silence
the front bench of the House of Lords ; while Thurlow on

the wool-sack, though he often spoke, as often as not did
so in opposition to the Government. Never was there in
appearance, to use Charles Townshend's graphic phrase,
such a lutestring administration.

There was one remarkable omission; nothing was
offered to Shelburne. At first sight this can only seem
attributable to gross imbecility or to flagrant ingratitude.
That Pitt, who was gasping in a famine of capacity,
should pass by the ablest statesman available, savours
of insanity. That he should deliberately and without
any political difference ignore the Minister who had a
few months before given him the lead of the House of
Commons, on whom at the moment of resignation he
had passed significant eulogy, and who had been his
father's closest adherent in public life, seems so incredibly ungracious as to leave a stain on Pitt's memory.
But his action was deliberate : it had been determined
months before. To clear Pitt, one must understand Shelburne. And in any case it is not amiss
to pause a moment by the complex character of the
politician who introduced Pitt to official life; whose
fate it has been to be utilised as a political stage-
property by a brilliant novelist, who was also a prime
minister ; and who is variously represented as a popular
statesman crushed in the contest with a Venetian constitution, or a sinister schemer of unusual guile. But
he was neither a Canning nor a Dodington, though his
career presents strange complications.

The problem may be briefly stated thus. How is
it that a noble of high lineage and fortune, of great
talents, and of an intelligence superior to his talents,
who was a distinguished soldier before he was twenty-

four; who was a Cabinet Minister at twenty-five,
and a Secretary of State at twenty-nine, when Secretaries of State often represented a greater power than
the Minister nominally first; who was Prime Minister
at forty-five; and who, to pass beyond dignities, was
far beyond his age in enlightenment; a Free Trader, the
friend of men like Franklin and Bentham and Morellet,
the leader of men like Dunning and Barré; who, if not
the friend, had at least the courage to be the admirer, of
the successful rebel Washington, with whom he had to
sign peace;—how was it that this man, so rarely gifted
and with opportunities so splendid, should only have
touched power to see it vanish for ever from his grasp,
and to spend the remainder of his life under universal
detestation and distrust? These phrases are unhappily
not too strong. It is not too much to say that, during
the last decade of the eighteenth century, the greatest
reproach that could be directed against a statesman,
short of calling him a Jacobin, was to insinuate a connection with Berkeley Square, where Shelburne had completed the palace which Bute had been forced to forsake.

The key to the enigma seems to lie in the bitter
description which he penned of Chatham in his cynical
but priceless fragment of autobiography; when he con-
temptuously dismisses the popular conception of his
leader, and pronounces him to be a mere actor, incapable of friendship, anything but disinterested, studied
and artificial in all that he wrote or said or did. This
was what the man who had gloried in being Chatham's
right-hand man, wrote of Chatham when Chatham was
dust and his lieutenant forgotten. Elaborate and
picturesque as it is, it discloses the fury of a dis-

appointed man wreaked on the cause to which he attributes his failure. It is the sneer of a worshipper burning the idol which he thinks has betrayed him, and attempting to warm himself at the fire. He had ruined his life by a great mistake; he had misread his lesson and misunderstood his master; but the fault, as is usual, seemed to the pupil not to be with himself, but with his teacher. After a cool survey of Bute and Holland, and the politicians of that kidney, he had decided that Chatham was the grand type, and only discovered too late that it was also an impossible one. He could readily see that he must be satisfied with less eloquence and a paler fire; but what seemed within his reach was the patriotic spirit, the attempt to be above and aloof from party, the combination by which the popular prophet cringed before the King, easy to emulate were the mysterious retirement and the haughty demeanour; easiest of all, the pompous fawning style which befogged and bewildered Chatham's contemporaries. All this Shelburne compassed, but what he never understood, until it was too late, was that these were not Chatham's aids but Chatham's drawbacks. There was something in the man, who almost discovered popular feeling in England, which was akin to inspiration; at any rate there was the occasional flash lighting up all his nature—the low and the dark as well as the brilliant and the sublime, the purlieus as well as the majesty of the structure, — which dazzled the beholder into seeing nothing but a great splendour.

Chatham had and sought no friends. The only shadow of such a relation that he knew was in his wife's unamiable family. Shelburne was, like Camden and Grafton, merely the superior disciple, and he was slow in discovering the difficulty of treading in the teacher's steps. In the meantime, having earlier in life gravely compromised his reputation for sincerity in a transaction which the popular and plausible Holland loudly stigmatised as a fraud, he further confirmed the general opinion of his subtlety by his imitation of his master in a sort of stilted finesse. He himself indefinitely strengthened this impression by his constant professions of guileless simplicity, and of a candour so effusive as to compel him to live in retirement for fear of self-betrayal.

Lampoons and caricatures are unanimous on this point. The testimony of his friends is only different in degree. Bentham extols his heart at the expense of his understanding, and charitably attributes the ambiguity of his patron to confusion of mind. But he admits a " wildness about him," and that he "conceived groundless suspicions about nothing at all." Further, Bentham declares that Shelburne " had a sort of systematic plan of gaining people." The third Lord Holland, who avows his partiality, gives much the same opinion. Rose, who was naturally and officially a judge of character, speaks of his discomfort in acting with Shelburne, who was "sometimes passionate or unreasonable, occasionally betraying suspicions of others entirely groundless, and at other times offensively flattering. I have frequently been puzzled to decide which part of his conduct was least to be tolerated." Perhaps an even more curious confirmation is afforded by Rayneval, who visited England as an envoy during the peace negotiations. "Lord Shelburne," he writes, "is not ignorant

of the suspicions which have been, and probably still
are, entertained in France as to his straightforward-
ness, and he feels them the more in proportion as he
believes that he has not deserved them.   I venture to
be of the same opinion, and if I say so, it is because I
consider my personal acquaintance and conversations
with Lord Shelburne have placed me in a position to
know him perfectly," and so forth.   This was in the
middle of September 1782, and in December he writes,
"You will perhaps ask me how it is possible to reconcile
the character I gave you of Lord Shelburne with his
conduct relative to the equivalent for Gibraltar," and
then he explains.   There lies the whole matter—Shelburne's good faith was always exemplary, but always in
need of explanation.

Some people seem to think that a reputation worse
than his deserts unfairly encumbered his career.
But, had his name been as untainted as Bayard's, his
style both in writing and speaking would have
accounted for the most inveterate distrust.   The
English love a statesman whom they understand, or at
least think that they understand.   But who could understand Shelburne?   Whether from confusion of head or
duplicity of heart his utterances were the very seed of
suspicion.   The famous lines in the *Rolliad* are merely
the versification of a speech he actually delivered.

A noble Duke affirms I like his plan,
I never did, my Lords, I never can :
Shame on the slanderous breath which dares instil
That I who now condemn advised the ill.
Plain words thank Heaven are always understood,
I could approve I said—but not I would,

Anxious to make the noble duke content,
My view was just to seem to give consent
While all the world might see that nothing less was meant.

In 1792 the King asked his advice, and Shelburne gave it in a memorandum which may be commended to any student of the man. It is a mere labyrinth of stilted ambiguities. Take again his speech on the Irish Union, from which both parties to that controversy to this day extract the strongest opinions in support of their respective views. Even his personal appearance, his sleek countenance and beady eye, imply the idea which is conveyed to the ordinary Briton by the word Jesuitical: and the caricatures of the time represent the outer wall of Lansdowne House as a mere rampart to screen his plots.

The pity of it is that his son, with much the same abilities, but richer by the warning, and aiming lower, achieved the position within the father's reach so exactly as to offer a reproachful contrast: the splendid noble, the patron of arts and letters, playing with rare dignity a public part, from duty rather than inclination; sought, not seeking; a strength, instead of a weakness, to his associates; a pillar, not a quicksand.

It was because Pitt had so truly measured Shelburne's character that he preferred any risk and any reproach to including his late chief in his Cabinet. He thus earned Shelburne's undying enmity; but that, as things stood, was rather an advantage than otherwise.

The composition of the Government was, however, the least of Pitt's embarrassments. The majority against him in the House of Commons was not less than forty or fifty, containing, with the exception of Pitt himself and Dundas, every debater of eminence; while he had, before the meeting of Parliament to prepare and to obtain the approval of the East India Company to a scheme which should take the place of Burke's. The Coalition ministers were only dismissed on the 18th of December 1783; but, when the House of Commons met on the 12th of January, 1784 all this had been done.

The narrative of the next three months is stirring to read, but would require too much detail for our limits. Never was excitement so high; never were debates of more sustained and fiery eloquence. But these are like the wars of Marlborough and Turenne,— splendid achievements, which light up the epoch, without exercising a permanent influence on the world; to us at any rate the sheet-lightning of history. On the day of the meeting of Parliament, Pitt was defeated in two pitched divisions, the majorities against him being 39 and 54. His government seemed still-born. His colleagues were dismayed. The King came up from Windsor to support him. But in truth he needed no support. He had inherited from his father that confidence which made Chatham once say, "I am sure that I can save this country, and that nobody else can;" which made himself say later, "I place much dependence on my new colleagues; I place still more dependence on myself." He had refused, in spite of the King's insistence, to dissolve; for he felt that the country required time, and that at the first blush it could hardly be expected to support so raw a Government. But he was daily preparing for the inevitable dispersal of a House of Commons sworn to hostility. To gratify

the independent members, he dallied with some idle
negotiations for the conciliation of the Portland Whigs.
He was able to show that the House of Lords was
with him by a division in his favour of 100 to 53.
He displayed the confidence of the King, who had
refused to grant any honours at the instance of the
Coalition, by the creation of several peerages. The city
of London, then the stronghold of Liberalism, vindicated
him from the suspicion of being a mere tool of the
Court by giving him its freedom. The East India
Company spared no exertion. They established a
Committee of Vigilance that sate permanently in Leadenhall Street. To every borough in the country they
sent a copy of Fox's bill with this message, " Our property
and charter are invaded, look to your own."

Two accidental circumstances also occurred to Pitt's
advantage. On his return from his city triumph, he was
waylaid and nearly murdered by an ambuscade of black-
guards opposite Brooks's club. So low had Fox fallen as
to be accused of instigating this outrage,—an imputation
which no one otherwise would have credited a moment,
but against which he thought it worth while to frame
an indecorous alibi. This occurrence would, perhaps
unreasonably, serve to attract the sympathy of Englishmen to the mob's victim, but another secured it.
The Clerkship of the Pells, a sinecure office worth not
less than £3000 a year, fell vacant on the very day that
Parliament met. It was universally expected that Pitt
would take it as of right, and so acquire an independence, which would enable him to devote his life to
politics, without care for the morrow. He had not
£300 a year; his position was to the last degree

precarious.   If now defeated, it was clear that he would
meet with no mercy, and that the King and the country
would fall bound into the hands of the Coalition, who
might almost achieve a permanent oligarchy to his
permanent exclusion.   Pitt disappointed his friends and
amazed his enemies.   He gave the place to Barré, making it a condition that Barré should resign the pension
received from Rockingham.   To a nation inured to jobs
this came as a revelation.   They were familiar with
great orators, and they had seen most of them provided
at one time or another with sinecures and pensions.   But
here was a youth of equal ability to whom it did not
seem to occur to place his own fortunes in competition
with the commonwealth—to whom money that could
benefit the State was abhorrent.   Even Thurlow could
not refrain from a growl of admiration.

Above and beyond all was the fact that Pitt,
young, unaided, and alone, held his own with the
great leaders allied against him.   Exposed to the
heaviest artillery that wit and fury and eloquence could
bring to bear, he was never swayed or silenced.   In
face of so resolute a resistance, the assailants began
to melt away.   Their divisions, though they always
showed a superiority to the Government, betrayed
notable diminution ; and, large or small, seemed to produce no more effect on the administration than if they
were the votes of a college debating society.   Worse
than all, they had an uneasy consciousness, ripening
daily into certainty, that the country was not with
them.   Addresses were pouring in, to applaud the conduct of the King in dismissing the Coalition.   Fox,
moreover, found that his party would not join him in

stopping the supplies. His one resource was a short
Mutiny Bill, which would prevent sudden or premature
dissolution. The current Bill would expire on the 25th
of March. Ministers were in a state of perplexity and
alarm. Burges, then Under Secretary of State, who
was, however, too vain a man to be a perfectly trust-
worthy authority, relates that they were relieved by a
simple expedient. It was found that more than once
the Mutiny Bill had been introduced into the House of
Lords, and coming thence had passed without question
in the House of Commons. Such a solution would not
be possible now, but it was adequate then. Pitt enclosed the paper of precedents in a note to Fox, asking
what course he intended to take. His answer is not
known, though sufficiently indicated by the result.
When the Committee on the Mutiny Bill was moved,
only two members showed themselves in opposition.

This was on the 9th of March. On the 25th of
March Parliament was dissolved, the announcement being
retarded by the unexplained theft of the Great Seal.
When the elections were over, the party of Fox, it was
found, had shared the fate of the host of Sennacherib.
The number of Fox's martyrs—of Fox's followers who
had earned that nickname by losing their seats—was
160. He himself had to await, in the constituency of
Orkney, the result of a scrutiny at Westminster, for
which he had been chosen. Conway and Lord John
Cavendish, two Whig princes, succumbed. Coke, the
Lord of Norfolk, shrank before the storm. The unknown and plebeian Wilberforce triumphed over the
Whig aristocracy of Yorkshire. Pitt himself forsook
the inglorious security of Appleby, and stood in the van

of the battle as candidate for the University of Cambridge, which had before rejected him. He ousted the two Coalition members, and secured the seat for life.

He won all along the line, but watched the last and longest contest with undisguised anxiety. Fox was carrying on one of those interminable combats which gave a singular celebrity to the constituency of Westminster. The poll was open for forty days. No effort was spared. Promises and menaces and drink and cash were all lavishly given; the proudest ladies stepped into the purlieus of the ancient city to secure highly flavoured votes; the Heir to the Throne himself took an animated part. In this respect the contest was unequal. On the side of Fox's opponent Lady Salisbury took the field; but her haughty canvass was easily routed by the energy, spirit, and grace of Georgiana, Duchess of Devonshire. At last, the first ministerial candidate headed the poll; but Fox easily distanced the second.

It was his only solace. On the other hand, he was excluded from office, with the exception of a few dying months, for life; more bitter still, he had to witness the complete triumph of the youth whom he could hardly yet consider a rival. Pitt, with the entire confidence of the King and the Legislature, was entrusted with a power such as no minister had ever wielded since the Revolution. And he was not yet twenty-five.

It is well here for a moment to pause and, with an undazzled eye, take stock of this splendid occasion. To idle observers it may appear that Pitt occupied his place by mere prerogative, aided by popular aversion to the Coalition. This is only a fraction of the truth. Fox, who had lately been the idol of the people,

would have been supported by the constituencies against
the prerogative, never popular, and against the King who
had not then attained popularity, had the case been so
simple; for they would have forgotten the Coalition in
resentment against the arbitrary authority of the
monarch.   But, as it was, the unpopularity of the King
was obliterated for ever by the odium of the Coalition.
Nor was North personally an object of aversion.   After
his resignation, he made a tour in the country, during
which he received ovations at once unexpected and
unusual.   The truth lies much deeper.   The King and
Pitt were supported on the tidal wave of one of those
great convulsions of feeling, which in Great Britain
relieve and express pent-up national sentiment, and
which in other nations produce revolutions.   "The
Public," says a shrewd contemporary observer, "and the
Public only, enabled Pitt to defeat the powerful phalanx
drawn up against him."

The country was sick of the "old lot"—the politicians who had fought and embraced and intrigued and
jobbed among themselves, with the result of landing
Great Britain in an abyss of disaster and discomfiture,
such as she had never known since the Dutch ships sailed
up the Medway.   For eight years there had been war
against scattered plantations of our own race, war ending in complete discomfiture; to which had been super-
added the perhaps more poignant humiliation of being
compelled to yield, not merely to the colonists, but to
the French.   And as, when the Dutch were insulting
and threatening the metropolis, the memories of men
recurred to the supremacy of Cromwell but a few years
before, so now there was an additional sting to those

still alive who remembered the glories of Chatham. Since then, at an expenditure of a hundred and forty millions, through eight agonising years, Englishmen had seen their armies in a constant condition of capitulation or defeat. They had hired Germans by the thousand to shoot down American Englishmen in vain. They had employed Red Indians to tomahawk their brethren without effect. Paul Jones had harried the coasts of Scotland, and people long remembered how the pious folk of Kirkcaldy had watched and prayed while his ships hove to within a mile of their shore. That night, by an interposition which the least devout hailed as a direct result of intercession, a gale arose and drove the flotilla away; but far in the Firth of Forth the traveller can still perceive, almost lost in a gaunt pier of the great bridge, the little simple fortification, which was erected against the audacious privateer. They had seen the fleet of England retiring before the squadrons of France and Spain, and yielding to them the dominion of the British Channel. Even the splendour of Rodney could not atone for this; while his instant supersession increased their distrust of the Government. They had seen their ambassadors suing for assistance at European courts in terms almost abject, and repulsed in terms of candid contempt. It was universally admitted that Great Britain had sunk to be a second, if not a third, rate Power. And if they were thus considered abroad, what was there to console our forefathers at home? They had beheld their capital half burned to the ground by mobs, which the Ministry seemed as unable to control as the people of New England. They had seen Government, in the sheer shame of impotence,

obliged to cede to Ireland whatever of independence the
Dublin Parliament demanded, from the impossibility of
sending a regiment to defend the island. What might
have been an act of grace, was only another abasement.
There was not a drop wanting to their cup of bitterness.
Was it for this they had spent their treasure and their
armies? There was something rotten in the State, and
the rottenness seemed to begin in their politicians.

The English mind moves slowly, but with exceeding
sureness, and it had reached this point at the election of
1784. The people had looked for a cause of these mani-
fold effects, and had found it in their rulers. Any doubts
they may have entertained would have been dispelled by
the speeches of Burke on economical, and of Pitt on parliamentary, reform. At the beginning of the reign they
had fancied that the Scots were at the root of the evil.
But, though Bute had long passed away from the political scene, matters had grown worse. And now they
found it authoritatively declared how deep the gangrene
of jobbery had eaten into the House of Commons ; how
one member received a large income as turnspit to the
King ; and how eight were purchased and nominated by
an Indian prince. Taxes might grow, and armies might
disappear, and the gazettes might reek of disgrace :
still, war loans and war contracts swelled the spawn of
corruption : still, successive ministers and their friends
filled their bottomless pockets, and found a solid set-
off to national dishonour in the pickings of national
profusion. Under North, political degradation seemed to
have reached its climax. There had been hope, indeed,
of Fox, who had denounced North in terms of masculine and indignant invective. But now he too had

embraced North; the accuser had sat down with the accused, and both were involved without nice discrimination in the common system of turpitude. As to the Whig figure-heads, they were possibly honest but certainly wooden. In their despair, men looked round for a saviour of society, who should cast the money-changers out of the temple of Government, and restore to Britain, not her former glory indeed, but a decent and honourable existence. At this moment, there appeared before them a young university student; rich with lofty eloquence and heir to an immortal name; untainted in character, spotless in life; who showed the very first day that he met Parliament as Minister a supreme disdain for the material prizes of political life. The auspices under which he obtained power were not indeed popular, but less odious than the combination he succeeded. To a jaded and humiliated generation the son of Chatham came as a new hope and a possible revelation. Here was one who would not be easily corrupted; nay, one who might stem the tide flowing so fast against us at home and abroad. In a few months, the elder Pitt had raised England from the ground and placed her at the head of Europe. Might not something be hoped of his son?

The change was thus not merely an epoch in the life of Pitt, but in English politics. It was hailed by the nation as a new departure. Nor did the situation lack the irony inseparable from great events; for there were piquant elements of miscalculation and anomaly. The anomaly lay with Pitt, the miscalculation with the King. Pitt, who had entered Parliament as a foe to prerogative and the friend of reform, was to become Prime Minister by a violent exercise of the one, and to lose sight for ever, with a faint exception, of the other. On the other hand, the risk run by the King had been immense: and it is only fair to say he had made proof of rare and signal courage. For he had played on the throw all that to him made a throne worth having. The general election of May, indeed, condoned his absolute action of December. But, had it fallen differently, he must have become as much the prisoner of party as Louis XVI. on his return from Varennes. And yet, while he stood to lose so much, his winnings, as he computed them, were small. He had reckoned on finding a minister who would execute his wishes, and be the pliant agent of a powerful monarch. But there is little doubt that in ridding himself of the tyranny of the Whigs, with the assistance of Pitt, he only exchanged one bondage for another. He had worked to procure for Pitt the majority which was henceforth to make Pitt independent of himself. There is evidence to show that from the first he dreaded, and in the end disliked, his too powerful minister. In their correspondence we find none of the fondness with which George III. addressed Addington or Eldon. The King's tone is rather that of a man in embarrassed circumstances, corresponding with the family solicitor. He was sensible that Pitt had him in his power, and that, should Pitt desert him, he must fall bound into the hands of Fox. Later on, he was suspected of meditating a possible resource in Grenville. But we doubt his seriously contemplating an emancipation from Pitt so long as Pitt, and indeed so long as Fox, should last. For the peculiarity of the position was that, apart from his own great qualities, the strength of Pitt lay in the aversion

of both King and people for Fox. Just as in the
opinion of the shrewd Auckland the opposition of Fox
had kept North in office, so now it largely helped to
sustain Pitt. Incapacity could not long have reposed on
mistrust; but so able and honest a Minister was served
to the end of his life by the generous extravagances of
Fox and the undying memory of the Coalition.

CHAPTER IV

FIRST YEARS OF ADMINISTRATION

THE first days of Pitt's power are not altogether pleasant to contemplate. His demeanour was unendurably
cold and repellent. He felt perhaps that it was necessary
for so young a minister to hold mankind at a distance;
or what had before been called shyness was now called
pride. At any rate, as the kind Wilberforce regretfully
notes, he did not make friends. His father had kept
two generations in a state of subjection and awe, but
Chatham was a consummate actor, and Pitt was not.
It is told of Chatham that when he met a bishop, he
bowed so low that his nose could be seen between
his knees. So appalling a suavity of demeanour inspired probably even more terror than his intolerable
eye. But Pitt's haughtiness was less sardonic; at any
rate, it was of a different kind.

His unfortunate bearing did him no good. A graver
charge against him at the moment of elevation is his
behaviour to Fox. Fox had been returned for Westminster. But the High Bailiff, instead of making a
return, sent in a statement of the number severally polled,
and an intimation that he had granted a scrutiny;—

a proceeding which could not be constitutional, as it might have excluded Westminster from representation for a whole parliament, should the scrutiny be prolonged into a measure of obstruction.   Pitt, however, under the influence of Sir Lloyd Kenyon, Master of the Rolls, sustained the action of the High Bailiff, and met with a well merited rebuff.   Nor was his action a mere incident of party warfare.   He threw into it all his energies, and the passion of a personal cause. Throughout the general election he had concentrated his attention on Westminster; he had been defeated, and now endeavoured to cover his repulse by proceedings which, as they were not adequate to prevent his powerful rival from sitting in the House of Commons, bore the appearance of personal rancour or personal mortification, and the even baser suspicion of an attempt to finally crush that rival's wrecked fortunes. On this issue Fox put forth new resources and splendours of eloquence.   He exceeded himself, by delivering what is often considered as the best of his speeches; and, more remarkable still, so well reported that Lord Holland declared in reading it, he fancied he heard his uncle's voice. But the Minister's resolution was worthy a better cause. Every omen pointed to disaster; the most sinister parliamentary portents and the marked hostility of public opinion failed to deter him.   In the face of shrinking majorities, of lukewarm friends, and a reluctant King, he persevered.   The result from the first was discouraging, and soon ended in collapse.   His majority on the address had been 168.   But in the first division on the scrutiny it fell to 97.   Within three weeks it sunk to 78, at the very moment when his majority on the India Bill was 211.

In the next session he fared worse, for on the 9th of February 1785 it had dwindled to 39. On the 21st of February it was but nine; while on the 4th of March Pitt found himself defeated by 38 votes; and the High Bailiff was compelled to make an immediate return. Pitt had mistaken the temper of the nation, and the complexion of his party. Englishmen delight in a fair fight and a fair victory; but nothing is so revolting to them as anything which bears the semblance of ungenerous treatment of a fallen enemy. The feeling of the country was reflected in his followers, who displayed more independence than Pitt had conceived possible. In this particular case, the demonstration against him was manly and justified. It is one of the rare occasions on which his parliamentary tact failed him; perhaps the only instance of personal pettiness to which he ever condescended. If it is not a surprising lapse of judgment and temper in a man of twenty-four, it is amazing when the general tenor of his character and career is considered.

If Pitt sustained humiliation on the scrutiny, it was forgotten in the general lustre of his statesmanship. In the interval between the 19th of December and the 12th of January he had not merely formed his Government, but he had prepared and procured the consent of the East India Company to a new India Bill. It had met, of course, with no mercy in debate, but had only been rejected by a reluctant majority of eight. He now reintroduced substantially the same measure, and obtained a division of 271 to 60 in its favour. It instituted that complex system of government and that Board of Control, which endured till the Act of 1858.

But in comparing it with Fox's notorious Bill, it is fair
to make one remark.   Fox had proposed to hand over
the patronage and power of India to irremovable
Commissioners for four years.   It was urged against
this scheme that by it, Fox, in or out 'of office, would
have through his appointed Commissioners all the
patronage of the East; and that for four years, whoever
might rule in England, he would rule in India.   The
same objection might, however, be urged against any
new body of Commissioners appointed under party
government; and so far as patronage was concerned, it
could hardly have been exercised in a more partisan
spirit for four years under Fox's arrangement, than it
was under Pitt's for eighteen.   Wielded by Dundas in
dexterous combination, he so arranged it, no doubt for
the mutual benefit of both, that the Eastern Empire of
which he was the trustee should be enriched by an
unceasing immigration from his own kingdom of Scotland.

Pitt's chief cares and eminent success of this session
were, however, connected with finance.   He had in a year
of peace to bring forward a war budget, having been left
with a deficit of six, and a floating debt of at least fourteen
millions, besides a debt of two millions to the Bank of
England and the usual deficiencies on the Civil List.
Moreover, smuggling had grown to such a height that it
required immediate and drastic remedies.   The leading
features of his financial operations were three.   Smuggling
was chiefly carried on in tea; it was calculated that the
consumption of illicit was double that of duty-paying tea.
To meet this, apart from more stringent regulations as
regards search, he lowered and varied the tea duty so as
to take away the smuggler's probable profit; while he

met the deficiency of revenue thus caused by an increase
of the window tax.   He calculated the population of
England to be six millions; four millions of whom, by
paying an increased window tax, should bring up the
revenue to at least the seven or eight hundred thousand
provided by the old tea duty, although they would pay
less for their tea, even with the new window tax thrown in,
than under the actual tea tax; while the remaining two
millions, consuming the cheaper teas and living in houses
of less than seven windows, would get their tea duty-free.

The second feature of his financial policy was that, for
the loans required to meet the deficit and the floating
debt, he accepted the lowest tender by public competition, thus abolishing for ever the corrupt and costly
favouritism which had disgraced previous loans.   By this
single measure he probably did more to purify Parliament than he could have effected by his Reform Bill.

The third was the variety of tax by which he raised
the additional revenue required.   Hats, raw silk, horses,
linens, calicoes, candles, licenses for dealers in excisable
commodities, bricks, tiles, shooting certificates, paper,
hackney coaches, gold and silver plate, the export of
lead, ale-licenses, race-horses, and postage were all taxed
to produce some £900,000.   On the night of his budget
(June 30, 1784) he moved 133 financial resolutions.
Some of his proposals, among them a coal tax, had to
be modified or withdrawn, and they are here stated in
their ultimate form; but Pitt's conciliatory method of
explanation produced scarcely less impression than the
capacity which he displayed in unfolding them.

The recess, after this busy and eventful session, he
spent between Putney and Brighton, studying, in con-

junction with Irish ministers and British merchants, the proper measures to give effect to his Irish policy. This period was marked by two incidents—one of transient, the other of permanent importance. The first was the entry into the Ministry of the cautious Camden; the other was the postponement of the opening of Parliament from the usual date at the beginning of November till the end of January.

The Houses met (January, 1785) under the cloud of European disturbances, evolved by the restless ambition of Joseph the Second in the Netherlands; a cloud soon dispelled. As regards domestic affairs, Pitt was able to point to the success of his financial measures. The revenue was displaying unwonted buoyancy; it was advancing by leaps and bounds; and the minister was able to promise the early creation of a sinking fund, so soon as he should have been able to dispose of the floating debts which he had inherited from the war. As to the measures for the suppression of smuggling, Fox himself acknowledged their efficacy. Pitt's reputation as a peace financier was established, and was to suffer no abatement.

His other measures were less successful. He suffered his final rebuff on the Westminster Scrutiny. For the third and, as it proved, for the last time, he brought forward (April 18, 1785) the question of parliamentary reform. He proposed to give seventy-two seats to London and the largest counties; these seventy-two seats to be obtained by the voluntary and compensated surrender of their franchise by thirty-six petty boroughs, while permanent provision was made for the future surrender of such boroughs under similar conditions of compensation and transfer. This last enactment would, he conceived,

make his measure final, self-adjusting, and complete, and
obviate all necessity for any further reform.

He displayed extraordinary zeal and ability on this
occasion. He personally canvassed his friends. He
summoned Wilberforce from the Riviera. He adjured
the Duke of Rutland to influence from Ireland York-
shiremen of weight in its favour. He declared to this
intimate friend that he regarded the success of his plan
as essential to the credit, if not the stability, of his
administration, as well as to the good government of the
country hereafter. Nay, he even implored the neutrality
of the hostile King, which was promised with the saturnine
comment that "The conduct of some of Mr. Pitt's most
intimate friends on the Westminster Scrutiny shows
that there are questions men will not by friendship be
biassed to adopt." The motion was defeated, whether
owing to the reluctance of members or the significant
silence of the monarch it is difficult to say.

But the capital measure of the session of 1785 concerned Ireland. Pitt's Irish policy was at this time
repeatedly defined by himself. It was large and statesmanlike. He accepted as irrevocable the settlement of
1782, which gave Ireland parliamentary independence ;
and he sought to unite the two countries on the sure
basis of commercial intercourse and common interest.
Were this accomplished, it would, he believed, remove
all possible danger and inconvenience from the duality
of legislatures. Nor was it a work that admitted of
delay ; it had to be done while the new institutions in
Ireland and their under-growth of tendencies were still
plastic, before gristle had hardened into bone. His aim
was to follow up this, the most urgent, with two other

measures; one a reform of the Irish Parliament, the other the conversion of the volunteers into a militia. But all hung together, all fell together.

His commercial scheme was embodied in eleven resolutions, concerted in the vacation, and passed by the Irish Parliament just before Pitt presented them to the House of Commons. Their object was to allow the importation, without increase of duty, of all produce from other countries, through Ireland into Great Britain and through Great Britain into Ireland; to reduce the duties on the produce and manufactures of both countries to the scale of that country where the duties were lowest; and to provide a contribution from Ireland to the imperial navy by enacting that, whenever the gross hereditary revenue of Ireland (which then stood at £652,000) should rise above £656,000, the surplus was to be applied to that object; only in a saving clause, introduced in Ireland, this last provision was not to take effect in time of peace, unless there was a just balance between income and expenditure.

Their general scope, however, was tersely embodied in the first resolution: "That Ireland should be admitted to a permanent and irrevocable participation of the commercial advantages of this country, when the Parliament of Ireland shall secure an aid out of the surplus of the hereditary revenue of that kingdom towards defraying the expense of protecting the general commerce of the Empire in time of peace."

Pitt's exposition of his policy was worthy of the subject. He denounced in the strongest terms the past treatment of Ireland by England. Until these last very few years, he said, the system had been that of debarring

Ireland from the use and enjoyment of her own resources; of making that kingdom completely subservient
to the interests and opulence of this country; without
suffering her to share in the bounties of nature, in the
industry of her citizens, or to contribute to the general
interests and strength of the Empire. This system
had counteracted the kindness of Providence and suspended the enterprise of man. It had been a policy of
keeping the smaller country completely subservient and
subordinate to the greater; to make the one, as it were, an
instrument of advantage; and to force all her efforts to
operate in favour, and conduce merely to the interest, of
the other. But this "system of cruel and abominable
restraint" had been exploded, and he aimed at a better,
a more natural, and a more equitable relation—a participation and community of benefits and a system of
equality and fairness which, without tending to aggrandise
the one or to depress the other, should seek the aggregate
interests of the Empire. On this general basis he moved
his resolutions; he had anxiously searched for the "best
means of uniting the two countries by the firmest and
most indissoluble bonds"; and this was the result.

As to the equivalent to be received from Ireland in
exchange for the commercial advantages conceded to
her, it was to be in exact proportion to the benefit she
derived from them. From the nature of the Irish
hereditary revenue, it would be an ingenious measure of
the success of the proposal and the advantage that Ireland
would reap from it; while, on the other hand, it would
be, by the same process of self-adjustment, scrupulously
fair towards England. For it consisted of certain
customs-duties, imposed on almost every species of goods

imported ; an excise duty upon some articles of the most
general consumption ; and a house tax levied on the
number of mouths in each. It was obvious, therefore, that
this revenue would necessarily increase, as soon as the new
arrangement began to take effect, and in exact proportion
to that effect : every article of which it was composed
being so closely connected with commerce, wealth, and
population. So much for the solace of Ireland. And for
the satisfaction of England he pointed out that, if little
should be given to England, it was because little had
been gained in Ireland ; so that, whether much or little
should be gained from it, England would have no cause
to be dissatisfied ; if much should be got, she would be
a gainer ; if little, it would be a proof that little of the
commerce of England had found its way to Ireland, so
that there would not be room for jealousy.

The policy and the speech were alike ingenious,
fruitful, and statesmanlike ; but in England the opposition of apprehensive interests was sustained and bitter.
Two months were spent by the House of Commons in
the examination and discussion of commercial representatives, headed and guided by Wedgewood. As a result,
Pitt found that he could not carry his original propositions. On the 12th of May (1785) he introduced a
score of remodelled resolutions. But the amendments
added to secure English, hopelessly alienated Irish support. All the new, as compared with the original, articles
were restrictive of Irish trade ; but the fourth resolution
attempted a restraint on the Irish Parliament. It en-
acted that all laws, which had been or should be passed
with reference to navigation in the imperial legislature,
should also apply to Ireland by laws to be passed

by the Irish Parliament. Fox saw his opportunity. He could not now defeat the propositions in England; but he could secure their rejection in Ireland. With extraordinary power and ability, he thundered against the surrender of legislative independence that the minister was demanding from Ireland. Where ministers, he declared, had not betrayed their imbecility they had been insidious; where they had not been insidious, they had been treacherous. It would have been more manly and more honourable to have plainly told the Irish, "that however desirous and happy we should be to serve you, yet, in justice to our own country, we find we cannot grant what we offered. Without being the ruin of many here, we cannot serve an equal number of you. Without exposing our own country and its manufactures and manufacturers to ruin, or without your yielding up the independency of your Parliament, we cannot grant the participation offered to you." And he bade farewell to the resolutions with the impassioned exclamation, "I will not barter English commerce for Irish slavery; that is not the price I would pay, nor is this the thing I would purchase." In that pithy sentence with consummate dexterity he combined the objections of both the English and the Irish. The note he struck readily resounded in Ireland. Grattan denounced the English propositions in a speech which the Viceroy described as incredibly eloquent, seditious, and inflammatory. Orde, the Chief Secretary, did not venture to proceed with them, and Pitt abandoned them for ever.

So passed away another of the rare and irrevocable opportunities of uniting the two countries. It is impossible to blame the Irish, jealous of any reflection on

their new legislative independence, and who had seen the
resolutions which they had passed suspiciously transmuted
in this direction. Nothing, again, can be more admirable
than the energy, the foresight, and the disregard of
popular clamour displayed by the young minister. There
is also some excuse for the opposition of Fox, because
Fox openly professed that he had never been able to
understand political economy. But when we consider
the object and the price; that the price was free trade
and the object commercial and, in all probability, complete
union with Ireland; that there was, in fact, no price to
pay, but only a double boon, to use Pitt's happy
quotation, "twice blessed; it blesseth him that gives
and him that takes," it is difficult to avoid the impression that there has been throughout the past history
of England and Ireland a malignant fate counteracting
every auspicious chance, and blighting each opportunity
of beneficence as it arises.

At any rate, Pitt, though he at first preserved the
confident language of persistence, abandoned hence-
forward this wise and kindly Irish policy. He felt that
the jealousy and prejudice which had driven Burke from
Bristol had abated little of their rigour; and that Irish
national sentiment, rooted deeply in the past, regarded
with classical apprehension the very gifts of the English.
His impressions were excusable, and even natural, in
view of the circumstances of the time. But all parties
may well regret that Pitt did not display on this occasion something of the same pertinacity that he did with
regard to his later Irish projects. In 1786 he included
Ireland in his commercial treaty with France, and Ireland
made no objection. This, however, did not encourage

him to resume his larger scheme. From this time forward, he appears to have turned his attention from Ireland, or at any rate to have looked more to that legislative union for which his most intimate friends, such as Rutland and Wilberforce, openly expressed their anxiety, and to which another juncture was soon to point.

But the abandonment of the Irish commercial propositions suggests a curious question. Why were they relinquished, and why were so many of the principal Government measures abandoned or defeated? We have seen that in May 1784 the Opposition lay crushed and almost obliterated at Pitt's feet. Since then, he had sustained defeat on the Westminster Scrutiny, on Parliamentary Reform, and had first to remodel and then to withdraw his Irish resolutions; he had also been compelled to take back his coal tax. In 1786 he was defeated on the government scheme of fortifications. In 1788, on the East India Declaratory Bill, he was again run hard, and thought to be in actual jeopardy.

Why was this powerful minister exposed to these rebuffs, in a Parliament elected so entirely for his personal support? The reason is partly special, and partly general. "It is a very loose Parliament," notes Eden, than whom there was no more acute observer, "and Government has not a decisive hold of it upon any particular question." Pitt soon made the same observation. "Do not imagine," he writes this year, "because we have had two triumphant divisions, that we have everything before us. We have an indefatigable enemy, sharpened by disappointment, watching and improving every opportunity. It has required infinite patience, management, and exertion to meet the clamour out of doors, and to prevent it infecting our supporters in the House. Our majority, though a large one, is composed of men who think, or at least act, so much for themselves, that we are hardly sure from day to day what impression they may receive." It is probable that, in view of Pitt's youth, his plans were not at first received with the confidence to which they were entitled, nor does it ever seem to have occurred to his supporters that any number of defeats of this nature could bring about his resignation. There can be no doubt that he bitterly felt these miscarriages; but it is also clear that no thought of resignation crossed his mind. This in itself would show how different was the condition of the House of Commons of those days from the House of Commons of these.

But the difference lay much deeper. The composition of a parliamentary majority at that time was that of a feudal or a Highland army. It was an aggregate of the followings of a few great chiefs, of whom the King himself was the principal. A powerful leader would make a sign and his followers disappear; one bugle call would be followed by another, until one day the whole array would have melted away, and the general be a lonely fugitive. What Clanronald or Lochiel had been in a military, Lord Lonsdale or the Duke of Norfolk were in a political campaign. And of those who were not at the beck of great mongers, fewer then than now feared the loss of their seat as the consequence of their parliamentary vote. Some sate for family boroughs; some who had paid four or five thousand pounds for their seat, knew that for the same price they could always secure another.

Public opinion, in so far as it existed, was a subtle and
indirect influence. The cohesive force of a party lay,
not in the power of the people, but in the patronage of
the minister. And so we shall find in those days many
more instances of a sort of personal independence in the
House of Commons than now, and a minister much
more frequently at the mercy of Parliament, of the
personal pique of some baffled noble, of a Duke of
Greenwich alienated by a Lord Oldborough's unsealed
letter, of a Temple resentful of withheld dignities. In
recent times a government, clearly designated by the
result of a general election, can generally remain in office
for the duration of a Parliament; as the pressure of the
majority, instant and weighty, not merely supports but
guides. But, in the last half of the last century, a
minister obtained comparatively little assistance from
public opinion, while he had to struggle with the secret
currents of royal and jobbing intrigue.

A curious illustration of parliamentary government
at this time is to be found in an analysis of the House
of Commons dated May 1, 1788, which has been recently
discovered among the papers of one of Pitt's private
secretaries. In it the "party of the Crown" is estimated
at 185 members. "This party includes all those who
would probably support His Majesty's Government under
any minister not peculiarly unpopular." "The independent or unconnected members of the House" (a party
which seems to have corresponded very much with the
Squadrone of the old Scottish Parliament) are calculated
at 108; Fox's party at 138; and that of Pitt at 52.
Even this unflattering computation is further discounted
by the remark that "of this party, were there a new

Parliament and Mr. P. no longer to continue minister, not above twenty would be returned." No document has thrown more light than this on the political system of this period.

In these days, too, a minister would expect some help from his colleagues. But Pitt could depend on no one but Dundas. Timidity at first made able men hold aloof. Afterwards, when Pitt had secured his mastery at the polls and in debate, it may, perhaps, be charged against him that he determined, during eight or nine years, that he should be sole and supreme minister, and that none should be admitted who would threaten that predominance. The ordinary vacancies in his Government were filled by men like Jenkinson—"Jenky," the subterranean agent of the King, who divided his studies between courts and commerce, and well understood both; —or Pitt's brother, Chatham, whose indolence swamped the superiority of his talents and the popularity of his manners. Grenville and Wellesley were not exceptions; for Wellesley only held a lordship of the Treasury, and no more than Grenville, Pitt's first cousin, in any degree menaced the minister's monopoly of parliamentary power. It was not till the stress of the French Revolution was upon him, that he summoned to his aid all the men of capacity that he could collect.

Pitt found some consolation for his Irish defeat, which he at first regarded as but temporary, in the purchase of Hollwood: an agreeable imprudence, which marked the beginning of his pecuniary embarrassments. There he planted and planned with all the enthusiasm which had marked his father's operations at Hayes and Burton Pynsent. But the Hollwood of Pitt has long disappeared.

The house he built has been demolished, and the woods
he planted can no more be traced.　There remains, however, an ancient, memorable oak ; stretched under which,
Wilberforce and he resolved on that campaign for the
abolition of the Slave Trade, which gave honour to the
one and immortality to the other.

CHAPTER V

In 1786 Pitt returned to a January meeting of Parliament, when the Duke of Richmond brought forward a scheme for the fortification of Portsmouth and Plymouth. This, as has been said, was defeated. On the other hand, the minister reached the culminating point of his financial fame by his plan for the redemption of the National Debt, which his contemporaries regarded as his highest claim to renown, and which is accordingly inscribed on the scroll to which he is pointing in Lawrence's majestic portrait. The merits of his plan were twofold. He created an independent Board of Commissioners for the reduction of the debt, to whom a million was to be annually paid; they were to be officials of the highest character and distinction: the Speaker, the Chancellor of the Exchequer, the Master of the Rolls, the Accountant General, the Governor and Deputy Governor of the Bank of England; and in this form the Board exists to this day. With the million allotted to them they were to purchase stock. This stock was not to be cancelled, and so would continue to bear interest; and this interest would be received by the Commissioners, and applied to the purchase of stock, in addition to the annual million placed at their disposal for the same purpose.

The signal merit of this scheme was that by these means the Sinking Fund so formed was in the hands of a permanent and substantive body, whose action could only be controlled by the direct interference of Parliament, and could not be tampered with for the passing needs of a ministry. There was this further indirect advantage, that there was extracted from the pockets of the taxpayer for the redemption of debt not merely the annual million, but also the amount of the interest of the stock purchased. These were the real benefits; of which the second was not merely subordinate, but kept in the background. The attractions held forth were far more dazzling, but absolutely fallacious. The great discovery was supposed to be the accumulation of the fund at compound interest. This was the golden vision held out by Dr. Price, with the fanaticism of an alchemist; a fanaticism which culminated in the declaration that " war, while such a scheme was going on, would increase its efficacy." The error was not merely fundamental, but disastrous; for the nation was deluded into the belief that it mattered little what was spent in war, if only the Sinking Fund were regularly maintained. As a matter of course, however, the compound interest, as it was called, was only the produce of taxation or loans. To grow of its own virtue and essence, in the manner described by Price, the Sinking Fund should have been invested in some remunerative form of productive industry, with a constant reinvestment of the profits; as it was, it only represented the sums, whether in the

shape of annual capital or of the interest paid on the stock
purchased, that Parliament chose to set apart for the
payment of debt. All the money, in fact, came from the
same source. Its real value lay in the fact that it was
an honest and steadfast method of paying off debt; and
experience tells us that debt is in reality only reduced
by the patriotic resolve of Parliament; which is rendered
doubly efficient when, as in Pitt's scheme, the Fund
devoted to debt redemption is placed beyond the casual
interference of a needy minister, and when its operations
are scarcely perceptible to a public, justly if sometimes
ignorantly, impatient of taxation. It is probable that
Pitt grasped this truth, and was not for long the
dupe of Price's fantastic calculations. Frere, at least,
says that this was so, and that Pitt mainly valued his
Sinking Fund as a means of inducing the nation to
submit to the irksome and unpopular operation of paying off debt.

The most striking feature of the session is the opening
of that long campaign against Warren Hastings, which,
as regards its duration and the forces brought into play,
resembles rather some historic siege of ancient times
than a judicial investigation into the conduct of an
individual. That great man had returned in 1785,
conscious of eminent services, of having strengthened,
if not preserved, our Indian Empire; conscious also
of having committed acts which might be easily condoned by Eastern morality and by the pressure of
dire necessity, but which could hardly bear the most
indulgent inquisition of a British Parliament. He had,
however, powerful allies; the Court, the East India
Directors, and, it was believed, the Ministry with its

majority. Indeed, with the exception of the leaders of the Opposition, his only enemy seemed to be his own intolerable agent. But he was ambushed by the undying rancour of Francis, and the sleepless humanity of Burke.

The episode may be said to have occasioned more eloquence (including Macaulay's), than any event in history. But we touch it only as regards Pitt's connection with it. On the first charge, that relating to the Rohillas, Dundas was spokesman of the Government, and defended Hastings, though he had once bitterly attacked him with regard to this very transaction. Pitt sate silent. On the second, that relating to Benares, one of less gravity, Pitt's support was confidently anticipated by the friends of Hastings, and he spoke mainly in Hastings's defence. But towards the end of his speech he astonished the whole House by declaring that, while he approved the demand for aid and a fine for non-compliance, he thought the fine too large, and should therefore vote for the resolution ; not thereby, he expressly stated, pledging himself that there should be an impeachment, but only, if there were to be an impeachment, that this should be included as one of the articles. The sensation was immense. There was open revolt. Both Paymasters, Grenville and Mulgrave, rose from his side to speak and vote against him. But he maintained his majority. For the Rohilla charge, which he had allowed to be opposed, there had voted 67 against 119 ; for the Benares charge there voted 119 against 79.

About few incidents of Pitt's long administration has there been so much controversy. Hastings had made so sure of his support, and had, indeed, received it on a

more damning charge; the point on which he gave his
vote seemed so comparatively insignificant; the occasion
for putting himself in direct antagonism, not merely to
the King but to his own subordinates, was so small,
that a score of reasons have been discovered for his
behaviour. He was jealous of Hastings; he wished to
draw a red herring across the path of the Opposition;
he had had a midnight interview with Dundas; Dundas
was jealous of Hastings : we can imagine the hum and
buzz of political insects. But there is no necessity for
any explanation, except the straightforward one that
after a detailed examination of the charges and answers,
completed after the Rohilla debate, and discussed at
length with Dundas, Pitt was led to the conviction that
he could not defend Hastings, or risk the reputation of
his Government by associating it with the acts of the
Hastings administration. Indeed we now know that this
was so. The debate on the Rohilla charge was on the
2d of June; that on the Benares charge on the 13th of
June. On the 10th of June Pitt writes to Eden : "I have
hardly hours enough to read all the papers necessary on
that voluminous article" (Benares). And Dundas writes
to Lord Cornwallis, speaking of Pitt and himself : "The
truth is, when we examined the various articles of
charges against him with his defences, they were so
strong, and the defences so perfectly unsupported, it
was impossible not to concur." That Pitt was not
deeply chagrined at seeing his great foes absorbed in a
different campaign, which should engross their energy
of attack, may readily be believed; but such a consideration is totally insufficient to explain a course which
implied a rupture with his own friends, infinitely more

distressing to him than a daily renewal of his accustomed
conflicts with the Opposition.   It may even be said without extravagance that, habituated as he was to these contests, and confident of success in them, he would have
regretted rather than promoted their cessation.

The recess was uneventful but for the signature of a
commercial treaty with France, on which Pitt employed
the polite perfidy of his most recent convert William
Eden.   When Parliament met on the 23d of January
1787 its conclusion was announced, and two days afterwards it was laid upon the table.   It was at once
made the subject of bitter attack by Fox, for reasons
which increase our admiration of the superhuman parts
that could obliterate such amazing vagaries.   In the
very language that he reprobated most strongly six
years afterwards, he thundered against any connection
or friendship with France.   It may be said that in one
case he was attacking a monarchy, and in the other
defending a republic.   But it was not a question of
government, so far, at any rate, as this speech was
concerned.   " Past experience proved that whenever
France saw this country weak, and thought her incapable
of effectually resisting, she seized the opportunity, and
aimed at effecting her long-desired destruction.   If the
minister would look over the correspondence in the
Foreign Office he would find the warmest assurances of
friendship from France up to the very moment of
breaking with us and joining America against us.   It
was idle, therefore, to hope that she would forget her
resentment, and abandon a purpose she had so long and
uniformly endeavoured to achieve."   This was not the
random rhetoric of faction, but the expression of his

matured and deliberate opinion.   In November 1785 he
had written to Fitzpatrick : "The worst of all is that I
am far from sure whether the country in general would
not like a good understanding with France (from the
vain hopes of a durable peace) better than anything.   I
am sure that any minister who can like it must not only
be insensible to the interests of his country, but to any
feelings of personal pride : for, depend upon it, whenever you are in such a situation the French will make
you feel it enough."

This strange opposition, though supported by the
heaviest artillery of Burke and Sheridan and Francis,
was absolutely futile ; and the address in favour of the
treaty was carried by 236 to 116.   Nothing in all Pitt's
career is more remarkable and more creditable than the
bold disregard of narrow prejudices and the large
conciliatory spirit which he displayed in framing
and concluding this treaty.   But the hostility of Fox,
though unavailing, was unrelenting and persistent, and
indeed, with the charges against Hastings, took up the
greater part of the session.   The operations with regard
to Hastings, so far as they concern the subject matter of
this book, may be dismissed in a sentence.   After the
most famous of all English orations had been delivered
by Sheridan, Pitt had spoken in support of the Begum
charge.   This made the impeachment inevitable.   A
formal resolution to this effect was unanimously carried,
and taken up to the House of Lords by Burke.   The
episode illustrates in the highest degree the power and
probity of Pitt.   He had held Hastings in the hollow of
his hand.   He, and he alone, had pronounced judgment;
and pronounced it against his own interest.   All the forces

of politics, with the exception of a small Opposition, were in favour of the great governor.   There can be little doubt that had Pitt given his vote for Hastings, he would have done what many men, as honest as he, were able conscientiously to do, and would have gratified the Court, the Company, and the mass of the Commons.   But his amazing authority was not more conspicuous than the purity of his rectitude.   He declined to associate himself with those who held that the end could justify the means, even for the construction of an empire or in the atmosphere of the East.   He gave his decision as calmly as a judge in chambers ; while Britain and India abided meekly by the decree of this young gentleman of twenty-eight.

Probably the most useful work of the session was a plan for the consolidation and simplification of the various duties levied for purposes of revenue.   These had gradually lapsed into a condition of confusion and complexity, involving great difficulty in collection and some loss to the Exchequer.   The intricacy of the subject may be judged from the fact, that the remedial resolutions were numbered by the hundred, and even the thousand; and the success of the proposal by the eulogy extorted from the truculent hostility of Burke.   Further detail is beyond the limits of a sketch like this.   So, too, is the scandal with respect to the Prince of Wales—his debts, his lies, and his marriage—which engrossed much of the session, and probably all the attention that what is called Society had leisure to devote to politics.   It is merely necessary to observe Pitt's stern attitude, and absolute refusal to agree to any parliamentary address to the King for the payment of the Heir Apparent's debts.

He had not long to wait for the result of his action in this matter.

The health of George III. seemed to promise a long life. As a young man, he had been warned by the precept and example of his uncle, the Duke of Cumberland, that the danger of their family lay in a full habit of body, and he had struggled against the hereditary tendency to corpulence with energy and success. He spent days in the saddle. His passion for exercise wore out his stoutest equerries. The simplicity of his daily fare was such as to excite scarcely less mirth among the wags and wits of London, than the cool solitude of Richmond's kitchen. But he had overdone his remedy. Already, in 1765, he was said to have been attacked by mental aberration. In the autumn of 1788 he was again stricken. Of all imaginable accidents the death or incapacity of the sovereign seemed the only one that could affect the position of the minister. It was known that, in either of those events, the Prince of Wales would at once dismiss the statesman, who had not merely withstood the proposal for the payment of his debts, but who was the foe of all his personal and political friends.

It seemed clear that a regent would have to be appointed, and the question at once assumed several different phases. Pitt maintained that it was for Parliament to name a regent, and to fix his powers; that it was the absolute and undeniable right of the two Houses, on behalf of the people, to provide for the revival of what he erroneously called the Third Estate. Fox improdently declared that "in his firm opinion the Prince of Wales had as clear, as express a right to assume the reins of government, and exercise the power of sovereignty during the continuance of the illness and incapacity with which it had pleased God to afflict His Majesty, as in the case of His Majesty's having undergone a natural and perfect demise;" an opinion which the Prince of Wales was compelled to disavow. The Parliament of Ireland saw in this difficulty an opportunity of asserting its independence; and, without waiting for the action of the British Legislature, accorded an unconditional regency to the Heir-Apparent.

At Westminster the limitations proposed were strict, but not unduly so when the nature of the case is considered. The view of the Ministry, as stated by themselves, was that, "while they considered the temporary exercise of the royal authority on His Majesty's behalf and during His Majesty's illness as essentially different from the actual possession of the Crown, they have at the same time been anxious to extend that authority which they could conceive essential or necessary for the temporary administration of the King's power." Pitt has been accused of attempting to maintain an authority independent of the sovereign and Parliament, because his Bill handed over the royal household, involving an expenditure of some £200,000 a year, and vast patronage, to the Queen, and therefore presumably to his own control. It was contended that his action was analogous to that of Fox in framing his scheme for India; and that similarly he would retain an irresistible influence and patronage, which could be affected neither by prerogative nor vote.

Those, who argued thus, ignored the keystone of this policy—the opinion of the best experts that the King's disorder was only temporary. No doubt, when the King's madness was declared, the first impression of his physicians was that it was incurable, and under those circumstances Pitt prepared for a prolonged exclusion from public life. But these doctors spoke with almost absolute ignorance of insanity; and, before the Bill for a regency was introduced, Willis, who spoke with almost absolute authority, predicted a speedy convalescence. The regency, then, for which Pitt was making provision, was not one for an indefinite number of years, but for at most a few months, or even weeks. Would it then have been well for the minister to hand over the King's household, his personal surroundings and personal associates, to the caprice of the Prince of Wales; that his old servants might be sent about their business to make way for the pimps and the blacklegs, the Jack Paynes and the George Hangers, who formed the Prince's Court, so that the King's first returning rays of reason might rest upon the faces that he most detested—on the parasites and boon companions of his debauched son? Such a state of things might have renewed the disease of the Sovereign, and was, at any rate, wholly unsuited to a fleeting and temporary regency.

The restrictions, however, such as they were, the Prince accepted, though with the worst grace in the world. The appetite of the Opposition was not such as could afford to wait. "I think it certain that in about a fortnight we shall come in," writes Fox, who counted eagerly on obtaining office by the prerogative of the new regent in disregard and defiance of Parliament; the very proceeding which had inspired him with such piercing philippics against his rival five years before. The

Minister prepared to fall with dignity. He had been, indeed, for the last two years, less a prime minister than a dictator; he ruled England, and loomed large in Europe. He now made unostentatious preparations to resume his practice as a junior at the bar. The merchants of London met, and voted £100,000 to place him beyond the accidents of politics. Pitt might without cavil have taken this offering, so honourable to both parties. But he would not even entertain it. He waved it aside with disdain. "No consideration upon earth," he said, "shall ever induce me to accept it." And yet, at the time, he was insolvent.

One may be permitted to regret that he was not allowed to pass for a month or two from his seat of power to a cell in Lincoln's Inn. History, however, was denied so picturesque an episode. While the Regency Bill was passing, the King was recovering. Before it was out of committee in the Lords he was receiving his ministers. The situation was almost ludicrous. A week later it would have been his duty to give his royal dissent to the Regency Bill. The Ministry of Fox, already overdue some weeks, melted into space. English rats, like Aubrey and Queensberry, cursed their evil star. The rats of Dublin Castle endeavoured to return, not wholly without success. As if to show that the humour of the scene was inexhaustible, there arrived at this juncture the luckless Irish deputation with an absolute offer of the regency to the Prince of Wales. They were received with universal hilarity, which their keen sense of the ridiculous made them, we may be sure, the first to feel. Their appearance was the crowning mortification of the discomfited Heir Apparent. The dignity of the delega-

tion in the presentation of their address, which had to
be accomplished, was indeed preserved by his genial
grace.   But no charm of manner could disguise the fact
that Pitt once more reigned supreme, and that the
Opposition had once more relapsed into outer darkness.
For the Minister enjoyed at once the gratitude of the
King, the enthusiasm of the masses, and the almost
blind confidence of Parliament.   It was his highest
point of fortune and power; an elevation that no other
minister has attained.

Fortune, moreover, had not exhausted her irony.
She seemed determined to show how entirely this
puissant minister was her plaything.   He had found in
the plenitude of his power that he held it by the precarious tenure of the King's health.   He was now to
realise that there was another frail life to be reckoned
in that lease of office.   While London was illuminating
for the King's recovery, Lord Chatham lay mortally ill.
So grave was his malady that the hunters after Providence had fixed on Grenville as the new minister.   For
Lord Chatham's death, by the grim humour of our constitution, would have removed Pitt from the Commons
to the Peers.   In the prime of life and intellect, he
would have been plucked from the governing body of
the country, in which he was incomparably the most
important personage, and set down as a pauper peer in
the House of Lords.   It would have been as if the
Duke of Wellington in the middle of the Peninsular
War had been transferred by the operation of constitutional law to the government of Chelsea Hospital.
The system, in which Burke could find no flaw, had
ruled that the lack of an elder brother should be

thus punished, and that the accident of an accident should have power to blight this great career. Fortunately for Pitt and for the country, Lord Chatham recovered. Strangely enough, in this very year, Fox was nearly overtaken by a similar calamity. He was indeed actually addressed as Lord Holland, under the belief that his nephew was already dead.

And elsewhere the fates were spinning new threads, weaving new combinations, and shifting in their most tragic mood the circumstance and destiny of the world. The cauldron was simmering into which all parties and politics and Pitt himself were to be plunged, to emerge in new shapes. Within three months the guns that were fired in London for the King's recovery were echoed in Paris as the first signals of the long agony of a King's downfall; the Bastille had fallen, and the French Revolution had begun. Outside France that event most deeply affected Englishmen, and of all Englishmen Pitt, the spoiled child of fame and fortune.

CHAPTER VI

THE FRENCH REVOLUTION

WHILE the eyes of all Europe were fixed on Paris, Pitt ostentatiously averted his gaze. He was deaf to the shrieks of rage and panic that arose from the convulsions of France. He determinedly set himself, to use the phrase of Candide, to cultivate his own garden and ignore all others. Let France settle her internal affairs as she chooses, was his unvarying principle. It is strange to read the uneventful record of the flat prosperous years as they passed in England from July 1789 to January 1793, and to contrast them with the contemporary stress and tumult in Europe.

The history of England and of Pitt during this period hardly fills a page. Pitt's budgets—to him the most important events of the year—are, with one exception, brief. The salient questions are questions of emancipation. There are two personal episodes, great but not equal: the final dismissal of the intolerable Thurlow, and the heroic quarrel between Fox and Burke. Thurlow had, as Pitt's Chancellor, both publicly and privately, led the opposition to Pitt's Government. The origin of the grudge that produced this scandal cannot now be

ascertained: some unguarded phrase had probably
rankled. Thurlow relied absolutely on the King, and
thought himself royally impervious to ministerial change.
He had been Chancellor with North, with Fox, and with
Shelburne; he could well afford to snap his fingers at Pitt.
He was therefore taken by surprise, but blurted out the
cynical truth: "I did not think that the King would
have parted with me so easily. As to that other man
(Pitt) he has done to me just what I should have done
to him if I could." The schism between Fox and Burke
is not merely one of the most dramatic scenes and one
of the most interesting personal passages in history, but
it marks a great epoch in party growth. A thick crust
of Whiggism was sloughed off, and there appeared a first,
raw, callow germ of the Liberalism that was to grow
in silence for forty years, and then assume a sudden
and overwhelming preponderance. There were some
revolutionary symptoms in the country, notably in
Scotland, where they were most justifiable; but system-
atised repression had hardly yet begun. It was difficult
to listen to Pitt, and believe that there was anything
more stirring in the world than the tax on female servants,
or the subjection of tobacco to excise. There was indeed in
1790 a dissolution of the Parliament which had now lived
six years; but it was uneventful, as it fully renewed the
mandate to Pitt. Tranquillity was only occasionally interrupted by the sonorous voice of the Minister, proclaiming, as from a muezzin's minaret, the continued
peace and prosperity of the Empire. Historians have
hardly done justice to the dogged determination with
which Pitt ignored the French Revolution.

So far from this being a period of coercion, it was one

of almost competing liberalism.   Attempts were made—reluctantly opposed by the Minister under the pressure of the bishops—to repeal, in the interest of nonconformists, those obsolete clauses of the Test Act which still remained on the statute-book.   The demand of Roman Catholics for the abolition of some of the disabling enactments by which they were oppressed, was actually acceded to. Fox introduced a Bill, substantially the same as one that had been ineffectually proposed by Chatham, for enabling juries to give a verdict as to the character of an alleged libel as well as to the fact of its publication.   He naturally received the warm support of Pitt; and the warm support of Pitt as naturally ensured the bitter hostility of Pitt's chancellor.   Thurlow, however, was only able to delay the measure for a single session.

On an even nobler stage than that of domestic emancipation, Fox and Pitt were able to display a generous rivalry in the cause of freedom.   In 1788 the physicians declared that Wilberforce could not live a fortnight.   On his death-bed, as he believed, Wilberforce exacted from Pitt a solemn promise to undertake the cause of the abolition of the Slave Trade.   In May, therefore, of that year Pitt, ardently supported by Burke and Fox, induced the House of Commons to resolve unanimously to take the question of the Slave Trade into consideration during the next session; and a Bill for its provisional regulation was actually carried.   In 1789 Wilberforce was able to exert his own mellifluous eloquence in the cause.   But it was in 1792 that Pitt set an imperishable seal on his advocacy of the question, by the delivery of a speech which all authorities concur in placing before any other effort of his genius; and certainly

H

no recorded utterance of his touches the imaginative flight
of the peroration.   He rose exhausted, and immediately
before rising was obliged to take medicine to enable him to
speak.   But his prolonged and powerful oration showed
no signs of disability ; indeed, for the last twenty minutes
he seemed, said shrewd critics, to be nothing less than
inspired.   He burst as it were into a prophetic vision of
the civilisation that shall dawn upon Africa, and recalled
the not less than African barbarism of heathen Britain ;
exclaiming, as the first beams of the morning sun pierced
the windows of Parliament, and appeared to suggest the
quotation—

> Nos . . . primus equis Oriens afflavit anhelis,
> Illic sera rubens accendit lumina Vesper.

Fox was loud in his generous admiration.   Windham,
an even more hostile critic, avowed that, for the first time,
he understood the possible compass of human eloquence
Sheridan, most hostile of all, was even passionate in his
praise.   Grey, who ceded to none in the bitterness and
expression of his enmity, ceded also to none in his
enthusiasm of eulogy.   To those who consider Pitt a
sublime parliamentary hack, greedy of power and
careful only of what might conduce to power, his
course on the Slave Trade, where he had no interest
to gain, and could only offend powerful supporters,
may well be commended.

It is now, however, necessary to turn from the recital
of home politics to the position abroad, where Europe
was watching with awe and apprehension the gathering
portents which presaged some unknown horror of
convulsion.

It is doing Pitt no injustice to say that, in the earlier years of his administration, his mind was given rather to domestic questions than to foreign affairs. The peace of 1783 found the vessel of the State, to resume the ancient and imperishable metaphor, in so grievous a condition that the first object of the captain was neces- sarily to repair and refit her, so that at some future date she might once more take the seas, though with a less imperial bearing. He had, indeed, to restore vital warmth and consistence to the shattered fragments of empire. He had, therefore, at once applied himself to place on a permanent and workable footing those novel relations, which had been hurriedly adjusted with Ireland under the pressure of calamitous defeat. He had strained every nerve to restore the ruined finance of the country, which was always the darling object of his political life. And, moreover, at the head of a passive and silent host, he had to maintain his position against the most powerful artillery of debate ever directed against a Treasury Bench. What wonder, then, if he had but little attention to give to those ex- ternal complications in which Great Britain could at the best play so subordinate a part? Even during the grave crisis in Holland, which first forced foreign affairs upon his notice, the only letter for months that he addressed to our minister at the Hague was to inquire as to the operation of the Dutch succession duties, in the hope that an analogous tax might furnish him with a new financial resource. At the same time it would be unfair to Chatham to suppose that foreign policy, on which he so largely built his own fame, occu- pied a secondary place in the training of his favourite

son. It cannot be doubted that Pitt would learn from
his father that a foreign policy required firmness and
purpose; that in that, as in other things, vacillation
was the one unpardonable sin; but that the arm of this
country should never be put further forward than it
could be maintained. Even in those days of exhaustion,
our means were less inadequate to our ends than now;
we were less scattered over the world; and our army,
relatively to the armies of the Continent, was respect-
able, and even powerful. Nevertheless Pitt, as we
shall see, had to draw back, although his first steps on
the Continent were marked with something of the happy
audacity of Chatham.

It was in Holland that his first complication arose.
On that familiar board all the great powers of Europe
were moving their pawns—the fitful philanthropist,
Joseph the Second, who had opened the game with his
usual disastrous energy; the old fox at Berlin; the French
monarchy, still bitten with its suicidal mania of foment-
ing republics against Great Britain; and the crafty voluptuary of St. Petersburg. The game lay ultimately
between England and Prussia on one side, and France
on the other, though it is hardly worth recalling now.
Harris, afterwards Lord Malmesbury, represented the
English interest with consummate dexterity, but the
final success lay with the big battalions of Prussia.
Nevertheless, honour is due to the firm attitude of the
British Government; and the treaties of alliance
between Great Britain on the one side, and Prussia and
Holland on the other, marked the first diplomatic
success that England had achieved for a generation.

We obtain, too, in this transaction an interesting

glimpse of Pitt's policy. Lord Malmesbury has preserved for us the minutes of a cabinet held on the 23d of May 1787. Pitt then said that, though war was only a possible and not a probable result of the affair, yet that the mere possibility should make England pause, and consider whether anything could compensate for arresting the growing affluence and prosperity of the country —a growth so rapid as to make her in a few years capable of grappling with any force that France could raise. He was, in fact, nursing England through the convalescence after the American War for the possibility of a great effort; and it was difficult, by any allurements of foreign success, to induce him to forsake the course which he had marked out, until the fulness of time should come.

A second complication arose with Spain. That great country seemed in the last state of decrepitude. Her monarchy and her religion, the bases of her former splendour, were fast rotting into superstitions; but she abated no jot of her highest historical pretensions. Her court was the common ground of priests and gamekeepers; her army, navy, and finance were a vast scene of ruin. Her princes burlesqued even the Bourbon passion for the chase, and shrank from no extravagance in the name of sport. One day they would bombard with artillery the 100,000 head of large game that haunted the vast domains of Aranjuez; on another they would have a solemn battue of all the little birds that fluttered through the gardens and pecked at the fruit. And yet Spain was taken almost as seriously by others as by herself. Pitt himself, in giving his reasons for abandoning the Russian armaments, spoke of the gaining

Spain as one of the chief objects of the concession.
She was now governed by that king who was to hand
over Spain and the Indies to Napoleon like a dish
at breakfast, and vanish ingloriously out of history with
his queen and their favourite at Bayonne.   In 1789 an
English vessel was seized off Vancouver Island by two
Spanish ships of war, and her crew imprisoned on the
ground that a trespass had been committed against the
sovereign rights of Spain.   This was not a matter which
the most pacific minister could afford to ignore; one
who loved peace less might have easily fanned England
into as fierce a flame as was roused by the alleged loss
of Jenkins's ears.   But Pitt kept his negotiations as
secret as he could.   At last, in 1790, a vote of credit had
to be asked, and the usual measures taken as for a
possibly immediate war.   The situation was further
complicated by the French Government—then a government half-way between the Monarchy and the Terror
—fitting out a fleet as a measure of precaution.   This
menace had at least the advantage of showing the
anxiety of Pitt to avoid all interference or contact with
France.   He pursued a firm but conciliatory course, and
the Court of Spain, after one or two mysterious lurches,
agreed to a convention honourable to England and not
dishonourable to herself.

So far all had been well.   Without war the minister
had raised his reputation, and England had once more
raised her head.   It is true that peace had been preserved in the main by the interior complications of
France.   Spain had appealed to France for aid under
the Family Compact of 1762; but the French Assembly,
in considering the question, had wandered off into

constitutional discussions, which indirectly landed her in peace; to which conclusion a naval mutiny at Brest may also have contributed. On this abstention Florida Blanca, the Spanish minister, had grounded the necessity of his concession to England. It is also true that Pitt had spent over three millions in naval preparations. Yet it seems clear that the powerful fleet, thus produced "in the readiest and most perfect state ever known in the annals of Great Britain," as Auckland writes, was scarcely less effective than the neutrality of France in determining the attitude of Spain; and the heaviest peaceful expenditure of this sort is much less costly than the smallest European war.

So far, then, all had been smooth and peaceful and cheap. But now a change was to come. Pitt was to put out his hand too far, and to be compelled to withdraw it with some appearance of discomfiture. If there is one point on which history repeats itself, it is this: that at certain fixed intervals the Russian Empire feels a need of expansion; that that necessity is usually gratified at the expense of the Turk; that the other Powers, or some of them, take alarm, and attempt measures for curtailing the operation, with much the same result that the process of pruning produces on a healthy young tree. One of these periods had occurred in 1791. The war declared by Catherine II. was running the usual course. The Russians had gained several decisive victories, and were preparing to reap the fruit of them. During the three years and a half that the war had lasted, Pitt had not been inactive. A main result of the operations in the Netherlands had been the conclusion of an offensive and defensive alliance between Holland,

Prussia, and Great Britain. In 1788 these powers had by their attitude averted the destruction which Gustavus III. of Sweden had brought on himself, at the hands of the Danes and Russians, in rashly attacking the Muscovite Empire. Again, in 1790, they had had no difficulty in detaching Austria, then governed by Leopold II., not merely a prince but a statesman, from the Russian alliance. And now, in 1791, their object was to induce Russia to content herself with a smaller share of recent conquests than was agreeable to her, and more especially to insist on the cession by her of the fortress of Oczakow at the entrance of the Dnieper into the Black Sea, which she had taken with an appalling loss of life at the close of 1788.

In this policy of the triple alliance, it is necessary to note that Prussia took an eager part, but Holland none. Pitt himself was strenuous. Chatham had avowed himself " quite a Russ," and the traditions of the Whig party had pointed in the same direction. But foreign policy necessarily varies with the varying importance of states. There is, indeed, no such a thing as a traditional foreign policy in the sense of its being necessary and inevitable, any more than, in all conditions of the atmosphere, a ship carries the same traditional sails, or a man wears the same traditional clothes. The instinct of self-preservation guides the European powers with the same certainty as weather moves sheep on the hill; it has at different periods produced combinations against the dominion of Charles V. and against the dominion of the Ottomans, against France and against Russia, against Venice and against the Pope. On this occasion there was no necessity for Whigs to be friendly to Russian policy. The

Empire of Catherine the Second was a very different affair to the Empire of Peter the Great. It was absorbing Poland, it was threatening the Mediterranean, it had swallowed the Crimea, it had become a European Power. Nevertheless, it might well be questioned, if war, without Austria, and with the aid only of Prussia and the disabled Porte; war which would certainly check the recovery of Great Britain and lose the gains of eight years; and which must be carried on in regions so remote, under circumstances so unfavourable, could be justified by any such exigency as had arisen. That the crisis should have overcome the passionate peacefulness of Pitt, his rooted economy, and his devotion to domestic policy, shows at least his overwhelming sense of its importance.

On the 28th of March 1791 a short message was brought from the King to the House, stating the failure of his Government to bring about peace between Russia and Turkey, and demanding an augmentation of the navy "to add weight to his representations." Fox received this announcement with unusual solemnity, and asked for further information. Pitt haughtily refused to afford more than was furnished in the message—an amazing reticence, when the circumstances are considered; and one which the Foreign Secretary, Leeds, himself denounced, after he had resigned. The next afternoon was fixed for the discussion; and before the dawn of another day Pitt had discovered his mistake. The country had had enough of war; the taste of the American campaigns was still hot in the mouth. It had never heard of Oczakow, and was not prepared to renew its sacrifices that that swampy spot might remain a

Turkish possession. More than that, the Baltic trade was of enormous extent; its annual value was computed at three millions sterling; the commercial classes were ablaze. Woronzow, the Russian ambassador, finding out from Leeds what was in contemplation, had gone to Fox and excited all the energies of Opposition.

Nor was the Cabinet by any means united. The measure, planned outside it, had, so to speak, been rushed upon it; and its ministerial opponents remained unconvinced. Richmond, one of Pitt's ablest colleagues, was hostile; Grenville, whose influence over the Premier appeared then to be on the increase, always cold, waxed colder; the mutes trembled and wavered. Pitt, his brother, and the Chancellor had been the strongest advocates for action. But Pitt, in spite of his enormous majorities on the message—97 to 34 in the House of Lords, and 228 to 135 in the House of Commons—resolved to recede. He had received some of the secret warnings that forebode the cyclones in which Governments go down. Camden, indeed, thought the Government would go down. Grafton made his sons, both members of Parliament, refuse their support. The action, so hurriedly determined, was as hurriedly withdrawn. On the 22d of March, 1791, the Cabinet had agreed to send fleets to the Baltic and the Black Sea, and to make a representation jointly with Prussia at St. Petersburg, stating that the two allies were under the necessity of at once taking part in the war against Russia, should satisfactory assurances respecting Oczakow not be received within a certain definite time. The messenger, with the joint representation, set off for Berlin on the 27th; the royal message was

delivered to Parliament on the 28th, discussed and
voted on the 29th. On the 30th the Cabinet met, and
showed a disposition to retreat. On the 31st two
Cabinets were held, at the second of which there was a
general collapse; so general, that Thurlow feigned sleep
to avoid being a party to it. It was determined to send
a messenger to Berlin to stop the joint representation.
Leeds with spirit declared that, if such a despatch must
go, it must go without his signature. This, however,
constituted the least of obstacles; the despatch went,
and Leeds resigned.

The whole transaction, from the very inception of
the policy to its withdrawal, including the parliamentary debate, had taken just nine days. Able
writers speak of Pitt's being warned to recede by
his declining majorities on this subject. Nothing can
be more erroneous. The rapidity of action with him
had been equalled, as we have seen, by the rapidity of
reaction. He resolved to recede in a space of twenty-
four hours, during which the one. division taken gave
him a crushing majority. The cool promptitude and
courage of his retreat, after a lease of power which would
have made most men headstrong, was rare and admirable.
Still, it was retreat, absolute and avowed. To drain the
cup of humiliation to the dregs, Fawkener was sent to
St. Petersburg to try what he could effect by expostulation. It needs no great experience of affairs to know
that, when menace has been attempted and has failed,
expostulation is only an opportunity for insult. It was
an opportunity that Catherine was fully qualified to
appreciate. Fortunately for her purpose, Adair, the
friend of Fox, happened to be at St. Petersburg. On

him she heaped every compliment and caress, while Fawkener was sent empty away.

The whole transaction is noteworthy for many reasons. The shortness of time during which the policy was framed and reversed is sufficiently remarkable. So, too, is the unreality of the great majorities in its favour. For it is clear that these votes were reluctantly given, and would have been turned against the Government had the pressure been less, or had the Government proceeded further. The weakness of the support was evidently due to the sudden force of public opinion; which acted with a celerity and a completeness rare in the eighteenth century, and amazing under the circumstances.

The most astonishing circumstance, however, is the undoubted fact that the Government, with all its overwhelming majority, was in imminent danger of dissolution. Storer, a keen watcher of men and events, wrote that, had not Fox been impossible, he could easily have got into office. Auckland, at least equally acute, thought the same : so, as we have seen, did Camden. Pitt himself acknowledged it. In a letter which he addressed to Berlin in explanation of his change of policy, he admits that, had he not receded, he must have fallen. So great, indeed, was the loss of prestige that nothing in all probability saved Pitt, but the fact that Fox was the only alternative.

What was the cause of this catastrophe? High authorities say the Prussian alliance. But it is clear that there was too much reluctance at Berlin itself for this explanation to be adequate. The real rival and enemy on which Prussian ministers kept their eyes fixed then and for near a century afterwards, reigned not at St. Petersburg but at Vienna. The cause was in reality twofold. Pitt saw the danger to the balance of power in Europe from the constantly growing strength of Russia; and emboldened by his pacific successes in Spain and in Holland, did not doubt that the armies of Prussia and the fleets of Great Britain would awe Catherine, then entirely without allies, into acquiescence. It is not impossible that his calculation was correct. Twice had he played the game of brag successfully, and on the whole he had a right to calculate on a third triumph. But his whole plan was nipped in the bud by the one element on which he had not calculated, the hostility of Parliament and of the country.

Why then had this not entered into his calculations? There lies the second cause of his disaster: it was his growing isolation. Always secluded, he had become almost inaccessible. Dundas and Grenville were alone admitted to his confidence. An inner cabinet, indeed, is not unfamiliar to us; and, as the numbers constituting cabinets increase, it must become a recognised institution. But Pitt had not the excuse of numbers; nor, indeed, that of impracticable colleagues. The real reason for the limitation of his confidences was probably his rooted distrust of Thurlow. It was scarcely worth while to summon a meeting of the Cabinet that he might be cursed and betrayed by Thurlow. Nevertheless, his solitude was a grave disability. He was not in touch with his colleagues, still less with the pulse of the people. Had it been otherwise he could scarcely have remained in absolute ignorance of the storm of opposition that his Russian policy was certain to evoke.

And so ends the Oczakow incident. Save a gigantic speech by Fox, it left little behind it. The place itself, like so many spots that have caused, or nearly caused great wars, is forsaken and forgotten. But as an epoch in Pitt's career, as an illustration of his weakness and his strength, the transaction possesses a vital interest, and deserves the most elaborate study. Its political effects endured for a considerable time. It relaxed if it did not dissolve that triple alliance of Prussia, Holland, and Great Britain, which had been so far Pitt's main achievement and object in foreign policy. It caused a grave disparagement on the Continent of Pitt's judgment and Pitt's power. Of this he reaped the fruits later. As Thurlow remarked with complacency of his chief, there could now be no danger of war while Pitt was in office; for, as he had swallowed this disgrace, it was impossible to conceive one that he could scruple to digest in future.

Pitt's reputation did not merely suffer abroad; it was gravely compromised at home. He had rashly menaced and hurriedly retracted. To his proud spirit the mortification was undoubtedly deep. Burges, then under-secretary for foreign affairs, has left a curious record of a conversation he had with Pitt at this time (April 19, 1791). Pitt assured him, " On my word of honour, that my sentiments, notwithstanding everything that has passed, are precisely the same as they were, and as the Duke of Leeds's are now. He has had the constancy and courage to act upon them in a manner which must ever do him honour. Circumstances, dreadful circumstances, have made it impossible for me to do the same. I am under the necessity of remaining

as I am, in order to avoid consequences of the most
unpleasant nature; but the Duke has acted nobly
both to the country and to myself." The exact import of these expressions it is not necessary to
seek; in the mouth of Pitt they are sufficiently remarkable.

Another result, as we have seen, was the resignation
of Carmarthen, who had succeeded to the dukedom of
Leeds in 1789. In itself the fact had no importance.
Leeds was a cypher. He had little capacity. He was
both vain and pompous. He was incurably indolent.
It is not, therefore, surprising to find that he had
become a mere channel and signature stamp for
despatches drafted by Pitt. The importance of his
retirement arises from the fact that his successor was
Grenville. Some have thought that Leeds was slighted
out of office, to make room for Grenville. But from the
conversation between Pitt and Burges just quoted, it
is clear that this is not so. Pitt was anxious to appease
Burges, and to confide to him the name of his new chief.
But Pitt expressly declared "that from the variety of
difficulties that have occurred, from the number of
claims and interests to be discussed, and the multitude
of things to be taken into consideration, it was impossible for him to tell with any certainty what that
arrangement was likely to be."

Grenville, who played so considerable a part, has
dropped out of history from sheer want of sympathy.
It is due to that fatal deficiency, congenital and hereditary with him, that he is now barely remembered as a
transient and unnoted premier, as the writer of an
obsolete pamphlet, as a partner in a sumptuous edition

of Homer, and for his behaviour to Pitt. He was not
merely one of Pitt's nearest relations, being by birth his
first cousin, and having married a Pitt, but he owed
everything to his great kinsman. Yet he pursued
Pitt with the most truculent hostility, to the very
death. What human feeling he possessed was reserved
for the jobs and sulks of his brother Buckingham. It
is strange to read his letters to that most contemptible
of human beings, who daily required incense or consolation or gossip or apology. It was a grievance against
Grenville that, when Prime Minister, he did not daily
pay his respects to the brother whose vassal he
remained. Buckingham frowns; and Grenville's pro-
testations of anguish and contrition and devotion rend
the air. It was a grievance against Grenville when
he did not, regardless of his oath, transmit cabinet
secrets to this benignant relative; and again he has to
kiss the dust. Great potentates have been found
after death to have always worn some mortifying gar-
ment next the skin; Buckingham was Grenville's hair
shirt.

Grenville was, or became, the typical Whig of his
day; for Fox and Burke, with their blaze of passion and
genius, were hardly Whigs; they were extremists, one
way or another, and the pure Whig hated extremes.
They were the gladiators and associates of those sublime
personages; they were with them, not of them. Fox
perhaps was rather a Liberal than a Whig; and Liberalism represents less the succession to, than the revolt
against Whiggery: Burke was a unique and undefinable
factor in politics, for both parties may claim him, and
both with justice. The Whig creed lay in a triple divine

right : the divine right of the Whig families to govern the Empire ; to be maintained by the Empire ; to prove their superiority by humbling and bullying the sovereign of the Empire. Grenville was an admirable embodiment of this form of faith. By accident rather than by choice, he became the leader of the Whigs, and Fox's superior minister ; he and his brothers each lived on enormous sinecures, Buckingham's amounting, it is said, to £25,000 a year ; while his tactless treatment first of the King, and then of the Regent, had much to do with the long exclusion of the Whigs from office. His pride and his principle were so equally unbending that he was apt to confound the two. It is fair to say that it was not only kings that he treated like dirt ; for, as he himself acknowledged, not prematurely, when he was Prime Minister, he was utterly incompetent to deal with men ; and when he was Secretary of State our foreign relations suffered from that deficiency. Fox, when in the closest alliance with him, groaned under his impracticability. By 1797 it is clear that Pitt found him extremely difficult to deal with. Wilberforce notes in July 1797, "Grenville and Pitt very like breaking friendship." The familiar allusions to Grenville in Pitt's private letters to Wellesley amply confirm this view. Most significant of Pitt's experience of him is the fact, that, in the sketch of a combined administration which he drew up in 1804, he substituted Fitzwilliam as Secretary of State and relegated Grenville to the Presidency of the Council.

It was not only impediments of temper and character that caused Grenville to remain so long out of office. From the time of Pitt's death, it is clear that he ceased to care about politics. Perhaps that blow had really cut deeper than appeared on the surface. Be that as it may, Grenville was obviously not reluctant to leave office in 1807, and certainly never showed any wish to re-enter it. He was not in harmony with his party as to the war. He had achieved all that his ambition sought. He was so amply, but so strangely, provided for by the State, that the very nature of his sinecure, the holder of which was supposed to audit the First Lord of the Treasury's accounts, was an obstacle to his holding the Premiership; while its income made life too easy. More than that, to so proud a man, the Buckingham system, of which he was a part, must have made politics unendurable. To so guide a flying squadron of borough nominees as to compel the change of a marquis's coronet into a duke's, was more than Grenville could stomach, but more than he could avoid. The enchanting shades, the rare shrubs, and the rare books of Dropmore became to him what St. Anne's had been to Fox. Poor devils like Sheridan might groan, but they were of no account. The oligarchy had made up its mind to remain in the country. "Lords Grey and Grenville" had issued their decrees, and would hardly deign to come to London to pick up the seals. It is to Grenville's freezing indifference that we mainly owe the long monopoly of the Tories; disastrous in training to the Whigs, and in loss of power to the country. To him we owe it that Horner never served the public as a minister; that Brougham never knew the cares and responsibilities of such service until too late to benefit by them; that Grey (though he himself was also to blame) was unable to complete his second year of office until he was sixty-six; and that a fair growth of political buds never blossomed at all. With many talents and some qualities, Grenville's career cannot be pronounced fortunate, either for himself or his country.

CHAPTER VII

THE SHADOW OF THE FRENCH REVOLUTION

AFTER the affair of the Russian armament Pitt turned his back upon Europe; and he had good reason for doing so. He had been compelled to swallow a mortification that his proud spirit could not easily forget; he had learned that in foreign affairs Parliament is an unknown quantity; and that in Great Britain the immediate certainties of trade generally outweigh the most elaborate views of ultimate advantage. Moreover, he saw the storm-cloud overhanging France—no man could say where it would break or how far it would extend—and that it was obviously the interest of this country that it should pass over our islands and spend itself elsewhere.

No English minister can ever wish for war. Apart from the inseparable dangers to our constitution and our commerce, his own position suffers sensible detriment. He sinks into a superior commissary; he can reap little glory from success; he is the first scapegoat of failure. He too has to face, not the heroic excitement of the field, but domestic misery and discontent; the heavy burden of taxation, and the unpopularity of

the sacrifice which all war entails. If this be true of
every minister, with how much greater force does it
apply to Pitt. The task that he had set himself was to
raise the nation from the exhaustion of the American
war; to repair her finance; to strengthen by reform the
foundations of the constitution, and by a liberal Irish
policy the bonds of Empire. At this very moment he
was meditating, we are told, the broadest application of
free-trade principles—the throwing open of our ports
and the raising of our revenue entirely by internal
taxation. He required, moreover, fifteen years of tranquillity to realise the fulness of the benefit of his
cherished Sinking Fund. His enthusiasm was all for
peace, retrenchment, and reform; he had experienced
the difficulty of actively intervening in the affairs of
Europe; he had no particle of that strange bias which
has made some eminent statesmen believe themselves to
be eminent generals; but he had the consciousness of a
boundless capacity for meeting the real requirements of
the country. Had he been able to carry out his own
policy, had France only left him alone, or even given him
a loophole for abstention, he would have been by far the
greatest minister that England has ever seen. As it was,
he was doomed to drag out the remainder of his life in
darkness and dismay, in wrecking his whole financial
edifice to find funds for incapable generals and for
foreign statesmen more capable than honest, in post-
poning and indeed repressing all his projected reforms.

To no human being, then, did war come with such a
curse as to Pitt, by none was it more hated or shunned.
What made his position the more galling was that there
could not have been a more inauspicious moment for

war. Strangely enough, the fourteen years from the
outbreak of the French Revolution to the Peace of
Amiens—from 1789 till 1802—formed an almost unbroken succession of bad harvests, and that of 1792 was
one of the worst of the series. There was, moreover, a
commercial crisis of the first magnitude, unconnected
altogether with any prospect of hostilities. For, indeed,
up to within a few weeks of the actual declaration
there was no sign of apprehension of war in any branch
of trade; the country had rightly judged Pitt, and was
confident of his determination to preserve peace. From
other causes, however, there were, in November 1792,
no fewer than 105 bankruptcies—almost double the
number recorded of any previous month. And whereas
the number of such failures in 1791 had been 769 and
in 1792 934, in 1793 there were 1956; of which as many
as twenty-six were those of country banks. In April
1793 Parliament had to intervene, and authorise advances
amounting to £5,000,000 in Exchequer bills to leading
merchants on good security. It was, then, at a moment
of acute commercial and agricultural crisis that this most
pacific and commercial of ministers found himself con-
fronted with a war of the very first magnitude.

It is probable that on the continent of Europe he
still stands higher than any of his contemporaries and
successors as having headed the great league against
France. Never was there a more involuntary distinction.
If we can fancy Lord Eldon complimented for his per-
formance of the Carmagnole, or Wycherley upon his
theology, we can form some idea of the feelings with
which Pitt up to 1793 would have regarded such a
reputation. It is true that, when he was driven to

fight, he fought with all his might and main; no
prudent minister could do otherwise : that is a matter
of conduct and of method, not of principle. But the
supreme and salient point is that there was no man
in England more resolutely determined on peace and
non-intervention ; and that he pushed his ostentatious
ignorance of the proceedings in France, and indeed of
the proceedings of Europe, to the verge of affectation.

Let us see how this matter stands ; and take the
positive evidence of his own pen and of his own lips.
At first it is quite clear that Pitt considered the French
Revolution as a matter which concerned France alone ;
but which by, disabling her, made a peaceful policy more
easy for England. On the day of the taking of the
Bastile, in ignorance of course of that event, he writes :
" This scene, added to the prevailing scarcity, makes that
country an object of compassion even to a rival." Fox
too in February 1790 delivered a great speech against
any augmentation of the peace establishment. " Had
France," he cried, " remained in that formidable and
triumphant state by which she was distinguished in the
year 1783, I should have been the first to applaud such
an augmentation." He described her as now, however,
" in a state which could neither fill us with alarm nor
excite us to indignation." " If fortune has humbled
the pride and ambition of this mighty empire, if
the anarchy and confusion incidental to such a
revolution has struck her people with inertness and
inactivity, why should we dread her sudden declaration of hostilities ? " Small blame, perhaps, attaches
to Fox for this extremely imperfect appreciation
of an unprecedented situation ; on the other hand,

in the teeth of such declarations it is unwise to claim for him any superior policy of prescience. Pitt's reply was no less remarkable. "The present convulsions in France must sooner or later terminate in general harmony and regular order, and though the fortunate arrangements of such a situation may make her more formidable, they may also render her less obnoxious as a neighbour. I hope I may rather wish as an Englishman for that, respecting the accomplishment of which I feel myself interested as a man, for the restoration of tranquillity in France, though that appears to me to be distant. Whenever the situation of France shall become restored, it will prove freedom rightly understood, freedom resulting from good order and good government; and thus circumstanced France will stand forward as one of the most brilliant pioneers of Europe: she will enjoy that just kind of liberty which I venerate, and the invaluable existence of which it is my duty as an Englishman to cherish. Nor can I under this predicament regard with envious eyes an approximation in neighbouring states to those sentiments which are the characteristic features of every British subject." "And," he concluded, "we must endeavour to improve for our security, happiness, and aggrandisement those precious moments of peace and leisure which are before us." It will be observed that the tone of the minister is one of almost patronising friendship. Yet within a year or two he was to be universally denounced as the ruthless and inveterate enemy of the new state of things in France.

In October 1790 he writes to Hugh Elliot: "This country means to persevere in the neutrality which it has hitherto scrupulously observed with respect to the internal dissensions of France, and from which it will never depart unless the conduct held there should make it indispensable as an act of self-defence. . . . We are sincerely desirous of preserving peace and of cultivating in general a friendly intercourse and understanding between the two nations." Again, in July 1791, he writes to his mother : "We are all anxious *spectators* of the strange scene in France," and by underlining the word "spectators" he emphasises the attitude he was determined to maintain.

It is, however, in February 1792 that we obtain the most remarkable view of his mind on this subject. It was then that he delivered that famous survey of the finance of the country which has been noticed as the exception to his commonplace budgets of these four years. In it he repealed taxes, he added to the Sinking Fund, he reduced the previous vote for seamen by 2000 men—from 18,000 to 16,000—he declined to renew the subsidy for the Hessian mercenaries. And to raise hopes of further reductions he declared that : "Unquestionably there never was a time in the history of this country when from the situation of Europe we might more reasonably expect fifteen years of peace than at the present moment." This, it may be said, is a random expression in debate. Even in a budget speech, an eloquent and sanguine Chancellor of the Exchequer may be betrayed into a flash of extravagance by the high hopes that he entertains and excites. On the contrary, this was a speech as to which extraordinary means were taken to supplement the imperfect reporting arrangements of that day. Moreover, this unusually accurate result was submitted to Pitt, and the speech is one of the two, or at most three, which he corrected for publication. So far, then, from this being a haphazard utterance of impulse, it may be considered, delivered as it was after three years of watching and waiting, specially reported and personally revised, as one of the most mature expressions of Pitt's most deliberate opinions. Nothing, perhaps, can more than this impress the reader who remembers that within twelve months the great war between France and England had begun. But Pitt's letter of the 13th of November 1792 to Lord Stafford is, if possible, still more remarkable. He was writing within ten weeks of the commencement of hostilities, and says : "However unfortunate it would be to find this country in any shape committed ; " and further : "Perhaps some opening may arise which may enable us to contribute to the termination of the war between different powers in Europe, leaving France (which I believe is the best way) to arrange its own internal affairs as it can." It will be perceived that he still speaks as a mere spectator of the war in Europe, and as a supporter of the sound and wholesome policy with regard to France which he had always advocated : this but a few days before France had declared the Scheldt open, and her readiness to overturn every established government in Europe.

Grenville's language is even stronger. He was at this time, it will be remembered, Pitt's Foreign Secretary. Six days before the letter last quoted, (November 7, 1792), he writes : "Portugal and Holland will do what we please. *We shall do nothing.* . . . All my ambition is that I may at some time hereafter . . . have the inexpressible satisfaction of being able . . . to tell myself that I have contributed to keep my own country at least a little longer from sharing in all the evils of every sort that surround us. *I am more and more convinced that this can only be done by keeping wholly and entirely aloof* :"—and he continues in the same spirit.

This language was fully embodied in action, or rather inaction. In spite of many provocations, the Government preserved a severe neutrality. They would have nothing to do with the expedition of Brunswick, towards which they preserved rather an unfriendly than a friendly attitude. They indeed recalled Gower, the ambassador in Paris, after the events of the 10th of August 1792, but that was because the King to whom he was accredited was actually suspended, and soon afterwards deposed; so that his mission had terminated, and he had no longer any functions to discharge; while the fact that an insult to his person or domicile was possible in the convulsed condition of Paris, made his presence there an actual danger to peace. They ordered Chauvelin, the ex-envoy of France, to leave England after the execution of Louis XVI.; but public sentiment left no choice in that matter, and Chauvelin had been actively employed, since his official character had ceased, less as a diplomatic than what is known in police language as a provocative agent. On the other hand, they saw Belgium, and what is more, Antwerp, seized by France, but they determined not to make either event a cause of war. It may safely be said that few ministries would have remained so passive. They witnessed the promulgation of a policy of universal disturbance, which culminated in the decrees of the 19th of November and the 15th of December 1792.

The first of these decrees promised assistance to all nations that should revolt against their governments, and was accentuated by the constant reception of English deputations to whom the Convention promised early "liberty"; while the second compelled all territories occupied by the French to accept the new French institutions. As the French had seized Savoy and Nice, the Low Countries, and the Rhine Provinces of Germany, there was an ample area for its execution.

By these decrees the French Government had not merely placed all monarchies on their defence, but goaded them into war. Nor were they merely abstract declarations; they were accentuated by constant promises of action. A few days after their promulgation a deputation from Great Britain, which came to intimate its intention of overturning the British Government, was received with rapture by the Convention, which assured the delegates that the day was at hand when France would be able to congratulate the National Assembly of England. These deputations were numerous and frequent, and were invariably received with the same incendiary assurances. France, in fact, would not leave other countries alone—would not leave England alone. By so doing she disarmed the most ardent and powerful advocate in England for peace at almost any cost—the Prime Minister himself.

It can hardly be denied that the Government pushed their neutrality to an extreme point. On the publication of the decrees, however,—these being the open declaration of a proselytising policy which was at the moment being carried into effect by arms,—and when the navigation of the Scheldt was thrown open, this imperturbability began to give way. The navigation of the Scheldt had been assured to the Dutch by the treaty of Westphalia. It had been repeatedly guaranteed by the Powers; by France herself in 1785; and by Pitt in the name of Great Britain more solemnly and specially in 1788. The French now declared these provisions abrogated by the law of nature, and the Scheldt to be an open river. It was impossible for Pitt to pass by his own treaty of 1788, without a violation of good faith, so signal as to be remarkable even at the time of the second partition of Poland. But, on wider grounds, the danger to Europe was more universal. To allow that the French Government were in possession of a law of nature which superseded all treaty obligations, and the copyright and application of which rested exclusively with them, was to annihilate the whole European system. On this point, however, the French were firm. They were ready to explain away the decree of the 19th of November, but on the question of declaring the Scheldt open, and open by the operation of natural law, they would give no satisfaction at all. Moreover, it was certain that an invasion of Holland was being prepared; and the treaty of 1788, barely four years old, compelled Pitt, without any possibility of evasion, to come to the assistance of the States.

It became clear now, even to those most unwilling to see, that war was inevitable. Then came the execution of Louis XVI. A universal shudder ran through England. The nation went into mourning. The playhouses were closed. Maret, afterwards Duc de Bassano, who was secretly in London as a semi-diplomatic agent,

said that he could not leave the house for fear of being
exposed to the "insults and ignorant ferocity" of the
populace.   The King could not leave his palace without
being surrounded by crowds demanding instant war.
A fortnight before, Fox had been nearly turned out of a
vestry meeting at St. George's.   But the feeling then,
which this circumstance proves to have been sufficiently
bitter, was faint compared to the horror excited by the
death of Louis.   Yet Maret wrote days after that event
that Pitt was still sincerely anxious for peace.   There
is something pathetic in this flash of light thrown on
the lonely figure, clinging to hope with the tenacity of
despair.   As it fades, the darkness closes, and the Pitt of
peace, prosperity, and reform disappears for ever.

While Maret was writing his report, war was already
decreed.   On the 1st of February 1793 the French Convention—moved, as Maret said, by stockjobbers, or as
Roland said, by the necessity of finding employment for
armed desperadoes—declared war on the rulers of Great
Britain and Holland.   Pitt cherished one last sanguine
belief.   He was confident that the condition of her
finances would make it impossible for France to wage war
for more than a short time; just as a few years later he
is said to have assured the House of Commons that he
could see his way to one more loan of twenty millions,
but that then the credit of England would be exhausted.
Both forecasts were probably correct according to experience; but the French Revolution was destined to
annihilate the guidance of experience, and to elicit un-
suspected powers both in France and in England.   At
any rate, Pitt entered on the contest under the firm
faith that any war with France must necessarily be brief.

Two points remain to be noticed. Why, if Pitt was so much opposed to war, did he not resign? The answer is simple. His resignation would not have prevented war in any case. He had, moreover, no excuse or colourable ground for resignation. He could not go to the King or to Parliament and say, "I have resigned because I would not go to war. The case for war has arisen under a treaty I concluded with infinite pains four years ago. Yet, rather than avert the very danger against which it was framed, I wish to resign and let others fight for my treaty." The bare statement of the case needs no further demonstration; he would simply have been succeeded by a minister much more warlike and much less capable than himself.

The other matter is this. A wearisome busybody called Miles has left it on record that George III. bullied Pitt into war. But this story is on the face of it untrue; has, indeed, not the remotest plausibility. The date given for the transaction is 1791. If the story be true, Pitt ought to have been dismissed in that year, for it was not until November 1792 that the bare possibility of going to war occurred to him. The authority given for this preposterous statement is Moira, who declared that he was to have succeeded Pitt at the Treasury. That George III. should dismiss Pitt to take to his counsels the bosom friend of the Prince of Wales, would seem to reveal a fit of lunacy of which we have no other record. The relations between Pitt and George III. were very far from being of this nature. It is no disparagement to either to say that the King would not have ventured to send such an ultimatum to Pitt; nor at first did he feel any great hostility to the popular

movement in France.   The royal sentiments with regard
to the war were transparent enough.   It does not need
a Rochefoucault to understand that the first humiliations
of that French Court, which had so largely contributed
to secure the independence of the United States, were
observed without poignant displeasure at St. James's.
And, up to the last moment, the King, as Elector of
Hanover, maintained an absolute neutrality.   But when
monarchy was abolished, and the monarch a prisoner,
the drama became unrelieved tragedy.   Then, no doubt,
the King was anxious for war; and at the end of 1792
Pitt had lost every weapon by which he could oppose it.
That, however, is a very different matter from the King's
sending word to Pitt that he must either go to war or
make way for Moira.

It is, then, abundantly manifest from every source of
evidence that war was forced on the English Ministry;
that Pitt carried to an extreme his anxiety to avoid it;
that his resignation could not have averted it; and that
in any case it was impossible for him as a man of honour,
or a serious statesman, to resign.   We shall see, when
war had begun, his constant endeavours to put an end
to it.   Whether he was a great war-minister, as he is
generally considered, or an incapable war-minister, as he
is called by Macaulay, he is certainly the most strenuous
peace-minister that ever held office in this country.

CHAPTER VIII

WAR

IT does not seem necessary in a sketch of Pitt's career to enter at large into the incidents of the war that raged from February 1793 to the preliminaries of the Peace of Amiens in 1801. Its first incident as concerns Great Britain was that an army was sent to Flanders under the Duke of York, to act in conjunction with an Austrian army under the Prince of Coburg. From February to August, (1793), the French sustained an unbroken series of disasters. Dumouriez was defeated at the battle of Neerwinden, and deserted to the enemy. Belgium fell into the hands of Austria. Mayence with a garrison of twenty, and Valenciennes with a garrison of eight thousand men surrendered to the allied forces. Toulon admitted an English fleet. But the French were stimulated and not cowed by these reverses. They called the whole population to arms. They set in array a million of soldiers. Naturally brave, but now inspired with the last heroism of patriotism and despair, they turned the tide of fortune. York was driven from Dunkirk with the loss of all his heavy artillery. The Austrians were defeated at Wattignies. The internal

K

enemies of the Republic were ruthlessly crushed. Lyons fell, and Marseilles. The royalists of La Vendée were scattered and slaughtered. Toulon was taken and introduced Napoleon to the world ;—a heavier blow to the allies than the loss of a score of fortresses or armies. A few months later, by a strange freak of fate, he became a subject of the King of Great Britain, when Corsica proclaimed herself a monarchy under the sovereignty of George III. Prussia began to withdraw from the war, preferring the tangible advantages of an immediate share of Poland to the much more doubtful possibilities of a problematical partition of France. The Austrians were overthrown on the historical battlefields of Worth and Weissenburg; while Brunswick once more displayed his sinister strategy in a retrograde movement.

In the succeeding year (1794) the battle of Fleurus, followed by a retreat of the Austrians, which is explained less by that defeat than the policy of their government, put an end to the campaign of Flanders ; Belgium and Holland fell into the hands of the French. The German Emperor, who had come to witness victory, returned to Vienna. Coburg and York were recalled. On their eastern frontier the French repelled the Prussians, and on their southern, the Spaniards and the Portuguese. So great was the effect of their successes that, at the opening of the parliamentary session, on the 30th of December 1794, there were several motions urging negotiation, two of them brought forward by Wilberforce.

As some set-off to this picture, it may be recorded that the English had captured the French settlements in India and a few West Indian islands ; while, at the famous battle of the 1st of June 1794, Lord Howe secured a crushing victory over the fleet of France.

To the British Government also occurred a signal advantage for the future conduct of the war by the adhesion of a number of the principal Whigs. Portland, the ex-Prime Minister, and Windham, a brilliant but fantastic orator; Lord Spencer, an administrator of signal ability, and Lord Fitzwilliam, a great noble of less tact than character, joined the Government; and the moral effect produced by their accession was greater than any personal assistance that they could render. It gave a national character to the Administration and to the war. It reduced the Opposition in the House of Commons to something less than fifty; a little later, and they were able to travel with comfort in two hackney coaches.

As the war continued, the superiority of France increased. In April 1795 Prussia, in June Sweden, and in July Spain came to terms with the triumphant Republic. A limited consolation might perhaps be derived from the fact that the Court of Vienna continued its readiness to receive subsidies from England; but in other respects it showed little activity, though its armies under Clairfait gained some unfruitful victories in the autumn. Pitt's Government displayed a singular but luckless energy. Windham, the new War Minister, built his greatest hopes on an expedition of French aristocrats and malcontents to Quiberon Bay; but this force, sumptuously provided with money and munitions of war, and supported by a powerful fleet, was pulverised by Hoche as soon as it landed. In the West Indies the English arms lost ground. On the other hand, the Empire was enriched by the splendid acquisitions of the

Cape of Good Hope and Ceylon. Pitt's hopefulness was in no degree diminished. He wrote to Addington (October 1795) that he trusted to open his budget before Christmas. "If that goes off tolerably well," he added, "it will give us peace before Easter."

In 1796 a general election refreshed Pitt's majority. While it was proceeding, he sent on his own responsibility a subsidy of £1,200,000 to Austria,—a grave act, fiercely censured by the Opposition, and only condoned by a devoted House of Commons, on the express stipulation that it should not be considered a precedent. He was rewarded by the recall of Clairfait and the substitution of the Archduke Charles,—a young prince whose consummate generalship was sometimes crippled by physical disabilities, and more often by the pedantry or jealousy of his own Government, but who stands forth as one of the most brilliant opponents of Napoleon. He at once defeated Jourdan, and drove the French back across the Rhine. In the West Indies, Great Britain also secured some advantages. But all was darkened and eclipsed by the Italian campaign of the irresistible Bonaparte; while Spain and Prussia entered into distinct alliance with France.

This year (1796) began and ended with determined overtures for peace on the part of Pitt. In the previous December (1795), the minister had brought a royal message to Parliament, declaring that the establishment of a new constitution in France (that of the Directory) offered facilities for negotiation. In March, Pitt made an earnest and genuine overture for a general pacification, through Wickham, our envoy in Switzerland; but it was ungraciously received, and was rejected.

Again, in October, Lord Malmesbury, a diplomatist of the highest distinction, was sent to Paris. But as had happened in March, the envoy's instructions to insist on the evacuation of the Netherlands by France rendered negotiation fruitless. On the 19th of December (1796) he was ordered to leave France within forty-eight hours. Four days earlier, a French fleet, with an army under General Hoche, had sailed for the invasion of Ireland. The expedition was, however, wholly unsuccessful. The weather was unfavourable; the fleet was scattered; Hoche was in one portion, the army in another; both returned separately to France, and the hopes of Irish discontent were postponed. A slighter enterprise of a filibustering character directed against south-western England completely failed. A far greater effort was, moreover, crushed in its inception. It had been calcu lated that by a junction of the Dutch, the French, and the Spanish fleets, another and more fortunate Armada might effect the invasion of England. But the great victory of St. Vincent, fought on the 14th of February 1797, by which Jervis and Nelson crushed the Spanish contingent, blighted these hopes.

The year 1797, which opened so brilliantly, was destined to be the darkest and most desperate that any British minister has ever had to face. In April, Austria, England's last ally, laid down her arms and concluded a preliminary treaty of peace at Leoben (April 7, 1797). France was now free to turn her victorious armies and her inexhaustible resources to the destruction of England; and she was determined to do so.

At this moment Great Britain was paralysed. The

Navy, that had just given fresh courage to the nation, was now to deal a blow which struck at the heart and stopped the circulation of the Empire. In the middle of April, the crews of the Channel Fleet at Portsmouth rose in rebellion, dismissed their officers, and hoisted the red flag. Their grievances were great, their demands were moderate; and these had to be conceded with a full amnesty. By the end of April the mutiny was over. At the beginning of May, however, it broke out again and spread to Sheerness. Here it assumed a graver aspect, and bore all the marks of being inspired by revolutionary agencies outside. There was, indeed, no sympathy between the two movements. The sailors at Spithead sent word to the sailors at Sheerness that their conduct was a "scandal to the name of British seamen." Nevertheless, the Government was as much disabled by the one as the other. The fleet with which Duncan was blockading the coast of Holland joined the rebels, with the exception of two ships. With these the Admiral kept signalling as if to the rest of his squadron : a mild stratagem, on which, however, the safety of England depended, and which was happily successful. In these days the news would have been flashed to every nook of Europe, and Britain would have lain at the mercy of her enemies. Fortunately neither the French nor the Dutch had any idea of our condition.

The mutiny lasted five weeks and spread all over the world. It smouldered in the victorious fleet of Jervis ; who, however, suppressed it with a prompt and masterful hand. The crew of the *Hermione*, cruising near Porto Rico, outraged by the inhumanity of their captain, killed all their officers, and delivered their ship to the Spaniards.

At the Cape of Good Hope, the British squadron was in open revolt, but was brought back to discipline by the ready firmness of the Governor and Admiral. The artillerymen at Woolwich were tampered with. There was an attempt to seduce the army. What a position for a country engaged in a life-and-death struggle with a triumphant enemy! Never in the history of England was there a darker hour. The year had begun indeed with one great naval victory, and was destined to close with another. But these isolated successes formed the sole relief to a scene of perpetual gloom. Our generals and armies had been so uniformly unfortunate that we had no longer a foot on the continent of Europe. On land our great foe was everywhere triumphant. We were entirely on the defensive. Two invasions of our islands had been attempted. A third was impending; it might at any moment take place, and could scarcely be opposed.

The war had lasted over four years; and had added a hundred and thirty-five millions to the National Debt, or about as much as the whole cost of the American war, for scarce any corresponding advantage. The Funds had fallen to a lower point than in the worst depression of the American war. In December 1796 it had been necessary to propose a further loan of eighteen millions, and three millions and a half of new taxes. The loan, though issued at a price which produced $5\frac{5}{8}$ per cent, was at $15\frac{1}{2}$ discount in March 1797. There had been an unexampled run on the Bank of England. Cash payments had just been suspended. There was a terrible dearth. Not merely were the ports thrown open to foreign corn, but large bounties were paid on its importation. The last of our allies had just made her peace

with France ; and we were left to continue the contest
alone.   Our own efforts to come to terms had been so
received as to make all hope of truce indefinitely remote.
The worst of all wars was raging in Ireland.   Scotland,
though not harried into open rebellion, was scarcely
less discontented.   England was maddened by crimps
and press-gangs and unprecedented taxation.   Pitt was
grossly insulted in the streets ; he had to be brought
back from St. Paul's under an armed guard.   And at
this juncture our one efficient arm, to which alone the
nation could look for solace and even protection, was
paralysed by insubordination : the flag of lawlessness had
been hoisted ; and the guns of the navy were pointed
at British shores.   But the spirit of the minister was not
shaken, though his health had begun definitively to fail.
At the height of the crisis, Lord Spencer came to him
for instructions so pressing—(for it was said that the
marines had joined the revolt and were about to march
on London)—that he awoke Pitt in bed.   He received
them and left ; but in a short time he received a con-
tradiction, and returned.   He found the minister already
asleep.

This crisis has been dwelt on at perhaps disproportion-
ate length, because it represents not merely the darkest
period of the war, but the dauntless spirit which faced
it, and which enabled this country, in spite of incapacity
and blunders and debt, in face of the hostility of a
surpassing genius and of a world in arms, finally to
surmount its difficulties.   And we are thus able to understand why Pitt, with all his share of miscalculation
and disaster, remained long after his death the embodiment and watchword of British determination.

Once more this year did he make overtures for peace. "I feel it my duty," he repeated to Grenville, who urged that the French minister was treating him with scant courtesy, "as an English minister and a Christian, to use every effort to stop so bloody and wasting a war." Grenville formally dissented. But Pitt persisted, in spite of the disapproval of his Foreign Secretary and the anguish of the King. He sent Lord Malmesbury, whose instructions Grenville had the irksome task of drawing, to the town of Lille, which had been fixed for the meeting of the plenipotentiaries. These, however, had their eyes fixed on Paris, where a struggle was impending between the extreme and the moderate factions; on the issue of which, and on nothing else—for Pitt was ready for the most considerable concessions—peace really depended. On the 4th of September 1797 the party of extremes and of war gained the upper hand, and on the 16th of September Malmesbury was again ordered to leave the soil of France.

During the next month, (October 1797), the eclipse of the Navy was proved to be only temporary. In a bloody and obstinate battle off Camperdown the Dutch fleet, once so famous and so formidable, took its leave of history. It fought with a splendour of heroism worthy of its ancient renown, but was defeated by Admiral Duncan at the head of the fleet which had returned to discipline; and thus this black year ended well.

In the year 1798, the struggle had ceased on the continent of Europe, with the exception of a brief campaign in the kingdom of Naples. The genius of war in the shape of Napoleon was in Egypt; where

Nelson, by destroying the French fleet in Aboukir Bay (August 1798), seemed effectually to confine him. We were fully occupied at home by the rebellion in Ireland; which might, had timely succour arrived from France, have proved sufficient to tax the entire energies of the Empire. When it is remembered that the population of Ireland was then little less than one-third of the whole population of the United Kingdom; that it was largely in possession of arms, and almost wholly disaffected; it is not easy to calculate what would have been the extreme extent of the danger, had one of the many French expeditions, under such a general as Hoche, arrived to aid and discipline the revolt. Fortunately for Great Britain, the French force under Humbert, which landed in Killala Bay on the 22d of August (1798), came two months too late; for the battle of Vinegar Hill, in which the insurgent forces were completely routed, had been fought on the 21st of June. Moreover, Ulster, which had been the province most organised and eager for insurrection, held aloof—deterred by the religious character of the rising; and the rebellion spent itself in the isolated efforts of a war of banditti, distinguished by constant horrors of outrage and reprisal.

In this year Pitt himself engaged in single combat. Tierney had declared that the proposal to carry in one day the Bill for the more effectual manning of the Navy was somewhat precipitate. Pitt, in reply, charged him with a desire to obstruct the defence of the country. The taunt of obstruction, even of obstruction so mild as to be almost imperceptible to the palled palate of our generation, was then an insult to be wiped out with blood. The statesmen met and exchanged shots;

while Pitt's devoted friend the Speaker, Addington,
watched the harmless combat from the genial shade of
a gibbet on an adjoining hill. Addington was destined
to be Pitt's successor; but it is said that Pitt was asked
by Ryder, his second, on this occasion, who should
succeed him in case of the worst, and that he designated
Perceval. This nomination would be inexplicable, did
there not exist a letter of Pitt's which shows the extraordinary impression that had been produced on him
by a recent speech of Perceval's.[1] Pitt's own account of
the combat is still happily extant, in a letter to Lord
Wellesley. In it he lightly declares as to Tierney and
himself: "I believe we parted better satisfied with each
other, than on any other occasion in our lives."[2]

The duel seems childish to us now, and may have
seemed so then, for it was followed by a widely circulated report that Pitt was insane,—a rumour less
discreditable under the circumstances than such rumours
usually are. Though he was not insane, there is no
doubt that his health was seriously impaired, to which,
perhaps, we may attribute his loss of self-control on this
occasion.

The break-up of his constitution is so marked and
so important that it deserves a momentary reference;
as it marks an era in his career scarcely less critical
than the declaration of war in 1793.

It has been seen that Pitt was a delicate child. A
careful course of life, except in regard to the large
quantity of port that he was accustomed to drink, had
enabled him to get through his work and enjoy his
holiday without interruption up to 1797. In that year,

---

[1] See below, p. 205.   [2] See below, p. 210.

the death of his brother-in-law Eliot deeply affected him ;
and at that very time he began to complain of illness.
He suffered greatly from headaches. What is more
significant is that he began to speak of retirement, and
of Addington as his successor. It is clear that these
allusions were due to yielding nerves and broken health;
for the reasons which afterwards caused his resignation
did not then exist. His condition became worse in
1798. The passage with Tierney reveals a petulance
alien to his singular self-command. And when Wilberforce threatened a motion condemning the principle of
duelling, Pitt wrote to him that he considered it as one
for his own removal. The report of his insanity probably
arose from a continuous display of nervous irritability,
culminating in the duel. A few days after his letter to
Wilberforce, this last notes that his friend was seriously
ill. Wine began to produce an effect on his seasoned
head. In August 1798, Lord Auckland reports him as
much shaken in his constitution. It is clear that 1798
marks an evil crisis in Pitt's health, which accounts for
much in his subsequent career. The man is different
afterwards. His will seems to shrink ; he has less
self-control. The illness of princes and ministers is
always a subject of hard swearing ; and it will be
curious to watch if the archives of Pitt's contemporaries,
as they yield their treasures, will gradually clear up
a certain air of mystery that surrounds his health in
this year.

Meanwhile, Pitt was strenuously combining a second
coalition against France. He found in the Czar Paul,
who had recently succeeded to the throne of Russia, an
ardent if insane ally, who was able to contribute not

only great armies but a consummate general to the
common cause. The Porte, outraged by the French
occupation of Egypt, readily lent its aid. Naples,
alarmed by the French invasion of Italy, also prepared
for war. Austria, who had recently come to terms with
the French at Campo Formio, finding herself tricked,
was again arming. Thus, with powerful armies commanded by the genius of Suvaroff and the Archduke
Charles; with the fleets of Great Britain in absolute
supremacy at sea; and with Napoleon blockaded in
Egypt; the year 1799 opened with splendid prospects
for the new confederacy.

Had it not been for the strange oscillations of Austria,
all these bright presages might well have been realised.
But the brilliant victories, with which Charles and Suvaroff opened the campaign in Switzerland and northern
Italy, were rendered futile by the orders from Vienna.
Russia retired disgusted from the contest. Austria persevered for one year more, unequally matched with
Napoleon, who had succeeded in returning to Europe.
England's share of the war, besides subsidies, was to
send another expedition to Holland, then the favourite
theatre of English incompetency. It was commanded by
the Duke of York, and was, though the Dutch fleet was
finally captured, indecisive and even disastrous. Pitt,
ever sanguine, derived a whimsical consolation in its discreditable termination from the fact that "it ought to
be a great satisfaction to us to know that our valuable
army will be restored to us safe and entire." Against
this failure it is only fair to set off a great triumph in
the East. Tippoo, the sovereign of Mysore and the
relentless enemy of Great Britain, encouraged by the

presence of the French army in Egypt, had become a serious danger to our dominion in India. Under the command of General Harris, with the guidance of Lord Wellesley and his greater brother, a British army invaded Mysore, and after an obstinate combat stormed Seringapatam. Tippoo fell, and his kingdom was divided.

In the East, again, Sir Sidney Smith had held Acre against Napoleon's Egyptian army, which, after a pertinacious investment of sixty days, was obliged to retire : the sole check that he knew in his career, until he crossed the Pyrenees.

The last day of the year 1799 brought a letter from Napoleon, who had just become First Consul, with overtures for peace. It was scarcely six weeks since a revolution had placed him in power ; and Pitt, dogged though he was in his anxiety for a cessation of warfare, felt that the actual situation of France did not hold out any solid security to be derived from negotiation. He was anxious, however, to express this negative in terms of eagerness for peace, with a hint that that would be best secured by the restoration of royalty.

It was a pity that the task of answering the First Consul's letter devolved upon Grenville. The didactic despatch is unhappily familiar to us in the annals of British diplomacy. England has always assumed the possession of a European censorship, which impels her to administer exhortation and rebuke to the States of the continent through the medium of her Foreign Office, as well as by the articles of her press. It is this peculiarity which has constantly earned for her an unpopularity of the most universal and the most exquisite kind. No British minister or journalist has, however, carried this spirit further than Grenville on this occasion. He did not send any direct reply to Bonaparte's letter, but he enclosed to the Foreign Minister at Paris what was, though called a note, in reality a supercilious and arrogant lecture to the French nation. Harping on a "system" which he did not further describe, but which he said was the source of all the woes of France and of Europe, he informed Talleyrand that "His Majesty cannot place his reliance on the mere renewal of general professions of pacific dispositions." Some further guarantee was required. "The best and most natural pledge of its reality and permanence would be the restoration of that line of princes, which for so many centuries maintained the French nation in prosperity at home and in consideration and respect abroad," and so forth. There is a fine untutored insolence in this communication, addressed to the triumphant head of a victorious republic, that would be difficult to match. Even George III. could not stomach it. He wrote on the draft, "In my opinion much too strong, but I suppose it must go."

To the advice thus considerately offered, Napoleon despatched a conclusive reply. "The First Consul," he wrote, "of the French Republic could not doubt that his Britannic majesty recognised the right of nations to choose the form of their government, since it is from the exercise of this right that he holds his crown ; but he has been unable to comprehend how to this fundamental principle, upon which rests the existence of political societies, the minister of His Majesty could annex insinuations which tend to an interference in the internal affairs of the republic, and which are no less injurious to the French

nation as to its government, than it would be to England
and His Majesty if a sort of invitation were held out
in favour of that republican government of which
England adopted the forms in the middle of the last
century, or an exhortation to recall to the throne that
family whom their birth had placed there, and whom
a revolution compelled to descend from it." He concluded by proposing to put an immediate end to hostilities,
and to name plenipotentiaries to meet at once at Dunkirk
or some similar place. Grenville sent a bald and meagre
rejoinder saying, what was in fact untrue, that he had
no desire to prescribe to a foreign country the form of
its government, and refusing the offer.

We may assume from what we now know of the
character of Napoleon as it developed itself, that a
durable peace could not then have been concluded;
but it is melancholy that Pitt, who had grasped at
hopes so much more slender, should have declined even
to entertain this solid proffer. He was willing to
negotiate in the succeeding August; but in January
the French Government was not sufficiently established.
On this point Fox was especially happy. "We must
keep Bonaparte some time longer at war as a state of
probation. Gracious God! is war a state of probation?
Is peace a rash system? Is it dangerous for nations
to live in amity with each other? Is your vigilance,
your policy, your common powers of observation to
be relinquished by putting an end to the horrors of
war? Cannot this state of probation be as well undergone without adding to the catalogue of human suffering?
But we must pause. What! must the bowels of Great
Britain be torn out—her best blood be spilt, her treasure

wasted, that you may make an experiment?" After
pointing out that soldiers in other battles, such as
Blenheim, at least knew what they were fighting for,
he proceeded: "But if a man were present now at a
field of slaughter, and were to inquire for what they
were fighting, 'Fighting!' would be the answer, 'they
are not fighting, they are pausing.' 'Why is that man
expiring? Why is that other writhing with agony?
What means this implacable fury?' The answer must
be, 'You are quite wrong, sir; you deceive yourself;
they are not fighting; do not disturb them, they are
merely pausing! This man is not expiring with agony—
that man is not dead—he is only pausing. Lord help
you, sir! They are not angry with one another. They
have now no cause of quarrel, but their country thinks
there should be a pause,'" and so forth.

This volley of reason and pleasantry was all the
more stinging from being directed at what was, indeed, Pitt's real motive, (as we see in a letter to
Dundas of the 31st of December 1799), which was
to wait, or, as Fox would have said, to continue fighting until the French Government was firmly established. Nothing could be more impolitic than this
refusal, except the manner of it. If Bonaparte were
insincere, as was said, and only wished to make the
French believe that the wish for peace was on his side
and not on ours, the negative upon negotiation was
playing his game. If he were sincere, the responsibility
of the Government was unbounded. Moreover, there
was the advantage of dealing with a strong administration, even if its durability was insufficiently proved. It
must, however, be acknowledged that the reception of

peace proposals in France had hitherto been far from encouraging; that the dealings of the French with other nations even in the act of treaty did not inspire confidence; and that the course of negotiation in the succeeding August shows that Bonaparte rather desired to snap an advantage by parley, than to establish anything like a durable peace.

In 1800, the Austrians, after a succession of disasters, were compelled to conclude an armistice; and Pitt again made overtures for peace through Lord Minto, our ambassador at Vienna, so that a settlement might be arrived at in conjunction with Austria, and not by separate negotiation. But the preliminary conditions of the French stipulated that they should be allowed to send supplies, while negotiations were pending, to their army in Egypt, and to their garrison in Malta, which were blockaded by our fleets. This would have deprived the British Government of the only trumps in their hand. The opportunity, therefore, if it was one, again passed away. But it elicited a curious minute from Dundas, showing the fierce divisions that existed in the Cabinet on foreign policy. He traces no less than four factions in a cabinet of a dozen persons, ranging from Windham, the representative of Burke, the apostle of holy and eternal war with the Revolution, to the less exalted views of Pitt, who was anxious for peace on any decent terms. These differences were not abstract, but practical and incessant. It is clear, therefore, that Pitt must not merely have overridden some of his colleagues in his negotiations, but looked to a certain break up of his Cabinet, had they been successful. It is necessary to note that, while the negotiations were proceeding,

Malta fell into the hands of the English (September 1800).

Austria was more successful. She concluded peace at Lunéville in February 1801. That peace, which marks the termination of the Second Coalition, coincides with Pitt's retirement from office.

CHAPTER IX

PITT AS A WAR MINISTER

THE notable points of these years as regards Pitt's conduct of the war and of foreign policy are these :—his two endeavours to combine Europe against the common enemy; his constant anxiety for peace; the four direct overtures which he made with that object; the almost uniform success of the enemy on land, and the uniform triumph of our arms at sea; finally, the dictatorship with which the country wisely entrusted him, which enabled him to overrule the dissensions of the Cabinet and carry on war, if not triumphantly, at any rate with more success than would otherwise have been possible under the conditions royal, aristocratic, and traditional, which so hampered our efforts.

Pitt's war policy was twofold : it was a naval and colonial policy, it was also one of subsidy. His enterprises by land were neither numerous nor successful. There he spent himself in scattered and isolated efforts, costly both in money and life. It was calculated that these expeditions had, at the Peace of Amiens, cost us no less than 1350 officers and 60,000 men. But our fleet swept the seas; and swept all hostile colonies into our net. Something falls now to be said of his subsidies.

At first sight subsidies have a crude appearance, nor
have they agreeable associations. They are apt to recall
the time when degenerate emperors were buying off
hungry barbarians, or the doles that Charles and James
II. received from Louis XIV. But they must be judged
on their separate merits. A nation that conducts its
main operations by sea, and endeavours also to stimulate hostilities by land, has hardly any choice in the
matter. She has, on this presumption, no spare army to
send; and she must contribute something more substantial than goodwill or despatches. Pitt, it must be
remembered, was in the position of being at war with
an enemy of more than twenty-seven millions with
many vassal states, though the population of Britain
was little more than ten millions, while that of Ireland
at her side could only be reckoned to the enemy. His
policy of subsidies was, therefore, a necessity; for, while
the population of France was eminently warlike, that of
England was relatively rich. The essential point, however, in advancing money under these conditions, is to
receive in return the services for which the payment is
made. This is a precaution not free from difficulty; and
so Pitt found it.

His subsidies were of two kinds: guaranteed loans
or direct gifts, though they were only different in form,
as the result to the taxpayer was the same in either
case. Of the first description there were two. One
was a loan of £4,600,000, made in 1795, under an Act
passed to give effect to a Convention between Great
Britain and the Emperor of Germany, dated on the 4th of
May 1795. By this instrument it had been stipulated
that, in consideration of the maintenance by Austria of

200,000 troops in the war against France, Great Britain should guarantee the interest on this loan. As, after the first two years, Austria was unable to provide the requisite sum, the burden henceforth fell on the British Exchequer. This guarantee Fox describes as "the most imprudent measure, all things considered, that ever was carried through."

Again, a similar Convention was concluded on the 16th of May 1797, and a loan of £1,620,000 made on the same conditions. But the charge fell entirely on the British Exchequer, as Austria was unable to pay anything. Besides these loans, it may be of interest to add[1] a list of the subsidies which were gifts during Pitt's governments, as furnished to Parliament in 1815.

But the subsidies, though considerable, formed of course only a small fraction of the cost of the war. On this point something must now be said.

The total addition made to the capital liabilities of the State between the 1st of February 1793 and the 17th of March 1801 amounted in stock to £325,221,460.[2] Stock, however, did not constitute the whole liability. For, in addition to stock, subscribers often received, as part of their security, a certain amount of terminable annuities. These terminable annuities, (which expired in 1860), were known as the "Long Annuities"; and their capital value, if computed at a rate of 5 per cent interest, may be taken to amount to £9,323,976 at the end of the eighth year of war (1800-1). Thus Pitt increased the capital liabilities of the State for war purposes in the course of those years by a total sum of £334,525,436. But it must be remembered,

[1] See Appendix A.   [2] See Appendix B.

that, during all this period, Pitt's Sinking Fund was at work. While he was borrowing with one hand, with the other he was still setting aside large sums for the redemption of debt by the purchase of stock. The stock, therefore, acquired during this period by the National Debt Commissioners, amounting to £42,515,832,[1] must be deducted from the total liabilities, if it is desired to ascertain the burden that the war during these years laid upon posterity. The result of the deduction gives a net total of £292,009,604 as the war burden permanently imposed by Pitt in his first and main administration.[2]

Of these 334½ millions Pitt only received about 200 millions in cash. He borrowed in a stock of a low denomination; and, as in January 1797, for example, the 3 per cents fell to 47, it may readily be imagined at what a sacrifice of capital value the loans were raised. For this he has been much blamed. It has been said that he should have borrowed in stock of a denomination more nearly corresponding to the actual credit of the State; by which method the capital would not have been swollen to such an inordinate extent, and the generation responsible for the war would have borne a fairer share of the burden. The answer to this criticism, though convincing enough, would require too much spaciousness of detail to be given here. This much may, however, be said, that Pitt had no choice. He was borrowing on a scale unknown in the history of the world; and he had to borrow, not in accordance with his own views, but with those of the lenders. He made repeated attempts to borrow at 5 and 4 per cent, but

[1] See Appendix B.
[2] The further additions made to the debt by Mr. Pitt in his second administration will also be found in Appendix B.

met with no response. For his very first loan, raised
within a few weeks of the declaration of war, he received
tenders from only one set of persons, who insisted
on 3 per cents. When, again, he funded the Navy
and Exchequer Bills in 1796, he offered options in 3,
4, and 5 per cent stock. According to the market
price, the option in 5 per cents was the most favourable to the lender; but 85 per cent was taken in 3
per cent stock, and only 11 per cent in 5 per cent stock.

There is overwhelming evidence to show that he
repeatedly did all in his power to stimulate public competition, and to raise his loans in stock of a higher denomination. Such stock, however, not only commanded
less popularity, but had relatively a less marketable
value, owing to its liability to be redeemed on the
conclusion of peace and the return of better credit.
Consequently, it is open to question whether Pitt would
have done better for posterity, even if he had succeeded
in borrowing by methods different to those to which
he had to resort. Indeed, a high financial authority—
Mr. Newmarch—in an interesting monograph on this
subject, demonstrates, by actuarial calculations, that
borrowing in 3 per cent stock as compared with 5 per
cent stock was in reality an economy. However that
may be, the plain truth is, that, having to appeal to a
limited and abnormal market, Pitt was in no sense
master of the situation; and that, had he not offered
the temptation of stock which was certain to rise sooner
or later in capital value, he could not have secured the
requisite means for carrying on the war.

Another cognate objection is that he ought to have
raised more by taxation within the year and depended

less on loans.   There was no more strenuous upholder
of this doctrine than Pitt himself.   He explored and
attempted every source of taxation.   He added repeatedly
to existing taxes.   He even appealed to voluntary contribution ; by which he obtained more than two millions
sterling in 1798, and a further sum in 1799.   He introduced such fertile expedients as the legacy duty, which
he borrowed from Holland in 1796.[1]   In 1796 he took
the desperate measure of trebling the assessed taxes
(when the familiar phrase of the "pleasure horse" made
perhaps its first appearance) ; and when this impost fell
short of expectations, finding that "the resources of taxation were failing under him," he boldly carried through
an income tax of minute and complicated graduation in
an oration "which," said a competent French writer,
Mallet du Pan, who heard it, "is not a speech spoken by
the minister ; it is a complete course of public economy ;
a work, and one of the finest works, upon practical and
theoretical finance that ever distinguished the pen of a
philosopher and statesman."

Mr. Gladstone demonstrated in a speech fully worthy
of this description that, had Pitt imposed the income tax
in 1793 instead of 1798, there need have been no debt at all.
But he would be the first to admit that what was possible
in 1798 would not have been possible in 1793 ; that what
was practicable in the fifth year of war would not have
been practicable in the first ; and that it was not until all
other possible sources of taxation had run dry that he
could have persuaded the country to accept a severe

[1] There are no fewer than three claimants for the honour of
having called Pitt's attention to these duties : Miles, Harris, and a
Mr. Lamb.

and graduated income tax. It was only when the trebling of the assessed taxes had failed, that he determined to attain, by a direct impost, his avowed object, of taking a tenth of the income of the country. The net of the tax was extremely wide, and the mesh extremely small. It operated on incomes of no more than £60 a year, which were mulcted at the rate of twopence in the pound. The tax proceeded by a minute and complicated scale; each £5 of additional income being taxed at a different rate until £200 was reached. From incomes of £200 a year and upwards Pitt boldly took his tenth. The imposition and acceptance of a tithe so novel and exasperating shows sufficiently that all that taxation could do was done, as well as the anxiety of Pitt and his genera- tion to bear the fullest possible proportion of the burden of the war.

Another criticism of a directly opposite import has been raised against him. He has been accused of unduly adding to that burden by keeping up the charge for the Sinking Fund. The main reason for his doing this is that which would have prevented his proposing the income tax in 1793. He was convinced that the war would be so short, that it would not be worth while to derange his scheme of redemption on that account. It is clear from his speech of the 11th of March 1793, as well as from other indications, that he thought it highly improbable that hostilities could continue beyond that year. This expectation was based entirely on the financial condition of France. It would, therefore, have been extravagant, in his judgment, to interrupt a beneficial sequence of fifteen years, for a few months of incidental warfare. Financially, his calculation was correct; but, politically,

he was trying to compute a tornado. Nor did these
sanguine hopes abate, as the war proceeded. Each year,
each month was to be the last. And even had it been
otherwise, it may well be that he would have been
reluctant to dispel that mirage, which induced the
population to bear taxation readily, under the belief
that a magic machinery was producing gold as fast as
it was spent. The Sinking Fund, in fine, inspired
confidence, and enabled the nation to endure with
cheerfulness the burden of what he believed would be a
short war.

It is, therefore, probable that, in spite of the large-
ness of the figures, Pitt's finance was well and wisely
managed ; that, looking indeed to the monetary and
political conditions of his time, he achieved as much
both in annual payment and in economy of borrowing
as could well have been accomplished. That he managed
this, too, without crushing commerce by taxation is evident from the fact that our imports and exports went on
mounting during the war, in spite of deficient harvests,
with reassuring elasticity. In the year ending January
5, 1793, the total value of all imports into Great Britain
had been £19,659,358; and on an average of six years ending at that date £18,685,390. In the year ending January
5, 1799, it was £25,654,000, and on an average of the
six years then ending £22,356,296, showing an increase
as between the two years of £5,994,642, and as between
the two averages of £3,670,906. The total value of the
exports of British manufactures in the year ending
January 5, 1793, had been £18,336,851; on the six years'
average £14,771,049. The comparative figures in 1799
were £19,771,510, and £17,154,323, showing an increase

of £1,434,659 and £2,383,274 respectively. Of foreign merchandise exported in the year ending January 5, 1793, the value was £6,568,000, and in the six years the average had been £5,468,014; the corresponding figures in 1799 were £14,028,000 and £10,791,000, showing an increase of £7,460,000 and £5,322,986 respectively. It might be said of him, as the grateful citizens of London recorded of his father, that under his administration commerce had been united with and made to flourish by war.

But it is not possible to discuss Pitt's war administration, which has been so bitterly attacked, merely by laying down general principles. It must be considered as a concrete record of achievement and failure. As regards the minor and military part, it may at once be admitted to be unsuccessful, and want of success may be held at once to damn it. But the circumstances must be borne in mind. Pitt's catamarans and martello towers must not be compared with torpedoes and Brialmont turrets. It must be remembered that he was dealing with dupes or invalids or self-seekers on the one hand; and with a cosmopolitan convulsion, embodied in a similar genius, on the other. The French Revolution, to borrow Canning's fine figure, was a deluge which submerged the ancient monarchies of Europe; it was long before their spires and turrets emerged once more above the subsiding wave. Most European Courts beheld it in the spirit of wreckers. While Pitt was planning how to check the torrent, they were speculating on the value of its flotsam and jetsam. His and their professed objects were the same; their real aims were totally different and incompatible.

Pitt was, as it were, heading a crusade with a force of camp followers. They took his money, and laughed in their sleeve. He could not believe that they were insensible to their real interest or their real danger. It is probable that some Pompeians saw in the great eruption an admirable opportunity for shop-lifting; so it was, but it cost the depredators their lives. Pitt saw the real peril, though he succeeded neither in averting it, nor in alarming the princes of Europe; they deceived him and themselves, and were overwhelmed.

Europe was rotten. The decay had been demonstrated in France, but the fact was universal. The old systems were moth-eaten. The Holy Roman Empire, never very puissant, crumbled like a corpse under the new light. Prussia, so arduously constructed by the unwearied vigilance of genius, had withered under the single reign of an extravagant voluptuary. Spain was a name, and Italy a geographical expression. Great Britain was neither sound nor particularly great. The nations were indeed a dominant force, but the governments which acted in their name were either unrepresentative or futile. Pitt recognised this after Ulm, when he said that nothing more could be hoped of the sovereigns—there must be a war of peoples. A few weeks afterwards, the overthrow of the Emperors at Austerlitz confirmed his opinion; Spain, then Russia, then Germany, were to fulfil his prophecy.

But it was the governments that Pitt headed. And, if he could not calculate on the selfish ineptitude, which distinguished, not the peoples, but the courts of the continent, still less could he calculate on Napoleon.

To that imperial intellect he had to oppose the state-craft of the Thuguts and the Cobenzels, the Lucchesinis and the Haugwitzs, men pitiful at all times, contemptible at such a crisis : and the military capacity of the aged Melas, the hampered Archduke Charles, the incom-prehensible Duke of Brunswick. He himself had no generals. "I know not," said Lord North, when a list of officers was submitted to him for the commands in America, "I know not what effect these names may have on the enemy, but I know they make me tremble." So with Pitt. He discovered the genius of Wellington, but did not live to profit by it. He was obliged to employ the Duke of York, or, as Lord Grenville said, "some old woman in a red riband." Nothing perhaps could have availed against Napoleon, for two Napoleons do not coexist. But Europe never had a fair chance.

It is also just to remark that, while Pitt's efforts on land were generally futile, he was uniformly successful at sea. If France held one element, England held the other. If the responsibility of the one be debited to him, the responsibility of the other must be placed to his credit. Even if it be said that these victories were entirely due to the incalculable genius of Nelson, which would not be true, it must be said that the defeats were due to the incalculable genius of Napoleon ; so that the one may be set against the other.

There was, however, another reason for the wide difference between the results achieved by the army and the navy in the last decade of the last century. The army was essentially an aristocratic, and the navy a comparatively democratic service. In the navy a man of obscure origin could rise, and the area of choice was

not limited by the circumstances of birth; but in the
army, purchase and favour and lineage gave promotion.
Our admirals were not born in the purple. Collingwood
was the son of a Newcastle merchant, Jervis of a
country lawyer, Nelson of a country parson. But
when our armies had to be sent into the field, it was
necessary that, if possible, a prince of the blood should
command them. A military command seemed to
require nothing more than exalted rank, or the seniority
which often spelt senility. It is difficult to apportion
the blood-guiltiness of this proceeding or tradition.
Pitt at any rate informed George III. that, so far as
the Duke of York was concerned, it could not continue. The King acquiesced with real anguish as a
father, and perhaps as a sovereign; but solaced himself
by telling Pitt that it was not his son, but Pitt's brother,
then at the head of the Admiralty, who was responsible
for our disasters. What chance had armies, thus guided
by indolence or hazard, against legions of veterans, to
whom war was a business and a passion, many of whom
had risen, and all of whom looked to rise, by merit? The
English generals were brave, and the Duke of York had
gallant qualities. But they were engaged in a struggle
where this was not enough. The disparity extended from
the leaders to the ranks. "The French system of con-
scription brings together a fair specimen of all classes;
our army is composed of the scum of the earth—the mere
scum of the earth," said the Duke of Wellington, with
more accuracy than gratitude. So it was, and so it was
treated. Largely recruited from the refuse of humanity,
it was scourged and bullied and abused as if outside
humanity. And these were the soldiers we opposed to

the regiments in which Ney and Hoche and Massena served as privates.

These explanations and reserves are not intended to prove that Pitt was a great War Minister. In that respect it may be said that he has been much under-rated without asserting that he was a born organiser of victory. He had dauntless spirit, he had unfailing energy, he evoked dormant resource, he inspired confidence; but his true gifts were for peace. The signal qualities which he had shown in administration did not help him on this new stage. Unsupported and over-weighted as he was, he could not in any case have succeeded. Nor in all probability could the greatest of War Ministers,—not Chatham, not Bismarck. It must be repeated again and again that, locked in a death grapple with the French Revolution, he was struggling with something superhuman, immeasurable, incalculable. We do not read that the wisest and the mightiest in Egypt were able to avail, when the light turned to dark-ness and the rivers to blood.

CHAPTER X

DOMESTIC POLICY

DURING these years of struggle, Pitt was compelled to allow all measures of social progress to remain in abeyance. The note of his domestic policy was to avoid any measure that could embarrass the efficient conduct of the war. That, however short it might be in his anticipation, would in any case require the undivided energies of the country. He had no choice, as has been seen, but to go to war. Suppose that, having done so, he had devoted his energies not to the war, but to measures of emancipation and reform, and had split Parliament, which in a war should be unanimous, into half a dozen parties, would he have done better? War is a hideous engrossing fact; it cannot be paltered with. Too much or too little, as Burke said of property, is treason against it; it must have all; every nerve, every muscle, every fibre. And the nation that gives its whole immediate energy to the war it has in hand will have an incalculable advantage over the nation to whom it is merely an expensive incident, dividing its attention with a number of other agitating and absorbing problems.

M

Parliamentary reform was, no doubt, loudly and
justly demanded. But, while, on the one hand, the
enthusiasm of the French Revolution would have demanded a larger measure than Pitt would have granted,
the far more general reaction against anything in the
shape of change would have denied anything. Reformers
then insisted on more than we, after a century of agitation, have attained. To move in the matter, then, could
only provoke irritating and fruitless dissension, perhaps
disabling anarchy, when the union of the nation was the
first necessity. It was absurd to discuss annual parliaments when the Gaul was at our gates. It was indispensable to check the French revolutionary propaganda,
of which these proposals were only an instalment, and
which were really aimed at the subversion of the entire
constitution of which Pitt was the official trustee.
Heavy taxation for war with little apparent result, and
the maintenance of a narrow system against a popular
and reasonable demand for reform, soon bear fruit in
what is called coercion. And to coercion Pitt was
compelled to resort.

It has been said that the period from 1789 to January
1793—the first part of the French Revolution—was one,
not of coercion, but of almost competing liberalism. It
is true, no doubt, that in May 1792 a royal proclamation
had been issued, warning the people against seditious
writings; and another in December of the same year
had called out the militia as a precaution against the
intrigues of "evil-disposed persons acting in concert
with persons in foreign parts"; but these edicts could
scarcely be considered as other than storm signals.
Even the Alien Bill, which was introduced in 1792

as a measure directed against revolutionary propa-
gandism, though severe and harassing to foreigners,
was not extraordinary, when the circumstances and
opinions of the time are considered. These measures
were, however, followed up by frequent press prosecutions; and juries competed in finding persons guilty of
sedition on the thinnest evidence, or on no evidence at
all.

More especially was this the case in Scotland, where
the judges hounded on the prosecutions; and where
Braxfield attempted, not without success, to rival the
fame of Jeffreys. The discontent here stopped little
short of rebellion. A Convention sate in Edinburgh,
which scarcely disguised revolutionary aims. So far as
parliamentary representation was concerned, the malcontents were fully justified; their grievance in that respect
was immeasurably greater than that of Ireland, for they
had lost their own parliament, and had no real representation in any other. But, had their complaints been
less founded, disaffection would have been justified by
the measures taken against them. A brilliant young
advocate named Muir, arraigned as a member of the
Convention and as a promoter of parliamentary reform,
was condemned to transportation for fourteen years.
Palmer, a clergyman, was sentenced to seven years'
transportation for circulating a paper in favour of
parliamentary reform. Skirving, for being concerned
in the same address and in the Convention, was trans-
ported for fourteen years. Margarot and Gerrald, the
London delegates to the Convention, received a like
punishment. These trials sank deep into the minds of
the Scottish people. Half a century afterwards, a

memorial was erected to the victims on one of the loftiest sites in Edinburgh; while Fox expressed in an ejaculation what is still thought of those who sentenced them: "God help the people who have such judges."

So far, these prosecutions had proceeded under the ordinary law. But, in May 1794, a royal message was communicated to Parliament, calling its attention to certain papers that were to be laid before it. A secret committee was appointed in both Houses. Reports were issued by each to the effect that a traitorous conspiracy existed for purposes of revolution. The Habeas Corpus Act was instantly suspended. In that year Watt, who had been a spy, was tried and executed in Scotland for high treason; nor, indeed, did he deny that his designs were rebellious, though the plot was on so small a scale that it might well have been treated as venial. In England, on the other hand, a few weeks later, Hardy, Horne Tooke, and others were brought to trial on the same charge and acquitted. Nothing apparently in the nature of treason was proved against them; they had merely combined for purposes of reform; and they derived an agreeable satisfaction from summoning Pitt and Richmond to testify to their own former participation in similar aspirations. These acquittals cleared the air. They showed, on the one hand, that the alarms of Parliament had been exaggerated; and on the other, that in England, at any rate, justice was still pure and unbiassed.

In 1795, the suspension of the Habeas Corpus Act was renewed, and it was continued till 1801. In this year the King, on the opening of Parliament, was shot at and pelted; his coach was wrecked. These outrages were followed by a Treasonable Practices Bill and a

Seditious Meetings Bill. Both measures were interfer-
ences with the liberty of a subject, which only the last
extreme of necessity could justify. The first indefinitely
enlarged the category of treasonable offences, and dispensed with proof of any overt act of treason; the
second forbade all public meetings of more than fifty
persons without the superintendence of a magistrate,
and contained other clauses of a similar tendency.
These bills were voted by great majorities. In 1799,
an Act was passed for putting an end to various
societies, and forbidding the formation of others under
specified conditions. Regulations and restrictions and
taxation were also imposed on the press. For some
years past steps had been taken with the special object
of restraining the circulation of cheap newspapers, of
which these burdens were the complement. These various
proceedings gave Fox a great advantage, of which he
nobly availed himself. Though he thundered in vain
against the enactment of such laws, his speeches remain,
and embody in the most exact and stirring terms the
large polity of a free people. In half a dozen words he
laid down the fundamental principle of liberal policy.
"Liberty is order," said he, "liberty is strength."

It is not easy in cold blood to defend these pro-
clamations and prosecutions and bills. Still less easy
is it for a generation that has so often resorted to
coercion to criticise them. Ever since the death of
Pitt, all English governments have at times adopted
those exceptional measures for which their supporters
are so apt to censure him. But he can only be held
partly responsible. In Scotland, the ruling and language of the judges were largely answerable. In

England, the early findings of juries under the ordinary law pointed in the same direction. For the extraordinary laws Parliament itself bears the burden. Its secret committees and reports made it impossible for any minister to refrain from proposing coercion bills. The scandal and terror caused by the assault on the King were the cause of others. But more must be acknowledged than this. These laws were passed, and these prosecutions instituted, under the ignorant ferocity of panic. The extremity and brutality of that panic can perhaps best be realised in the accounts of the Birmingham riots, of which Catherine Hutton, one of the chief sufferers, has left so graphic a narrative. The French Revolution was a new portent; none could measure it, nothing could be predicated with regard to it; its terrors consisted not merely in the success of its arms, but in the ramifications of its proselytism. Before any exceptional measures were taken, it was encouraging revolt in England, promising support to rebellion, and receiving disaffection with cordiality and honour. To this the English response took the form of some conspiracies, real, though no doubt exaggerated; but in the main of an intense reaction and dismay. "Repression and severity," says so stout a Whig as Erskine May, "were popular and sure of cordial support."

Mr. Massey supplies from secret records the exact moment when the masculine mind of Pitt succumbed to the plots and rumours of plots with which he was encompassed. In December 1792 three thousand daggers had been discovered at Birmingham; one of them had been flung by Burke on the floor of the

House of Commons. The Government had convincing
evidence, or evidence which at any rate convinced them,
that this was only a part of a vast and imminent conspiracy. The Cabinet sate till four in the morning.
When it had dispersed, Pitt still bent brooding over
the fire. Presently he asked the under secretary, who
was in attendance, what he thought of the situation;
and added, "Probably by this time to-morrow we may
not have a hand to act or a tongue to utter." Nor did
the gravity of his apprehensions diminish with time. He
told Wellesley and Wilberforce in 1795 that, were he to
resign, his head would be off in six months; and, shortly
afterwards, when Wilberforce borrowed Pitt's carriage,
he was informed that, were it recognised, its occupant
ran the risk of being murdered. When once Pitt yielded
to the public sentiment in this matter, there could be
neither pause nor limit. The public in its terror called
for more and more; Parliament passed every repressive
measure with something like acclamation; it was not
the coercion of a people by a government, it was the
coercion of a government by the people.

It must, further, be admitted that later ministries
have departed from the ordinary law with much less
reason. While we were struggling for bare existence
with the most formidable enemy that England has ever
had to face—an enemy fighting not with armies and fleets
alone, but with every art of seduction—we had one-third
of our population, that of Ireland, arrayed in avowed
disaffection; Scotland was combustible and explosive;
and it was impossible to speak with confidence of the
population of England. All that was known was an
enormous sale of the works of Paine, an extensive

manufactory of secret arms, a considerable and indefinable amount of furtive organisation. It was as usual
the unknown, the suspected, that was terrible. At any
moment we might find the very ground that we were
defending from France crumble beneath us. Discontent might burst forth somewhere; and once in view,
who could tell, with bad harvests and heavy taxes and
press-gangs to foster it, how far it might extend?
Making the best front we could against an overwhelming
enemy, we might find the country in flames behind us.
In so dark and desperate a juncture, men act and strike
blindly. In face of so present a peril, it is not the minister
who is master. He only attempts to keep his feet in
front of a tempestuous crowd; and his responsibility in
case of mishap is terrible. It may be that exceptional
measures of repression can never be justified. If they
can, the justification can only be concrete, can only rest
on a solid base of formidable circumstance. If they
ever can, a fair plea can be advanced for Pitt; for the
crisis was incalculable. And if they cannot, it is difficult for any extant political party in England to censure
him. But the truth, with or without apology, may be
best expressed by saying that, while the torrent of the
French Revolution demolished monarchy in France, its
back-eddies swept Pitt and England into reaction.

Even in this dire time of distress, he turned from a
state of war, external and intestine, to those eternal
problems where policy and humanity work side by side.
Whitbread had brought forward a Bill for regulating
and fixing a minimum of wages. Pitt recalled the
House to a juster view of political economy. He
believed that the true course was to allow the price

of labour to find its own level, and that this would
best be promoted by a reform of the poor-laws; more
especially of that law of settlement which prevented
the workman from taking his industry to the best
market. But, passing from this criticism, he proceeded
to deal earnestly and exhaustively with the whole
question of the condition of the poor. He admitted
a vast ill, and suggested various remedies, which on a
later day he embodied in a measure.

He had spared, he said, no pains to collect information on the subject; and there is a curious tradition as
to this. It is said, that on a visit in Essex, (probably to
the house of his private secretary, Joseph Smith, at
Shortgrove), he was descanting on the prosperity of the
country and on the comfort enjoyed by the working
classes. His host answered nothing; but took him
next day to the neighbouring town of Halsted. The
minister surveyed it in silent wonder, and declared that
he had no conception that any part of England could
present a spectacle of such misery. The scene produced
a deep impression on his mind; he at once addressed
himself to the question; and not long afterwards he
took the opportunity of Whitbread's motion to deliver
this sympathetic and thoughtful speech on the condition of the poor; through even the meagre reports of
which there breathes a warm spirit of earnestness and
humanity, unlike the political deliverances of that day.

He followed it up with a Bill, full of novel and comprehensive propositions: so novel and comprehensive,
indeed, that, after several alterations, it sank over-
weighted beneath the parliamentary wave. A vast new
system was to be created; a hierarchy of Justices and

Wardens and Guardians. In every parish or group of
parishes were to be established Schools of Industry,
which were in fact what we have since known as
Ateliers Nationaux. Their conditions were to be
settled to some extent by Parish Councils; but they
were in all cases to furnish work for the destitute poor.
The Justices and other authorities were to have nearly
the powers of a private employer of labour in regard to
them. They were to buy materials; they were to sell
the manufactured article; they were to fix the rate of
wages. They could build or hire warehouses; they
could buy or hire land. They could enclose and cultivate commons for the support of the workers in the
Schools of Industry. Moreover, in every parish or
union, a friendly society was to be established. Persons
also, having more than two children, or, in the case of a
widow, one child, were entitled to claim exceptional
relief. A certain amount of visible property was not to
debar a person from receiving parochial aid. There
were, indeed, some 130 clauses more or less. One—
perhaps the most daring in those days—provided that
money might be advanced, in deserving cases, for the
purchase of a cow or some other animal producing
profit. Bentham, in his criticisms on the measure,
urged that a cow required three acres of grass, and
asked whence these were to come. Though the question was not answered, the proposal will be recognised
as the germ of a proverbial policy.

There was a certain crudity in the measure, which
makes it all the more remarkable as a sterling and
strenuous endeavour to grapple with a great question,
without deference to tradition or precedent; and it

affords a view of Pitt's character which can nowhere else
be found.   To some of us it is the most interesting
view.   For in the boldness of this Bill, in its compre-
hensiveness, in its very immaturity, we see the desperate
effort of a man to break through the bonds of circumstance and tradition, through that thin red tape which
is mightier than chains, in order to raise his race.
Failures of this kind are sometimes more impressive and
more honourable than the most polished masterpiece of
the parliamentary draughtsman.

The Bill was constantly revised; but the mordant
animadversions of Bentham, which, though not published
at the time, were communicated and circulated, disheartened the Government.   It was probably felt that,
if to various vested interests the hostility of philosophical radicalism were added, there could be no hopes
for the measure, at a time when all novel propositions
were discountenanced as dangerous; but men will long
look back with admiration to the hearty spirit, the
freedom from conventionality or prejudice, and the
genuine sympathy which animate its clauses.

CHAPTER XI

IRELAND

BUT the greatest of Pitt's domestic difficulties has been left to the last. Throughout the whole period of the war, he had by his side the gaunt spectre of the Irish question in its most menacing and formidable shape; an aspect which it retains to this hour. It has never passed into history, for it has never passed out of politics. To take a simile from a catastrophe of nature less ruinous and less deplorable, the volcano that caused that eruption is still active; beneath the black crust the lava torrent burns; so that the incautious explorer who ventures near the crater finds the treacherous surface yield, and himself plunged in the fiery marl of contemporary party strife. No number of previous volumes will suffice to ballast or preserve the innocent investigator; his fate is certain and foreseen; for, the moment his foot rests on 1795 he irresistibly slips on to 1886; and rebounding from 1886, he is soon soused in 1891.

Happily, however, it is only necessary, for the present purpose, to consider the actual personal contact of Pitt with Irish affairs, and not to deal with their general phases and effects; although, even thus, there are episodes so controversial that they cannot be treated so concisely as those in regard to which there is less dispute.

It is needful to remember that Pitt, after the rejection of his commercial schemes in 1785, appeared to despair of a change of system. He sent over Viceroys and Chief Secretaries to occupy Dublin Castle and accept its traditions—Buckinghams and Westmorelands, Fitz-herberts and Hobarts ; but he turned his own attention, perforce, elsewhere. Then came the Regency question ; when the action of the Irish Parliament indicated dangerous possibilities under the settlement of 1782,— contingencies, which once more directed men's minds towards a Union, and furnished arguments in its favour not easy to meet in those times of perpetual apprehen-sion and peril.

The next stage in Irish politics is the emancipation of the Roman Catholics in 1792 and 1793 ; when measures were passed, which, by admitting the Catholic peasantry to the parliamentary suffrage and to juries, and by relieving them from all property disabilities, exhausted, for the time at any rate, their interest in that question. The delay in granting a full emancipa-tion subsequently gave the admission of Catholics to Parliament and to office, no doubt, considerable im-portance. But it was accompanied by a reversal of the enfranchisement of 1793, and was therefore so much the less a popular boon than the Acts passed by Pitt. To say that they were passed by Pitt is but the strictest truth ; for it was only owing to the persistent pressure of Pitt and Dundas that the violent hostility of the Irish Government was overcome. "I do not believe," writes the Viceroy with plaintive acrimony as regards even the minor measure of 1792, "there was ever an instance in any country of such a sacrifice of private judgment to the wishes of His Majesty" (meaning of course the British Government) "as by the Irish ministers in the present concession." While this was the act of Pitt and Dundas alone, it may be noted that, after the admission of the Whigs, the official protectors of the Catholics, to the Cabinet in the ensuing year, nothing more was done for their benefit.

It was in July 1794, as has been seen, that the Portland Whigs joined Pitt. The Duke, their leader, in this rearrangement obtained the Home Secretaryship; under which department Ireland was then directly, as it is now more nominally, placed. It was also arranged that, so soon as a new opening could be found for Lord Westmoreland, Fitzwilliam should succeed him as Viceroy of Ireland. In this way the two official heads of Ireland would be Whig, under of course the general superintendence of the Cabinet; but it was expressly stipulated that there should be no change of system; and that, in fact, Irish policy should be continuous with that previously pursued by the Government.

We are told that Fitzwilliam accepted the Lord Lieutenancy after long hesitation and with great reluctance. It must, on the other hand, be admitted that all the facts point to an immediately opposite conclusion. He discharged letters in every direction. He published his nomination everywhere. He wrote, three months before he was appointed, to offer Thomas Grenville the Chief Secretaryship. He wrote at the same time to solicit the support of Grattan, and to propose an immediate conference; so that Grattan came at once, accompanied by the Ponsonbys, and full of high hopes, to London. So much did he put himself in Grattan's hands that, after the disputes that ensued, he left to that statesman the ultimate decision whether he should undertake the Lord Lieutenancy or not. The news of his approaching Viceroyalty became common property in Ireland. This premature revelation, of an appointment in contemplation but not actually settled, was the first of Fitzwilliam's disastrous indiscretions. It gave a mortal blow to whatever reputation for prudence he may have possessed, and led directly to the unhappy catastrophe which followed. But he did not limit himself to words. He determined to remove Fitzgibbon, the Chancellor, the most powerful man in Ireland. He determined to find high offices, at all costs and by the violent displacement of some of Pitt's oldest adherents, for the two Ponsonbys, the most prominent of the Irish Whigs.

By this time it is clear that Pitt was becoming thoroughly alarmed at the precipitate proceedings of the reversionary Lord Lieutenant. He had told Westmoreland, the actual Viceroy, nothing of any alteration; he did not contemplate any immediate change of system; least of all, would he countenance the removal of the few devoted adherents who had stood by him during the Regency crisis of 1789. He now discovered to his dismay that Fitzwilliam had already formed his administration, was announcing his policy, and proclaiming from the housetops his future achievements, which included the dismissal of Pitt's principal friends. He uttered a despairing wish that the promised appointment could be annulled; but intimated that at any rate Fitzwilliam could only go to Ireland on the condition that he gave satisfaction on these vital points. The new Whig ministers declared they must resign. Pitt expressed his regret; but he declared that it was impossible for him to consent to the Chancellor's removal, or to leave "either him or any of the supporters of the Government exposed to the risk of the new system." "I ought to add that the very idea of a *new system*, (as far as I understand what is meant by that term), and especially one formed without previous communication or concert with the rest of the King's servants here, or with the friends of Government in Ireland, is in itself what I feel it utterly impossible to accede to; and it appears to me to be directly contrary to the general principles on which our union was formed and has hitherto subsisted." He had nothing to reproach himself with. If the worst came to the worst, "I must struggle as well as I can with a distress which no means are left me to avoid, without a sacrifice both of character and duty." Grenville, one of Pitt's two confidants in the Cabinet, was not less dismayed; for the talk of new systems and a new predominance was entirely strange to him, and resolutely repudiated by him. At last there was a general explosion; salutary, as it would seem, for it disclosed and appeared to settle the grounds of dispute. Pitt declared that Fitzwilliam, in his various communications with parties in Ireland, had entirely exceeded his powers, that nothing would induce him to consent to Fitzgibbon's removal, and that he could give no countenance to the idea that Ireland was to be treated as a separate province, outside the general control of the Government, under the exclusive dominion of the Whig party.

Fitzwilliam appears to have thought that Ireland was

made over to him, as were Lampsacus and Magnesia
to Themistocles for his bread and his wine; and that
Pitt would have no more to do with its government and
the policy pursued there than with Finland or Languedoc.
This hallucination was due partly to the idiosyncrasy of
Fitzwilliam himself, but mainly to the strange proprietary
principles of government, to which allusion has already
been made, which were held consciously or unconsciously,
though quite conscientiously, by the Whig party.

Burke intervened at this juncture with letters of
passionate eloquence and pathos. It is scarcely possible
even now to read them unmoved. He acknowledged
that he was ignorant of the terms on which Portland
and his friends had entered the Government. He had
the highest opinion of Fitzwilliam, whose virtues he
once described as the highest and the most unmixed he
had ever known in man. Nevertheless, he admitted
that Fitzwilliam had acted with indiscretion, and that
Portland and he had put themselves in the wrong. At
first, then, he was doubtful as to what they should do.
But at last his mind seemed to be made up. He
despatched a letter on the 16th of October, in which he
solemnly summed up the situation. He wrote, he said, as
a dying man, with all the freedom and all the dispassionate
clearness of that situation, and declared, with "infinite
sorrow," "with inexpressible sorrow," that the Whigs
must resign. Four days afterwards, he pronounced, in
a letter not less powerful or less pathetic, a directly
opposite opinion. If they went, they must be turned
out; they must not resign. "Oh! have pity on your-
selves," he broke forth, "and may the God whose
counsels are so mysterious in the moral world (even

more than in the natural) guide you through all these labyrinths." In truth, he himself was distracted by contending dreads and scorns : with a living loathing of the Irish system of corruption, but with that loathing overborne by his mastering horror of the French Revolution. Rather than that a schism in the Government of Great Britain should weaken the resistance to that pestilence, let even Ireland stand aside. He was, in fact, incapable of giving advice. That the terms on which the Whigs joined Pitt did not include any new system of men and measures was positively asserted by Grenville, who was not merely a man of rigid veracity and in the innermost secrets of the Cabinet, but a strong pro-Catholic. Nor is there a particle of proof, or even probability, that there was any such stipulation; for we may be sure that Pitt would never have agreed to part with so large and critical a part of his prerogative.

At last a settlement was arrived at. A final conference was held, at which Pitt, Portland, Fitzwilliam, Spencer, Windham, and Grenville were present; that is to say, Pitt and one follower with four Whigs. Every detail of patronage and policy was exhaustively canvassed and settled. The results were recorded in a sort of protocol, preserved among the Pelham Papers. Fitzwilliam was to go as Lord Lieutenant indeed; but on the explicit understanding that there was to be no new system of men or of measures in Ireland; that he should, if possible, prevent any agitation of the Catholic question during the present session; that, in any case, on that or any other important measure he should transmit all the information which he could collect with his opinion to the Cabinet; and that he should do nothing to commit the Government in such matters without fresh instructions. Thus, one would have thought, was removed all possibility of misunderstanding.

Here, however, was the fundamental mistake. It was impossible for Fitzwilliam, after his detonations and activities of the autumn, to prevent the agitation of the Catholic question; for he was the prime agitator. It would have been as reasonable for Sir Robert Peel to offer Cobden a seat in his cabinet on the condition that he should exert his endeavours to prevent all agitation for the repeal of the Corn Laws. Fitzwilliam for months past had done nothing but announce his approaching Lord Lieutenancy, and stir up the question. Naturally he found Ireland already in a flame.

Nor did his official action allay it. He landed January 4, 1795. The next day (Monday) he spent in bed. On the Wednesday he summarily dismissed Beresford, a powerful though subordinate officer, a main adviser in Pitt's commercial propositions, and one of Pitt's confidential agents; who was not officially under the Lord Lieutenant at all, but in the Treasury department, that is under Pitt himself. This act, Pitt, who did not speak at random, characterised as "an open breach of a most solemn promise." Other dismissals followed. Cooke, the Secretary for War, and Sackville Hamilton, the Under Secretary of State, were promptly removed. It was a clean sweep. Fitzgibbon alone remained; and he only because Fitzwilliam was specially pledged not to remove him. Every faction in Ireland was astir. One party was to be crushed; the other party was to rule. Those with whom Pitt had constantly co-operated in Irish administration were in consternation; for every

act of the new Government was directed against them.
It was a *coup d'état*, a stroke of State, justifiable and even
necessary on grounds of high State necessity, or on the
presumption of a revolution in policy; but only de-
fensible on such considerations, and even then to be
executed with care and judgment. It was, however,
wholly incompatible with the stipulation of Pitt that
there was to be no general change in administration or
of system; and with his declared, obvious policy to
keep clear of domestic embarrassment, when all his
energies were required for the war with France.

As to the condition with regard to the Catholics, it
would have been impossible to maintain it, even had
Fitzwilliam desired to do so. And from the day on which
he landed, he bombarded Portland with letters to press
for the immediate settlement of the question. To these
communications Portland for some weeks gave no reply
whatever. It is urged by Fitzwilliam's apologists that he
considered that silence gives consent: a proverb, doubtful at all times, but preposterous as a political plea; more
especially absurd, when it is relied upon for guidance in
defiance of definite instructions. Fitzwilliam asserted that
he was permitted to give the Catholic cause a "handsome
support," in case they were resolved to bring it forward.
The Government, on their side, declared that he was in no
way to commit them without fresh instructions. But, even
on the assumption that Fitzwilliam's interpretation was
correct, it is clear that such instructions would apply
only to a spontaneous movement, and not to one excited
by the Viceroy himself.

At last, on the 8th of February (1795) Portland wrote
to impress on Fitzwilliam the importance of giving no

encouragement to the Catholics, and of not committing
himself in any way : the importance, in a word, of his
not doing all that he had been doing for a month.
On the 9th, Pitt himself wrote, complaining of
the dismissal of Beresford. On the 16th Portland
wrote to declare at length his views on the Catholic
question, and his entire disapproval of the policy of
emancipation at that time. A passage from this strictly
confidential despatch Fitzwilliam was afterwards so ill-
advised, to say the least, as to publish, with the most
disastrous results. Even now he did not resign, but
answered these communications at length. In his letter
to Pitt, he made the unfortunate assertion that Beresford
had been guilty of malversation ; a charge for which he
never produced the slightest evidence, and which in any
case he could scarcely have examined judicially in the
forty-eight hours that elapsed between his landing and
Beresford's dismissal. To Portland he reiterated long ex-
postulations on the Catholic question. In reply, Portland,
who it must be remembered was his party leader as well
as his administrative chief, wrote a curt note of censure.
The next day (Feb. 19) Fitzwilliam was recalled.

Never was there so hopeless a misunderstanding, or
one, after the general exchange of views in October, more
incomprehensible. Fitzwilliam published two pompous
pamphlets, and declared in his place in Parliament that
his recall was due to his having connected himself with
Grattan. The Government refused to discuss the matter
But it must be admitted that, untoward as was that event,
the person most responsible for Fitzwilliam's recall was,
as is generally the case in such removals, Fitzwilliam
himself. He seems to have been a man of generous

sympathies and honest enthusiasm; but not less wrong-headed than headstrong; absolutely devoid of judgment, reticence, and tact. Two months before he set out, Pitt had discovered this, and deplored the decision to send him. His announcements of his appointment before it was made, his unauthorised propaganda, his rash dismissals, his speeches, his protests, his publication from confidential letters after his recall, betoken a man earnest, intrepid, and single-minded, but singularly destitute of the qualities required for a delicate and discretionary mission.

The importance of his recall may easily be exaggerated, although it was, in truth, a political calamity. Because it was followed by some miserable years, it has been held to be the cause of the misery of those years. This is surely a misstatement; it was rather a landmark. What in 1795 was called the Catholic question was rather a sign of grace than a measure of real importance. The mass of the Catholic peasantry already had the franchise under the Emancipation Act of 1792-93, and it imported little to them whether or not a number of gentry of their own persuasion went up to Dublin to be bought and sold at the Castle; it has, indeed, always been a matter of comparative indifference to them whether they were led by Protestants or Catholics. Nor can parliamentary reform, if we may trust witnesses so intelligent and well informed as Emmett and M'Nevin, be said to have been an object of enthusiasm to the mass of the population. What pinched the people were tithes and oppressive rents; with this distinction, that, whereas for rents they got something, though perhaps not much, for tithes they got less than nothing. And what excited them were the new prospects presented by the French Revolution. The importance of the recall of Fitzwilliam lies in the fact that he had, however unwarrantably, excited hopes, not of emancipation and reform alone, but of a completely new system; hopes which were shattered by his peremptory removal. So that the quick revulsion produced the blind fury of despair.

The affair still remains obscure; what is clear is that which alone concerns these pages—the part and responsibility of Pitt. It is evident that there was a total misunderstanding; that there was a hopeless discrepancy between the assertion of Fitzwilliam that the removal of Beresford had been tacitly sanctioned by Pitt beforehand, and Pitt's own statement that he considered it a grave breach of a solemn engagement; that the views, declarations, and policy of Fitzwilliam as to a new system of men and measures were irreconcilable with those of Pitt and his colleagues. It is only necessary, however, to produce one proof that Pitt was in the right, though others are not wanting. All Fitzwilliam's friends in the Cabinet, who loved Fitzwilliam, who disliked and distrusted Pitt; who had entered the Government reluctantly, and who would have embraced any fair opportunity of leaving it; who had been indeed on the brink of resignation with regard to Irish affairs three months before,—all these men, Portland and Windham, Spencer and Loughborough, three of them men of the nicest honour, and cognisant of the entire chain of agreements and events, all unhesitatingly took the part of Pitt against Fitzwilliam. Who, indeed, was the minister who, having obtained

special responsibility for Ireland by the threat of resignation, now recalled Fitzwilliam? Who but Portland,
himself Fitzwilliam's political friend and chief. In that
very letter to Grattan which has been mentioned, of the
23d of August 1794, Fitzwilliam says, "I shall look to the
system of the Duke of Portland as the model by which
I shall regulate the general line of my conduct." Portland's lethargy had been blamable in the earlier stages
of the transaction. But he showed none now. This is
a circumstance which appears to bar further controversy.
From the mouths of four unquestionable and unwilling
witnesses it establishes Pitt's good faith, and the fact
that the mistake lay with Fitzwilliam.

We should, however, beware of the slightest confusion
between the cause and the effects of Fitzwilliam's recall.
That he himself was the cause alters in no respect the
unhappy results of his removal. It seems, moreover,
clear that the objection was not so much to his policy as
to his methods. It was urged by Fitzwilliam that the
Catholic question had nothing to do with his removal,
but that his dismissals were the real cause. This statement seems accurate to the extent that the Government
was by no means averse to emancipation, but had a
rooted distrust of his administrative discretion. Pitt
was always ready for concession to Catholics; he showed
his readiness before and after, in 1792 and in 1797.
There was nothing in 1795 that should change his views.
The misfortune was that the Irish could not know his
real sentiments, or how he had pushed forward the great
emancipation of 1793. They could only surmise that
Fitzwilliam had been removed because he was a reformer,
and the Government hostile to all reform. Dublin shut

its shutters and went into mourning; while ardent patriots made up their minds that any amendment must come from France or from an appeal to arms.

It would seem at first, therefore, that it would have been far better, as it happened, to allow Fitzwilliam to fulfil his own promises, and to carry out his own programme. But a moment's reflection shows that this was impossible. There was the direst of all obstacles—a sunken rock. The King had been approached; his honour and his conscience had been moved by the most insidious and most impracticable of arguments. For he had been told that, should he consent to the admission of Catholics to political office, he would break his Coronation oath, and forfeit the crown. In that narrow, and obstinate, but scrupulous mind, this belief was now irrevocably imbedded. Fitzwilliam's policy would, therefore, have been shattered against the King's immovable and impregnable position on the Catholic question : immovable as regards himself, because he believed that emancipation involved the personal guilt of perjury; impregnable against opposition, because it was based on the passions and prejudices of the great mass of the people of Great Britain. And, as soon as he scented the Catholic question, the King urged Fitzwilliam's removal. So the impartial thinker can only once more lament that the mission of Fitzwilliam adds another instance of that curse of mischance that has always assisted the curse of misgovernment to poison the relations between England and Ireland.

And now things went from bad to worse. In September of this year (1795) the Orange Society arose. The Catholic organisation of the Defenders was already in

full operation. The United Irishmen availed themselves
of both these leagues. Agrarian outrage and the plunder
of arms abounded. In Ulster there was an organised
persecution to drive the Catholics out of the province—
"to hell or Connaught." In 1796 all these evils were
aggravated by the enrolment of the yeomanry, an undis-
ciplined and uncontrollable force. In December of
that year, a French expedition under Hoche invaded
Ireland, but effected nothing. In 1797, the state of the
North was hardly distinguishable from civil war. It
was placed under martial law. A population, which
had long been arming for rebellion, was disarmed by
harsh and summary methods. The Government had
some 60,000 soldiers and militia quartered in Ireland.
There were violent reprisals on the part of the military
for the outrages that had been committed by the United
Irishmen and Defenders.

The year darkened as it passed. The gaols were
full. Men under suspicion were crimped and sent to
serve in the fleet. Some even attributed the mutiny at
the Nore to the element thus introduced into the Navy.
Patrols pervaded the country all night. There was disaffection among the troops. The Catholics fled from
Ulster. On the one side there were murders, roastings,
plunder of arms, and a reign of terror; on the other,
picketing, scourging, hanging—half or whole—house-
burning, and a reign of not less terror. The miseries of
the Thirty Years' War were scarcely more appalling; for
it was civil conflict of the most terrible kind, the worse
because it was not declared; it was anarchy inflamed by
fanaticism; while the Parliament and the Government,
that should have remedied and appeased, were themselves

beyond help or hope.   The first could only acquiesce in
the proposals of the last; the last could only appeal for
more soldiers to England.

In 1798, the rebellion, in breaking out, lost something of its horror.   The rising was fixed for the 23d
of May; and on that day it flamed forth in the counties
of Dublin, Meath, and Kildare.   It does not come within
the compass of this narrative to describe that insurrection, its massacres and retaliations.   That it was not
even more formidable may be attributed to two causes:
Ulster held aloof, and the French came too late.   As it
was, the rebellion lasted barely a month, and was both
local and partial.

It is, however, worth noting here what Pitt wrote to
an eminent Irishman on this subject.   To the account
of the duel which he had sent to Wellesley he adds ·
"You will hear that in Ireland the Jacobins (after
many of their leaders being apprehended) have risen in
open war.   The contest has at present existed about a
week.   The Government have acted with great spirit, and
the troops of all descriptions behave incomparably.   We
cannot yet judge how far it may spread, but I trust
with the present force and some augmentation from
hence, the rebellion will be crushed, before any attempt
can be made from France: and we must, I think, follow
up such an event by immediate steps for a union."   As
to the behaviour of the troops Pitt was certainly ill
informed.   But in such a matter he would not be likely
to know much.   The internal administration of Ireland
was entirely independent of England.   There he had
neither knowledge nor control, unless specially appealed
to.   After all was over, after, as an Irishman said,

"rebellion and its attendant horrors had roused on both sides to the highest pitch all the strongest feelings of our nature," he may have heard of the atrocities in Ireland with much the same emotions that later ministers may have experienced in learning the horrors of the Indian mutiny and the horrors of its repression. We know this, that when Clare attempted in his hearing a defence of the malpractices of the magistrates and the militia, Pitt "turned . . . round with that high indignant stare which sometimes marked his countenance, and stalked out of the House."

At the close of the revolt a new Viceroy arrived. Cornwallis, whose career had been marked by one supreme military disaster, had obliterated it by his industry, his honesty, and his public spirit. He had not perhaps conspicuous abilities; but this deficiency only brings into greater prominence the sterling splendour of his character; and he remains a signal example of unsparing, unselfish, patriotic devotion to duty. But here his lines were cast in evil places. The one lesson of the rebellion was that the whole system of Irish government must be remodelled. What form the new experiment should take had long been tacitly admitted, and Cornwallis came over to carry a legislative Union between Great Britain and Ireland.

If the dismissal of Fitzwilliam may be said to touch the rim of a volcano, the Union is the burning fiery furnace of the crater itself. Something, however, is admitted with regard to it on all sides. The Parliament that passed the Scottish Union in 1707 had been elected directly in view of that question, which entirely engrossed the national mind. The Parliament that in

1800 passed the Irish Union had been elected in 1797, with no more reference to the question of the termination of its own existence than to free education or female suffrage. So far from the nation being consulted in respect to the obliteration of its legislature, there was not, even after the conclusion of the treaty, any popular election held for the members to be sent to London; but lots were drawn among those elected under such totally different circumstances and for such totally different purposes. Nor is it denied that this Irish Parliament, so wholly without mandate, and probably without power to terminate itself (though this is still subject of contention), was practically bribed and bullied out of existence. The corruption was black, hideous, horrible; revolting at any time, atrocious when it is remembered that it was a nation's birthright that was being sold. It was perhaps less questionable in those days to buy up the nomination boroughs, or most of them, as chattels at a fixed tariff. Pitt had made a like proposition for England in his plan of parliamentary reform. Close boroughs then represented not merely a vested interest, but property of the most tangible and recognised kind. But what stands without either shame or palliation was the remodelling, in the autumn and winter of 1799, of the House of Commons, after it had rejected the Union propositions.

Between the close of the session of 1799 and the beginning of that of 1800, between June and January, sixty-three seats out of a total of three hundred were vacated. Some of those who had held them were cajoled; some were bribed into office and out of Parliament; the mass departed because the patrons of their boroughs had been bought over to the Union. In this way, without a dissolution, the whole complexion and constitution of the House were changed. In the session of 1799 the Irish Parliament rejected the propositions of the Government for a Union. When Parliament was opened in 1800, there was not the slightest allusion to the measure of Union in the speech from the throne; but thirty-nine writs were at once moved. The entire patronage and terror of the Crown were employed to pack Parliament and purchase the patrons of Parliament. It rained honey and gall as occasion required—offices and peerages, or dismissal and disgrace. Castlereagh, now Chief Secretary, and the executive agent in this degrading traffic, pursued his task without flinching or remorse. Not Strafford was more thorough. Cornwallis expressed his loathing and disgust of the whole transaction. Castlereagh neither felt nor expressed any. He, in fact, hoped that corruption would die of a sort of surfeit; that it would perish by this final exaggeration; and that by one supreme, shameless, wholesale effort he could put an end to it for ever.

Under these circumstances and auspices, the measure was passed in 1800, both in Ireland and in England. The Irish debates produced much fine and significant speaking, in which Foster against, and Fitzgibbon (now Clare) for the Union, bore off the palm; many weighty predictions from such men as Parsons and Grattan, that a Union so forced on would inevitably imperil the entire connection between the two countries; some ominous prophecies of the sinister influence that the Irish contingent would exercise over British politics. Charlemont, indeed, had always opposed any Union, on the ground that no other measure could so effectually contribute to the separation of the two countries. In Ireland itself there was a comparative apathy, produced by the ruinous struggles of the last few years; only in Dublin, the dying capital, was there a last agony of patriotism. On the other hand, all the efforts of the Government, unrelentingly applied, could produce but a few thinly-signed petitions in support of the Bill—not a twelfth of those against it. It passed by purchase. "The whole unbribed intellect of Ireland," says an eminent historian, "was opposed to it." Of the members who composed the majority in its favour, it is computed that only seven voted for it without any "consideration." In the House of Commons the minority set their names to an address recapitulating the evils and ignominies of the measure; in the House of Lords it was followed by an eloquent protest headed by Leinster, the only Irish duke, and completed by such signatures as those of Downshire and Meath, and Moira and Powerscourt. After an easy passage through the British Parliament, it received the royal assent in July.

With regard to the Union two separate questions have to be considered. Firstly, were the means by which it was carried justifiable? Secondly, was it a right measure in itself? On both these points it is necessary to keep in mind the preliminary remark that has been made. It is easy on the brink of the twentieth century to censure much in the eighteenth; but is it candid to do so without placing oneself as far as possible in the atmosphere, circumstances, and conditions of the period which one is considering? Have Pitt's critics done this? Have they judged him by the standards and ideas

of his time, and not by the standards and ideas of their
own? That is the spirit in which History judges statesmen, and for a simple reason : had they attempted to
carry into effect in their generation the ideas of ours, they
would not have been statesmen at all. They would have
been voices crying in the wilderness ; they might have
been venerated as well-intentioned visionaries, or imprisoned as agitators, and even as lunatics ; but statesmen
they would not have been in name or in fact. A statesman measures the opinions and forces that surround him,
and proceeds to act accordingly ; he is not laying his
account with remote posterity, or legislating for it. The
politician who is a century before his time is hardly more
a statesman than the politician who is a century behind
it. The man who doses a child with colchicum, or who
attempts to cure atrophy by bleeding, is neither in name
nor in fact a physician. To apply what is wholesome
at one stage of growth or of disease to an age or an
ailment totally different is merely dangerous quackery.
To the man who attempts such mortal mischief in politics
is commonly denied the power ; and for this reason
doctrines in advance of the age, as they are called, are
usually the copyright of philosophers entirely dissoci-
ated from affairs. It is in this spirit that History, truly
and justly written, apportions blame and praise to men,
judging by contemporary canons and not by ours. It
is thus that History weighs in her balance Cæsar, and
Richelieu, and William III., and Ximenes, and Oxen-
stiern. Were it otherwise, she would hold the third
Duke of Richmond, with his universal suffrage and
annual parliaments, a greater statesman than Pitt, or
Burke, or any of his contemporaries.

To Pitt alone is meted out a different measure. He alone is judged, not by the end of the eighteenth, but by the end of the nineteenth century. And why? Because the Irish question which he attempted to settle is an unsettled question still. He alone of the statesmen of the eighteenth century, with the exception of Burke and perhaps Chesterfield, saw its importance and grappled with it manfully. Since then many ministers have nibbled at it whose efforts are buried in decent obscurity. But Pitt's career is still the battle-field of historians and politicians, because he is responsible for the treaty of Union; and because he resigned and did not do something, neither known nor specified but certainly impossible, to carry what remained of Catholic Emancipation.

Of the corruption by which the Union was carried something remains to be noted. It was, admittedly, wholesale and horrible. But it must in fairness be remembered that this was the only method known of carrying on Irish government; the only means of passing any measure through the Irish Parliament; that, so far from being an exceptional phase of politics, it was only three or four years of Irish administration rolled into one. No Irish patriot can regard the Union as other than the sale of his Parliament, justifiable or unjustifiable according to his politics; but, for an English minister of that day, the purchase of that Parliament was habitual and invariable. The quotations of the parliamentary market were as well known as the quotations of wheat and of sugar. It is scarcely possible to open a letter from an Irish Viceroy or an Irish Secretary of that time without finding a calculation for the hire, open and

avowed, of some individual or influence; or some cynical
offer by some hungry nobleman of his interest for a
determined price. It was the ordinary daily life of
Dublin Castle; it was the air which the Government
breathed; the nourishment which alone enabled it to
exist. No one condemned it, any more than the neigh-
bours of Washington condemned him for owning
slaves. And the reason is simple. The Irish Executive
was appointed in England solely with reference to
English considerations; the Parliament through which
this Executive had to pass its measures was an Irish
Parliament, elected, so far as it was freely elected, with
reference to Irish considerations. The Government and
its policy were entirely exotic; and the attempt to root
them in Irish soil was a perpetual strife with nature.
An artificial temperature had to be formed for them, and
that was corruption. A means of bringing the Government and the Parliament into relations had to be found,
and that was corruption. A means of carrying Government measures through Parliament had to be discovered,
and that was corruption. For a government which rules
in disregard or defiance of Parliament must resort to
bribery or resort to force. There was no force available; corruption therefore was the indispensable agency.
The absolute severance of the Executive and the Legislature both in nature and origin produced an unnatural and
unworkable condition of affairs; it was only by bribery
that the machine could be set going at all. The great
measure of Catholic Emancipation was only carried in
1792-93 by Castle influence; that is, by direct or indirect
corruption through a reluctant Parliament. Had Fitzwilliam been allowed to carry the complement of

these bills in 1795, he could only have done it by the
same means. The Executive was in no way responsible
to Parliament; had Parliament been unanimous in
opposition, it could not have changed a minister. Any
bill, therefore, that the Government wished to pass
was a subject of separate negotiation with the jobbers of
the country. These were generally recalcitrant in proportion to their power, and had to be purchased accordingly.
There were in reality no constituencies for the Government to appeal to. As out of the 300 members of the
House 124 were nominated by 52 peers, and 64 by 36
commoners, it was with the owners of the constituencies
that the Government had to deal.

It must be understood, then, that corruption was not
a monstrous, abnormal characteristic of the Union; it
was the everyday life and atmosphere of Irish politics.
Was it not better, it may be then urged, that this
system should end? Was it not better, at the worst,
and once for all, to make a regiment of peers and an
army of baronets, to buy the rotten boroughs at the
price of palaces, than to go on in the vile old way,
hiring, haggling, jobbing, from one dirty day to another,
from one miserable year to another, without hope or
self-respect; poisoning the moral sense, and betraying
the honest judgment of the country, in the futile, endless
attempt to maintain the unnatural predominance, and
the unreal connection, of an alien executive and a
sectional legislature? If the answer be Yes, the means
are to that extent justified, for there were no others.

It may, however, be said, that even if it be granted
that the system was vile and rightly ended, and ended by
the only practicable methods, it might have been replaced

by something better than the Union. To some of us now living this seems clear enough; but had we lived then, is it certain that our judgment would have been the same? We were engaged in a war, not of winter quarters and of summer quarters, and of elegant expeditions some way off, and of musketeers in laced gloves and periwigs saying, "Gentlemen, fire first," not a war of the eighteenth century : but naked men were fighting for life and freedom with despair; they were crossing the ice barefoot in rags; they were capturing fleets with cavalry; both we and our foes believed it to be a struggle between existence and extinction. Fortunately, it ended in existence for us, nearly exhausted and in terrible debt, but still existence.

At the end of the eighteenth century, however, such a result was by no means certain. We formed the main object of an enemy, who had conquered half Europe. Thrice had that enemy invaded Ireland, and it was certain that an invasion of England was only a question of time. In so appalling a crisis, a new arrangement had, by the admission of all parties, to be formed for Ireland. Grattan himself had tacitly given up his own Parliament as hopeless ; for he had withdrawn from it, and encouraged the discussion of Irish affairs in the British legislature. What wonder, then, if from the natural tendency to draw closer and closer and closer yet, in the presence of an overpowering danger, men's minds should have turned with rare unanimity to the idea of a Union. During a campaign even a single Parliament sometimes seems a superfluity, and a second a danger. What would happen, if in war, as on the Regency question, the British Parliament should take one line, and the Irish Parliament the other ? If, however, they became united, it would be safe, in view of the overwhelming Protestant majority in England and Scotland, to give concessions that otherwise would be impossible to the overwhelming Catholic majority in Ireland. Internal free trade would give Ireland material prosperity, but without a Union the British commercial classes would not hear of any such arrangement. Neither concession, neither Catholic relief nor internal free trade, would in the then temper of men's minds have had a chance of acceptance in England, so long as they were made to the independent parliament of a hostile nation. But on Catholic relief and on internal free trade Pitt's mind was set.

Again, if a Union were achieved, there would be no focus for French intrigue. The Executive of the two countries had always been practically one : to make the two Parliaments one would place the conditions of Government on a natural basis. But, above all, was the consideration that Great Britain would now face the world with a united front, with a single Parliament in which the elements of loyalty and stability would be in an incalculable majority.

These arguments, whatever may now be thought of their value, appealed with irresistible force to statesmen, for whom, struggling in a great war, unity and simplicity of government were everything. But Pitt never thought, as some seem since to have thought, that the Union could stand alone ; he never deemed it a divine instrument, admirable and venerable by its own natural essence. He considered it as only a part, and not even the most important part, of a great healing policy in Ireland ; and that, almost if not quite simul-

taneously, the other parts should be applied; the last
limitations of the Catholics removed; the clergy other
than those of the Established Church provided with
stipends; the oppression of tithe abolished. These
were inseparable constituents of his scheme. Had his
hands been free, he might have even dealt with the
evils of the land system, at least as regards absen-
teeism. Who will say that, followed up by large,
spontaneous, and simultaneous concessions of this kind,
the policy of the Union might not have been a success?
Had Pitt, in face of the difficulties that presented
themselves, temporarily dropped Catholic Emancipation,
and only carried a Tithe Bill in 1801, the Union might
at least have had a fair start. Frere, who knew
Pitt well, declared that it was not true that Pitt
ever regarded Catholic Emancipation as a sop to be
offered to the Irish to make them accept the Union.
On the contrary, he regarded, as Frere knew, the
Emancipation of the Catholics as the more important
measure of the two, and he would gladly have carried
it at any time. The Union was to pave the way and
conciliate British opinion. "The word Union," Pitt's
Lord Lieutenant wrote, as he was passing the measure,
"will not cure the evils of this wretched country; it is
a necessary preliminary, but a great deal more remains
to be done." That was Pitt's view. But on this
necessary preliminary or foundation succeeding ministries reared either structures he had never contemplated,
or no structure at all. He passed the Union with one
object; it has been diverted to another.

There was a curse upon it. It drove its very
author from office in the full plenitude of his authority,

in the very moment of the triumph of passing it.
Never did Pitt hold power again ; for his last two
years of suffering and isolation do not deserve the
name. And so all went wrong. The measure of Union
stood alone. And it was one of the drawbacks of
that luckless measure that it left all the remaining
machinery of independence when it took away the Parliament; every other characteristic of a separate state,
everything to remind men of what had been. It was
like cutting the face out of a portrait and leaving the
picture in the frame. The fragment of policy flapped
forlornly on the deserted mansions of the capital, but
there was enough to remind men of what had been.
It was impossible, for example, to destroy that Ionian
colonnade which remains one of the glories of Dublin.
So the Government transformed into a bank the noble hall
which had resounded with some of the highest flights
of human eloquence, which was indissolubly connected
with such names as Flood and Grattan and Charlemont,
and which was imperishably imbued with the proud
memories of an ancient nationality. Men as they
passed murmured that that was the home of their
Parliament, which nothing had obliterated and nothing
had replaced.

But all that man could do was done to obliterate
the rest of Pitt's policy. Addington's Irish Government went over with express instructions to do
nothing for the Catholics, nothing for the Dissenters, but to push and promote the Established
Church in every way. The Union alone remained even
to indicate what Pitt's plan had been ; and that was
a misleading indication. Catholic Emancipation waited

for thirty, and Tithe Reform waited for near forty, embittered and envenomed years. The time for ecclesiastical stipends provided by the State passed away for ever. The bright promises of financial improvement that had been held out to Ireland faded away into bankruptcy. Seventy years afterwards, the Irish Church Establishment, which it had been one of the main objects of the Treaty to preserve, suddenly toppled over and disappeared. With it went the keystone of the Union. And so it is Pitt's sinister destiny to be judged by the petty fragment of a large policy which he did not live to carry out: a policy, unhappy in execution and result, but which was, it may be fairly maintained, as generous and comprehensive in conception as it was patriotic in motive. It was at any rate worth trying, where so many had failed. But it had no trial; the experiment was scarcely even commenced; and the ruinous part that remains, exposed as it has been to the harshest storms of nine decades, is judged and venerated as if it were the entire structure.

CHAPTER XII

PITT AND WELLESLEY

IT may be well here to desist for a moment from the task of description, and to give the reader a glimpse of the true Pitt afforded by himself. His friendships were few, but they were close, and even tender, to a remarkable degree. Of Wilberforce and him it was said that they were like brothers. A scarcely less affectionate though a later intimacy was that with Lord Mornington, afterwards Lord Wellesley, the great Viceroy whose brilliant rule in India conferred such renown on himself, though it afterwards disabled him to a great extent for the rough and tumble of English party strife. To him the following letters were addressed.[1] The first was evidently written in 1796, when it may be presumed that Mornington was in Ireland.

DOWNING STREET,
Sept. 22*d* (undated, but evidently 1796),

MY DEAR MORNINGTON—I have waited from day to day by no fault of my own, much longer than I wished or expected, in the hope of seeing my way as to our official

[1] These letters, which are in some respects the most interesting that we have of Pitt's, have been made available for this little book by the generous kindness of Mr. Alfred Montgomery.

arrangements, and being able to write you something positive respecting yourself. I am happy now to tell you that there is no obstacle to accomplishing what I have from the beginning eagerly wished to find practicable ; and that I shall certainly be enabled to open for you either the office of Joint-Paymaster, or some other equally desirable. A very few days will settle the specific mode. We mean to chuse the Speaker on Sunday, but to defer opening the causes of calling the Parliament till after the members are sworn ; probably till Tuesday sennight. This will avoid the inconvenience of making or at least delivering the speech so long before it can be debated, which is very material, at a time that every day produces such important events. We have fresh accounts to-day of continued success up to the 8th, when the Archduke was advanced to Wetzlar. Nothing can equal the rapidity of his progress. "Nec vero disjunctissimæ terræ citius cujusquam passibus peragrari potuerunt, quam suis non dicam cursibus, sed victoriis illustratæ sunt." [1] Our overture has been sent to Paris above a fortnight, but we have got no answer, nor any late accounts of what is passing there yet.—Ever sincerely yours,

W. PITT.

The next two refer to Mornington's desire for a peerage of Great Britain before setting out for India. As regards that wish nothing need here be said, nor does Pitt seem able to comprehend the frame of mind in which such a desire could be formed. But his hearty zeal in his friend's cause is surely a pleasant feature. The second of these notes was written on the very day (October 4, 1797) on which Mornington was formally appointed Governor-General of India.

[1] Slightly altered from Cicero, pro M. Marcello, Oratio II. 5. The present reading is, I am informed, "lustratæ."

HOLLWOOD,
Tuesday, Oct. 3d, 1797.
½ p. 9 P.M.

MY DEAR MORNINGTON—I cannot easily say how much gratification I felt, in opening and reading your letter, from knowing that as far as depends upon me, I had anticipated both your reasoning and your wishes. I had written to the King some hours before, requesting as strongly as I thought myself at liberty to do, that you should be included in the List of Peers. I will not pretend to you that I had quite convinced my judgment; but I certainly felt it one of the occasions on which I had the best right to consult my inclination; and I could not reconcile myself to the idea of leaving to such uncertain chance as belongs to these times my hope of being able to contribute to the success of what seems with you so favourite a wish. You will of course know the result from me to-morrow. I have put it in the way I thought most likely to overcome objections, but I cannot venture to state the thing to you as what you can count upon till I receive the King's answer; as he seemed most strongly bent against every extension of the List, and it is one of the points on which he is most apt to adhere to his opinion.

I trust from what I hear from Dundas that there is very little chance indeed that the second part of your case (your not going to Bengal) will arise. As we shall know the result on that so soon, I will say no more about it.—Ever affly. yrs.,   W. P.

The King's resistance did not last long.

DOWNING STREET,
Wednesday, (evidently *Oct.* 4, 1797,) ½ p. 1.

MY DEAR MORNINGTON—If you happen to be disen-

gaged I shall be very glad to see you here at dinner to-day
soon after five.—Yours ever,   W. P.

I am most happy to tell you, the King agrees to your
peerage.

The next letter gives a long and elaborate account of
the state of affairs as it appeared to Pitt's sanguine
apprehension. His sarcasm on the Crown lawyers is
characteristically cold and cutting. The allusion to
Grenville shows that the somewhat crabbed character of
that minister was recognised by his colleagues as a
difficulty to be reckoned with. In this letter, too, occurs
that account of a speech by Perceval which so impressed
Pitt as to make him on the morning of the duel name
Perceval as probably the most available man to succeed
him. His genial pleasure over the young man's success
explains perhaps what the ordinary view of Pitt's
haughty reserve does not : the idolatry with which so
many of his followers, particularly the junior ones, regarded him.

WIMBLEDON,
Jan. 26*th*, 1798.

MY DEAR MORNINGTON—You will hear I trust from
various other correspondents who have more leisure, a
much fuller history of all that has been passing since you
left us, than I can pretend to give you. But I think you
will like to hear from me even if it is only to tell you as to
myself, that in spite of six weeks of more fatigue and
anxiety than have attended almost any other Parliamentary
campaign, I am greatly better than you left me, and I trust,
equal to fighting the battle as long as may be necessary.
Our great measure of the assessed taxes was for some time
apparently in great danger of failing, less from any real

difficulty or even general dislike to it than from the impression of local and partial clamour, and from the effect of a very great degree of panic which infected too many of those who are generally most free from it. It became necessary to shew that *at all risks* I was determined to persevere in it; and by those means alone I believe it was carried. Opposition I think added to the odium and disgrace of their secession by returning from it on this occasion, and by the whole of their conduct and language upon it. Our last debate (to my great joy) produced a speech from Perceval, which was in all respects one of the best I ever heard; and was an attack upon Fox pointed and galling enough to have drawn forth one of Grattan's warmest encomiums. It certainly sent him home very sick to his supper. Since this effort we have heard nothing of him but from the celebration of his birth-day two days ago, in which the two most distinguished traits were a speech from the Duke of Norfolk, which I think even the Crown lawyers will hardly prove to be much short of treason, and a public profession from Horne Tooke of reconciliation and coalition with Fox, with which I think you will be delighted. On the whole the line now taken by the whole of what calls itself Opposition (with the exception of Grey and Whitbread, whom we neither see nor hear of) and especially by Fox, is a compleat and undisguised avowal of the most desperate system ever acted upon, and I think it seems to be understood and felt as it ought, both in Parliament and in the country. The two great objects of our attention and exertion now are, to endeavour to raise spirit enough in the country to contribute voluntarily to the expense of the war, such a sum as in addition to the assessed taxes may bring our loan within a moderate shape, and next, to be prepared both by sea and land for the invasion which I have little doubt will be attempted in

the course of the year, tho' the latter is much the easier work
of the two. And I hope we shall have to make the option
between burning their ships before they set out, or sinking
them either on their passage or before their troops can land,
or destroying them as soon as they have landed, or starving
them and taking them prisoners afterwards. Indeed the
scheme seems so romantic (without the prospect of any
naval force to support it) that at any other moment it
would not be credible; and it can hardly be attempted on
any other notion but that it may be worth the enemy's
while to devote two-thirds of an immense army to immediate
destruction, for the sake of the mischief which the remainder
may effect before they share the same fate. In the meantime however (tho' on the whole I think the attempt will be
made) there are two possible events which may prevent it.
One is if there should be fresh confusion in France, which
seems not distant, and of which the issue cannot be even
conjectured. The other is, if the new King of Prussia and
the powers of the North should at last awaken, of which
there is just now some appearance, but it is not yet decided
enough to rely upon. The new decree aimed at our commerce but tending to annihilate a large part of the profit of
neutral nations may perhaps (added to the danger of Ham-
burgh and the North of Europe) bring Denmark at least if
not Sweden or Russia, to be ready to enter into an effectual
concert with Prussia. And this prospect may tempt Prussia
to take a decided part, which if it does, Europe will at last
be saved. On the measure of voluntary contribution you
will not wonder to hear that all our friends have not
thought alike. But at so extraordinary a moment I have
felt it so decidedly right, that I have determined as far as
depends on me, to push it to the utmost; and tho' it has
begun but languidly, I have now good hopes of success; as
I have been enabled to-day to announce to the Bank, the

King's intention of giving one-third of his privy purse ; and am besides furnished with such particulars as will enable me to satisfy the world, that he has *no other* fund from which he can command a shilling. We in office have thought it right to give an ample *fifth* of our income. And to my great satisfaction, Grenville has concurred very readily in giving his personal share, tho' very adverse in his general opinion to the whole measure. I am very happy to be able to add too, now that I mention his name, that I have not seen a cloud on his brow since the commencement of the session, and that every thing has gone on as pleasantly and cordially as possible. I have now mentioned all that I think it will be most interesting to you to learn. And you must at least for the present accept this picture of the times (which is as much as I can compleat at one sitting) as a substitute for that which I owe you from Hopner and which I hope will come one day or other. I conclude you will have heard from different channels of the anti-Jacobin ; and I hope you will sometimes wish you were within reach of supporting it by your voluntary contribution. I have desired a compleat set to be sent you, lest you should not otherwise receive it.—God bless you.—Ever affy. yours,

W. Pitt.

The next, dated three months later, is not less sanguine ; more especially in reference to finance and the French Invasion. It is noteworthy that Sheridan's speech in defence of the war was made after a good deal of private negotiation, to which in these years, at any rate during the Addington government, Sheridan seems to have been addicted. The use of the word "Plug" in this sense must be explained by more learned commentators. Grose and other kindred lexicographers throw no light.

WIMBLEDON,
April 22d, 1798, 9 P.M.

MY DEAR MORNINGTON—Lord Auckland has sent me
word, by a messenger who came just before dinner, that he
is sending (I know not how) some packet to you to-night.
I had just before learned that a neutral ship from the Cape
brings an account to-day of your arrival there and of your
being perfectly well, which I hope we shall soon have
verified by yourself. I have not time to write much this
evening; but I am very glad to have an opportunity of
telling you shortly how much the state of things has been
improving since I wrote to you last. The voluntary contribution has succeeded to a great extent. The spirit and
courage of the country has risen so as to be fairly equal to
the crisis. I am to settle my loan to-morrow, to the
amount of fifteen millions, which will leave us without a
single difficulty in finance, and I have no doubt of making
it on better terms than last year. The plan for the sale of
the land tax (which I think we talked of before you went)
is going on. The Bill is to be read a second time to-morrow,
and in spite of many *Plugs* from Sir Wm. Pulteney will
certainly pass, and there is every reason to think the effect
will be very considerable. In addition to these favorable
circumstances our traitors at home (those chiefly of the
lower class) have given us the means of seizing them to
such a number as I believe to disconcert effectually whatever were their plans; and the Habeas Corpus Act has been
suspended by a Bill passed in both Houses in one day.
Our division 183 to 5. Sheridan came (after long notice in
general conversation and some *private*) to make an excellent
speech against the French, and his own friends here. But
he was foolish enough to oppose the suspension, and divide
in the minority in which the little of opposition that was
in the House, left him and voted with us. He did us some

good, gained some credit to himself and not too much, and
added to the disgrace of the seceders. Of the last class,
Fox, Grey, and Whitbread remain, the first, I believe, for
ever, and of the latter I cannot judge. The French go on,
I believe in earnest, with plans and demonstrations of invasion ; but the effect here, is only to produce all the
efforts, and all the spirit we can wish. In addition to all
this state of things at home, there is a chance (and a better
than has appeared for a long period) that the monarchs remaining in Europe will awake before their thrones are
taken from under them, and will think it better to lay aside
interested jealousies among themselves than to remain any
longer a prey to their common enemy. We shall of course
encourage and incite this to the utmost, and if they are true
to themselves, Europe will still be saved. If this should
fail us, I think you may still count fully on finding England
a country to receive you when you return from India ; and
I think you will find our friend (who quoted Pompey upon
you at your departure) in better spirits and temper than
you left him. He is doing every thing that is right. I
have tried to tell you all I could in a short time, and
perhaps unintelligibly.—Ever yrs.,   W. PITT.

The next letter gives Pitt's account of the duel. To
us his reference to Irish affairs is more interesting than
his light-hearted account of the somewhat boyish
escapade.

PRIVATE.

DOWNING STREET,
Thursday, May 31st, 1798.

MY DEAR MORNINGTON—I have not time to write you
a very long letter; but as you will hear of me from others,
I think you will like to be told by myself that I was
under the necessity last Sunday of meeting Mr. Tierney in

P

consequence of some expressions I had used in the House
of Commons, on the Friday preceding, and which I did not
feel it right to explain.   I enclose you a short statement of
what passed, taken down by the seconds before we left the
ground.   The business has ended to my perfect satisfaction,
and I must say that Tierney conducted himself with the
greatest propriety.   I believe we parted better satisfied wit 1
each other, than on any other occasion in our lives.

You will hear that in Ireland the Jacobins (after many
of their leaders being apprehended) have risen in open war.
The contest has at present existed about a week.

The Government have acted with great spirit, and the
troops of all descriptions behave incomparably.   We cannot
yet judge how far it may spread, but I trust with the
present force and some augmentation from hence, the
rebellion will be crushed, before any attempt can be made
from France ; and we must I think follow up such an event
by immediate steps for an union.   The French will probably
try a magnificent project of invading Ireland from Toulon ;
but will be surprised at meeting Ld. St. Vincent in the
Mediterranean where they least expect him.   I have not
time for another sheet.—Ever yours,   W. PITT.

ENCLOSURE.

May 28th.

WE are authorised to state that in consequence of what
passed on Friday last, Mr. Pitt, accompanied by Mr. Ryder
and Mr. Tierney, accompanied by Mr. George Walpole, met
at three o'clock yesterday afternoon on Putney Heath.

After some ineffectual attempts on the part of the seconds
to prevent further proceedings, the parties took their ground
at the distance of twelve paces.   A case of pistols was fired
at the same moment without effect.   A second case was also
fired in the same manner, Mr. Pitt firing his pistol in the

air. The seconds then jointly interfered, and insisted that
the matter should go no further, it being their decided
opinion that sufficient satisfaction had been given, and that
the business was ended with perfect honour to both
parties.

The next contains the innocent offer of the Irish
marquisate which caused such dire offence.

DOWNING STREET,
Nov. 6th, 1799.

MY DEAR MORNINGTON—I was in hopes to have atoned
in some degree for my long silence by writing to you at
large on all the interesting subjects on which you will wish
for information, but I have been continually interrupted till
the last moment and must now confine my letter to a few
lines. They must naturally be employed in the first place
to tell you what however I trust you are sufficiently assured
of already, how warmly and sincerely I rejoice in all the
success and glory which has attended your Indian Government. In the midst of the agitations of Europe, the
remoteness of the scene of action has not prevented the
value of your services from being felt and estimated by the
public as your warmest friends would wish. An Irish
marquisate, which the King confers on you, by the title
of Marquis Wellesley of Norragh, (which is pitched upon on
Bernard's authority) will I hope be satisfactory as an
ostensible mark of approbation, and the further provision
which Dundas will have explained to you is in contemplation, besides operating as a further acknowledgment of
your services, is likely I trust to set your mind wholly at
ease in what relates to the interest of your family. I must
not attempt in the haste in which I write to enter into any
particulars on the wide field of politics, many of them, I
know, you will hear from Canning, and probably from

Grenville. In general, much indeed has been gained in the course of the present year, notwithstanding the failures and reverses of the latter part. If Austria can be made to act in earnest next year, and to aim at gaining her own objects thro' the medium of saving Europe instead of destroying it, everything we wish seems within reach of being accomplished in two campaigns more. The decision of Vienna is however wholly uncertain and our best comfort is that if it fails us we can return to our defensive system with unbroken spirits and resources, and trust to our own anchors to ride out the storm. I cannot end without thanking you for the particular accounts you sent me of our gallant friend Cooke, about whom I am more interested than I can express. We are at this moment in great anxiety about him, as the accounts we had received of his being perfectly out of danger, have been followed by others of a later date mentioning his death, but as these last come by Bombay and are only in general terms, I trust there is still some room left for hope.—Ever affectionately yours,

W. PITT.

Wellesley's reply to this letter is well known. It is dated April 28, 1800, and is printed, though not at length, in Lord Stanhope's *Life* (vol. iii. p. 232). He speaks in the bitterest terms of the anguish of mind he felt; that the impression produced in India would be fatally detrimental to his Government; and that the slur inflicted by this "Irish," "pinchbeck" reward affected both his health and his spirits. Pitt's letter in reply, here subjoined, is the most interesting of his that we possess. It seems to combine an admirable specimen of his persuasive power in debate with the soothing affection of a brother ministering to a sick and overburthened mind. It is in itself a final and conclusive answer to the allegations of haughty heartlessness.

HAMPSTEAD,
Saturday, Sept. 27th, 1800.

MY DEAR WELLESLEY—I received last Wednesday your letter of the 28th April, and painful as were its contents to me in many respects I had at least great consolation and satisfaction in the proof of your continued kindness and friendship which I derived from the unreserved communication of your feelings. You will I am sure wish me to use the same frankness in return. I certainly most deeply lament that the particular mark of the King's favor which you have received is so little adequate to your wishes and expectations, but I must fairly own to you that on the fullest reflection I cannot concur in your view of the subject. In the first place I have always felt that in every question of reward for services, the manner in which it is given, and that in which it is received determine its value in the eyes of the public much more than its own specifick nature. But you must allow me to state freely that independent of this general feeling there are particular circumstances in the present case to which you do not appear to have given the weight which I think they deserve. Nothing but the duty of stating to you exactly what I feel with the sincerity of a friend would bring me to refer to the topic I am going to mention. It was certainly to me a most sensible gratification to be able previous to your going to India, to secure to you an object on which you set so much value as the British peerage. But surely considering the circumstances under which the King was induced to give it, it must be considered rather as an anticipation to no small extent of the reward for distinguished service than as a foundation for higher claims when those services should have been actually performed. In this view of the subject to have given you an English marquisate would have been to have conferred in the short course of your Indian Government four steps in the British peerage; a scale of promotion certainly very unusual. The step in the Irish peerage was precisely the same proportional advancement as was given to Lord Cornwallis for his services in the same quarter; and from the manner in which you have yourself referred to them, I am sure you will join in the general feeling that to adopt such a proportion had nothing in it disparaging. The truth really is that in my mind and I believe in that of almost all your friends (all feeling the same cordial and zealous interest in your just fame and consideration) the natural question seemed to be whether to recommend to the King to give you an English earldom, or the Irish marquisate. From many quarters I was led to believe that you would prefer the latter; and particularly the circumstance of Barnard's being in possession of the memorandum specifying the title to which you had looked decided my opinion. I have hitherto confined myself only to the point of promotion in the peerage; but in estimating the value of the ostensible marks of approbation and honour which you have received, and by which the public both here and in India would judge of the sense entertained of your services, there are other circumstances to be considered much more important than either an Irish or English marquisate. The unanimous thanks of both Houses of Parliament, in the marked terms in which they were conveyed, if they had been accompanied by no other distinction, would in my judgment alone have placed you on ground on which few servants of the public have ever stood. In addition to this decisive testimony, the provision proposed to be made by the company independent of its intrinsic value to your family, is to be considered as a public tribute to your merits, which makes it impossible to suppose that they were depreciated in any quarter. The King's speech to which you refer (however you may perhaps consider it in India as with us in the House of Commons as the speech of the minister) is at least as direct an indication of the sentiment of the sovereign and as much his act, as any title which he confers. Combining all these considerations, I really cannot conceive how the public in India should feel (what I will venture to say the public *in Europe* have never felt, and never I believe will be brought to feel) that there has not been in every quarter (the *highest* included) the most cordial and liberal disposition to bear full testimony and do ample justice, to the extent of your claims upon the public. Still less can I imagine, that with all these marks of approbation from England and with the impression which your conduct must have made on the minds of those who were nearer witnesses of it, it can have been a question whether you were likely to continue possessed of that respect and estimation from all the civil and military servants in India which is necessary for the full support of your authority. Forgive me if I add, that if any such feeling has found its way into their mind or into their conversation, it can only, I believe, have originated from some suspicion of its being entertained by yourself. That idea is at any time enough to make any but the most real friends, admit that a man is mortified and ill used. But it will hardly ever happen (unless in cases very different indeed from the present) that the opinion and language of the person most interested and of those immediately connected with him will not decide that of the public. I have now fairly stated to you my view of the subject. I cannot hope to change an opinion which I fear has taken so deep a root in your mind. But I am sure you will give a candid consideration to what I have stated, and I trust that the plainness and sincerity with which I have expressed myself will appear to you the best proof I could give of real friendship. With these sentiments on the subject as it stood originally, you will not wonder if I do not see the possibility (however anxiously I wish it were possible) that anything should be now done to repair your disappointment. Indeed your own wishes do not seem to point at any additional mark of favor, unless it had taken place on our receiving the news of the final settlement of Mysore. That period is elapsed, and I think you will agree with me that (if no other objection were felt here) whatever was done now would want the *grace* which belongs to rewards of this nature only when they are *gratuitous*, and would be liable to a construction neither creditable to Government nor to yourself. I have said nothing on the little intrinsic difference under the present circumstances, between an English and Irish marquisate, because I conceive you look rather to the public impression than to the thing itself. But as far as in itself it may be an object, it will certainly not escape you that under the circumstances of the Union, the difference to any person already possessed of a British title is little more than nominal ; scarcely extending further than to a question of stile in the journals and debates of the House of Lords or of relative precedence as to four or five individuals; objects on which I do not believe such a mind as yours can set much serious value. I have not time to add anything more to this long letter, except the assurance of the cordial and unabated friendship and attachment with which I hope ever to remain.—Sincerely and affectionately yours, W. PITT.

Both Dundas and myself enter into and applaud the justice and delicacy of your feelings with respect to the particular fund out of which your grant was intended to be made, tho' the objection is rather in appearance than in substance. I am persuaded some other mode will be found of carrying into effect what was intended.

MARQUIS WELLESLEY.

The last two letters were written when Wellesley was at war with the Board of Directors, and are interesting mainly as showing the tender delicacy with which Pitt soothed the sore and sensitive spirit of his friend. The great Viceroy, it remains to be added, landed in England in January 1806 just in time to give a farewell grasp to the emaciated hand of the great Minister. The note in which Pitt writes to Wellesley of the inexpressible pleasure with which he had received the note announcing Wellesley's return is dated January 12, 1806, and is given by Lord Stanhope (*Life*, vol. iv. p. 373).

PRIVATE.

PUTNEY HILL, *August 30th*, 1804.

MY DEAR WELLESLEY—The letters which you will receive by this conveyance will inform you that the King has conferred a peerage on General Lake, and an extra red ribband on your brother Genl. Wellesley. I hope these marks of honour will prove that a just value is attached to the brilliant and extraordinary successes which they have obtained under your auspices and direction, and I congratulate you most heartily on the advantageous and honorable peace which has been the fruit of your victories, and on a series of events which has produced so large an accession of personal glory to yourself and of power and reputation to the country. You will have heard from others the

general history of our political situation at home, and will
have seen in what has passed and in the state of parties
which it has produced, much to regret, and much I believe to wonder at. I have very much wished to write to
you at large on the subject ; but you will not wonder that
I found it impossible during the session, and in the weeks
that have elapsed since to the present moment, the details
of military preparation under the constant expectation of an
immediate attempt at invasion, have in addition to the
common course of business furnished me incessant occupation. We are *now* I trust in a state in which we may meet
with confidence any enterprise to which even the largest
scale of French exertions is equal ; and I believe the thing
most to be wished is that they may speedily make the trial.
It seems probable from what I collect of the last letters
received from you, that you will be on your passage home
before any further accounts from hence can reach India.
Indeed unless any more time should appear to yourself to
be necessary for winding up compleatly the result of all
your labours, or unless any new or great scene should unexpectedly open for fresh exertions, I hardly think that you
would be tempted to prolong your absence. If either of
those cases, however, should arise it cannot be necessary for
me to assure you that every additional period for which you
remain in India, will be considered by us (I mean the
Government, for I certainly cannot answer for the Court of
Directors) as so much gained for the public ; and that everything of course will be done which is practicable on our
part, to give you the fullest and most effectual support.
With the knowledge of these sentiments, you will I am sure
decide on whatever may be the state of circumstances before
you at the moment, in the way most for your own honor
and the public service ; without suffering that decision to
be influenced by the sense you may naturally entertain of

the petty cabals, and narrow views and prejudices which
too often operate at the India House, and which frequently
lead to an ungracious return for the services they ought
most to value.—Believe me at all times, my dear Wellesley,
sincerely and affectionately yours,   W. PITT.

DOWNING STREET, *Dec.* 21*st*, 1804.

MY DEAR WELLESLEY—Your brother, I find, thinks it
most probable from the last letter he has received from you,
that before the present packet reaches India, you will have
embarked for Europe.   Even if that should not be the case,
what you will learn by the present conveyance of the
temper and disposition which prevails at the India House,
will naturally lead you to a determination not to remain
longer than you may find necessary to compleat such arrangements as you may think it most material to bring to a
conclusion before your departure.   Indeed the advantage
which the persons hostile to your measures have derived
from your long silence on some of the most important trans-
actions of your Government, and particularly from their
being now left without any communication from yourself
respecting the war with Holkar has made it difficult to
keep them within any bounds ; and things are brought to a
point at which it seems to be the clear opinion of your
brother and of Lord Melville and Lord Castlereagh as well
as my own that you could no longer have the means of
carrying on the Government in a way either creditable or
satisfactory to yourself, or advantageous to the public
service.   It therefore seems to us clearly desirable that you
should carry into execution the intention you have expressed of returning home (if you have not done so at an
earlier period) in the course of next year ; and on that
supposition it will probably be thought that whoever should
be pitched upon to be your successor, should sail from hence

so as to arrive about September or October. Our intention
of course is if possible to select for this nomination some
person of high rank and consideration at home ; which I
trust you will agree with us in thinking a much more
desirable arrangement, than letting the Government devolve
to a company's servant, even in the instance of one of so
much distinguished merit as Mr. Barlow. You will I trust
readily believe that it must be my earnest wish that you
should not take your leave of India without receiving some
additional public mark of the cordial sense entertained of
your very transcendent services. That which I should be
most anxious to obtain because I believe it would be most
agreeable to yourself, would be the blue ribband ; but partly
from personal wishes of the King, and partly from political
engagements which in these times it has been impossible to
avoid, I much fear that I may find it impossible. In that
case the English marquisate, seems to be the only other
mark of honor that can be proposed, and I hope in the view
with which it will evidently be given, it will not be unac-
ceptable. But whatever you may feel as to rewards and
honors for the past, I hope the termination of your Indian
career will restore you to us with health and inclination to
take as distinguished a share as your talents and exertions
entitle you to in the agitated and anxious state of politics
in which you will find us involved on your return. It is of
course impossible now to foresee how circumstances may
change or what arrangements may become necessary within
the next twelve months. But if the King's health should
continue unshaken (of which at present there seems the
fairest prospect) I am convinced we have nothing to fear
from all the activity and ability of the combined opposition tho' much indeed to lament in the description of some
of whom it is composed. And if on your arrival you should
be as much inclined as I trust you will to give your assist-

ance to my administration, and an opening can be found to
give you as active and important a share in it as I should
wish, I need hardly tell you that such a circumstance would
from every public and private feeling be more gratifying to
me than I can express.   At all events I look forward with
eagerness to the moment when I shall find myself again in
your society, and to a renewal of all the habits of friendship and confidence from which for so many years I derived
so large a share of happiness and comfort.—Believe me
always, my dear Wellesley, affectionately yours,

W. PITT.

CHAPTER XIII

FALL OF THE GOVERNMENT

THE Union was considered a great triumph for Pitt, but it was the cause of his immediate fall. He was anxious not to delay an instant in pushing forward the large and liberal policy of which the Union had only been the prologue. The Act of Union received the royal assent on the 2d of July 1800. At the first Cabinet (September 30, 1800,) after the summer recess, Pitt developed his Irish policy. It included the substitution of a political in lieu of a religious test for office, a commutation of tithes, and a provision for the Catholic and Dissenting clergy.

Pitt had now to learn that, in choosing a successor for the impracticable Thurlow, he had managed to find an even more treacherous colleague. Loughborough, as he sate at council with him, had already betrayed him. During this month of September, while staying at Weymouth, the Chancellor had received a confidential letter from Pitt with reference to these different points, and had at once handed it to the King, whose prejudice on this subject had already been revealed in connection with the Fitzwilliam episode. Thus fortified, the Chancellor at the Cabinet of the 30th of September proclaimed his virtuous

scruples. The question was adjourned for three months,
during which time it was hoped that the good man
would reconsider his objections and prepare a complete
measure on tithes. Loughborough had no idea of thus
wasting his time. He spent this interval in working on
that royal conscience of which he was the titular keeper.
He sought the congenial alliance of Auckland, a valuable
accomplice, not merely on account of remarkable powers
of intrigue, but as brother-in-law to Moore, Archbishop of
Canterbury. That prelate was now stirred by some
occult inspiration to address a letter of warning to the
King. Stuart, the primate of Ireland, was moved by a
simultaneous impulse to exert his pastoral influence on
his sovereign. Pitt was undermined. His colleagues
began mysteriously to fall away. Chatham and West-
morland, Portland and Liverpool commenced to side
against the Catholics in a Cabinet which had been supposed to be unanimous in their favour.

In January 1801 the mine was sprung. At a levée
in that month, the King stormed audibly against the
proposals, which neither the First Minister nor the
Cabinet had laid before him. He sent Addington, the
Speaker, to remonstrate with Pitt, who indeed could not
have failed to hear at once of the scene at Court. Pitt
immediately addressed a statement of his policy to the
King, tendering his instant resignation if he were not
allowed to bring forward these different plans as
Government measures. The King in reply begged him
to remain and be silent. Pitt at once resigned, and the
King with apparent anguish acquiesced.

The parting honour that he awarded his minister is
notable. He knew that it was of no use to offer Pitt

money or ribbons or titles. So he began a letter to
him "My dear Pitt": a circumstance which throws a
little light on the character of both men.

The transaction has brought bitter censure upon
Pitt; it is not easy to see why. What more could he
do? What war is to kings, resignation is to ministers:
it is the *ultima ratio*. He was, perhaps, open to censure
for not having himself prepared the King at an earlier
stage of the proceedings for the projected policy, instead
of leaving it to others with a hostile bias. But a
minister who had served George III. for seventeen years
may be presumed to have understood the King's times
and seasons better than any retrospective intelligence.
It must be remembered also that, after the adjournment
in September to promote union in the Cabinet, he was
obliged to wait, in order to speak on behalf of a united
Government. Further, it may well have been that,
from his knowledge of the King, he thought that the
best chance of obtaining his consent was to lay before
him a completed measure, and not a projected policy.
Nor could he foresee the black betrayal of Loughborough.

It is not, however, necessary to dwell on the charge of
negligence, for the real accusation is much graver than
one of negligence : it is one of treachery. The accusation,
so far as it can be ascertained, (for it is vaguely and
diffusely expressed), imports that Pitt held out hopes to
the Irish Catholics by which he secured their support to
the Union, and that, instead of fulfilling these pledges, or
doing his best to fulfil them, he resigned : a mock resignation which he endeavoured to recall. But when and
how were these hopes held out? There is absolutely no
trace of them—none, at least, of any Cabinet authority for

them. Cornwallis and Castlereagh were indeed strongly pro-Catholic. What they did on their own responsibility is not known, nor is it now in question. But the most recent and the best informed of historians of the Union, and the most hostile to Pitt, expressly admits that : "It is in the first place quite clear that the English Ministers did not give any definite pledge or promise that they would carry Catholic Emancipation in the Imperial Parliament, or make its triumph a matter of life and death to the Administration. On two points only did they expressly pledge themselves. The one was, that, as far as lay in their power, they would exert the whole force of Government influence to prevent the introduction of Catholics into a separate Irish Parliament. The other was, that they would not permit any clause in the Union Act which might bar the future entry of Catholics into the Imperial Parliament; and the fourth article of the Union accordingly stated, that the present oaths and declaration were retained only 'until the Parliament of the United Kingdom shall otherwise provide.'"

The actual hopes held out were these. Castlereagh on returning from London in 1799, where he had gone to gather the sentiments of the Cabinet on the Catholic question, had written to Cornwallis that he was authorised to say that the opinion of the Cabinet was favourable to the principle of relief, though they did not think it expedient to make any public promise or declaration to the Catholics, or any direct assurance to the Catholics ; but that Cornwallis would be justified, so far as the sentiments of the Cabinet were concerned, in soliciting their support. And, in his speech of the 5th of February

1800, Castlereagh had further said that "an arrangement
for the clergy, both Catholic and Protestant Dissenters,
had long been in the contemplation of His Majesty's
ministers." These were the pledges—what was the per-
formance? That at the very first Cabinet, held after the
passing of the Union Bill, Pitt produced his policy, which
more than embodied them; that he urged it on his
colleagues with all his influence; that the King learned
it surreptitiously, and opposed his veto to it; and that
Pitt thereupon promptly and peremptorily resigned.

It is difficult for the most acute critic to perceive
what more he could have done. It was impossible
to convince or compel the King; his mind was too fixed
and his position too strong. But, it is urged that,
had Pitt insisted, the King, who had given way to him
before, would have given way to him again. The answer
is simple; he did insist, and the King did not give way,
and would never have given way. For in this case, unlike
the others, George III. was convinced that he would incur
the personal guilt of perjury under his Coronation oath;
and he knew that he would be supported in his resistance by the great mass of his subjects.

Under the strain of this agony, for it was no less,
torn by the separation from Pitt and by the pangs of
his conscience, his mind once more gave way. The
new ministry was already formed; and so, clear
of all suspicion of interest, Pitt allowed the King's
physician to soothe his old master's shattered mind
by the assurance that the Catholic question should
never more be raised by him in the King's lifetime.
The promise was natural; George III. was old and
breaking fast (two years later he was in fact at

the point of death) ; the promise would probably not long be operative.   But it has been insinuated that this was a mere renunciation on Pitt's part of a high principle in order to retain office ; and that he was only too glad to be rid of an embarrassing pledge by a resignation which he hoped in this way to recall.   Those who take this somewhat paltry view omit to state that Pitt's successor was appointed, that he himself declined to lift his finger to return to office, and promoted in every way the strength and efficiency of the Government that replaced him.

Facts of this kind can of course be always dismissed by a knowing wink or a sarcastic smile.   But it is not possible even thus to dismiss the letter written, late in December 1801, by Bishop Tomline.   The Bishop tells his correspondent, with a groan, that he had just had a long conversation with Pitt ; who had told him that he looked forward to the time when he might carry Catholic Emancipation, and that he did not wish to take office again unless he could bring it forward.   "Upon the Catholic question our conversation was less satisfactory. He certainly looks forward to the time when he may carry that point, and I fear he does not wish to take office again, unless he could be permitted to bring it forward and to be properly supported."

This, the striking testimony of a most reluctant witness with regard to Pitt's innermost views, ten months after he had resigned and given his pledge to the King, must convince all those who are capable of conviction, that Pitt's Catholic policy and consequent resignation were not less steadfast and straightforward than the rest of his career.   It seems also clear from

this significant narrative that Pitt's promise to the
King was given under the persuasion that the King
had not long to live, though George III. survived
his great minister just fourteen years. So much
for human computation. On the other hand, if the
King's death or madness could be attributed to the
Catholic question, that reform would be indefinitely
postponed. If the mooting of the question renewed the
Regency discussions or produced a Regency, it would
be too dearly bought. Compassion, nature, and policy
pointed in the same direction.

So obvious was the necessity of the pledge that Fox
gave it at once and spontaneously on assuming office
in 1806; though he had ten months before pressed the
Catholic petition in a long speech, raising a fierce debate
and division. "I am determined," he said, "not to
annoy my sovereign by bringing it forward." This
promise on the part of Fox, after harassing his rival with
the question a short time previously, has always been held
to be venial, and perhaps chivalrous; but, given by Pitt,
it forms an item in this inscrutable impeachment.

Another is this. The resignation was a sham, because
Pitt urged his friends to join and support the new
ministry. The reason, however, is obvious enough.
We were at war, and the first necessity of that state of
things was to form the strongest possible government. It
could not be strong, for the best men of Pitt's Government were out of it, and the area of choice was in no wise
extended. But it was the only possible Government;
and as it was by Pitt's act that the Government of the
country was so weakened, a heavy responsibility lay
on him. His critics appear to think it was his duty to

have declared war on the new Administration; to have harassed it with Catholic resolutions; to have bidden his friends hold aloof; and to have presented to France the spectacle of a political chaos, of fierce faction fights for power at the moment of vital struggle with a foreign enemy. Fox was impossible. No sane minister could have recommended as his successor in the midst of a war the fiercest opponent of that war, a leader of some fifty or sixty followers at the moment when the most powerful Administration available was required, to a monarch who less than two years before had struck him off the Privy Council with his own hand. Pitt could only be followed by a Government formed out of his own party; one which he could support, putting the Catholic question aside. The choice lay between making his successors strong or weak. His paramount duty was to the war, and he preferred to make them strong. It surely requires a lively prejudice to blame him for this, and the mere formulation of the charge implies considerable ingenuity. As for Catholic Emancipation, that did not enter into the calculation; for, if Pitt could not carry it at that time, it would have been mere folly for any one else to attempt it. We may leave the whole transaction with the words in which Sir James Graham admirably summed it up: "Mr. Pitt was prepared to do the right thing at the right moment: but genius gave way to madness; and two generations have in vain deplored the loss of an opportunity which will never return."

Addington, the new Prime Minister, was a friend of the King's, and a sort of foster brother of Pitt's. The son of the respected family physician, who had prescribed

colchicum to the elder and port to the younger Pitt,
Addington carried into politics the indefinable air of a
village apothecary inspecting the tongue of the State.
His parts were slender, and his vanity prodigious. A
month after Pitt's resignation, but before he had given
up the seals, some of his ardent followers, cognisant of
his pledge to the King on the Catholic question,
attempted a negotiation to keep him in office. Among
them was Canning, who sang—

> Pitt is to Addington
> As London is to Paddington.

This was true, and the minimum of truth; but Addington
did not see the matter in that light. The emissaries
found him happy and immovable. After a short tenure
of high office, the holder almost invariably thinks himself
admirably fitted for it. But this was a strong case.
Addington had never held political office at all, not an
Under Secretaryship, not a Lordship of the Treasury;
and yet, before he had even received the seals, he felt himself a meet successor for Pitt. To counterbalance this
deficiency in modesty, he had a handsome presence and
warm family affections. It must also in fairness be laid
to his credit that he was, Heaven knows why, the favourite
minister of Nelson. All that can be advanced on his behalf has been forcibly urged in the valuable vindication
which Dean Milman addressed to Sir George Lewis.
But it amounts mainly to this, that many country gentlemen preferred him to Pitt, because he had bland manners,
and because they were not oppressed by his intellectual
superiority. It is lamentable to think that, if Pitt had
to resign his power, it should devolve on Addington and

not on Fox to succeed him. It is, however, pleasant to
know that Loughborough received his due reward. The
seals were taken from him. Still the wretched man
hung on. He continued to attend the Cabinet, until
Addington was forced to tell him plainly to begone.
He continued to haunt the Court, with the result that
on his death George III. composed this epitaph for
him : "He has not left a greater knave behind him in
my dominions."

Pitt's retirement from office lasted three years. His
first duty, like that of most ex-ministers, was to examine
his private affairs ; and, like most ex-ministers, with a
distressing result. He was heavily in debt. He had to
sell Hollwood. That Tusculum was heavily mortgaged,
and realised little surplus. His distress became known ;
for he was in danger of arrest. It was proposed to ask
Parliament for a grant. The merchants of London
offered him a free gift of £100,000. Pitt instantly put
an end to such projects. He could not hold office again
with the consciousness of such obligations. The King
begged him to accept £30,000 from his Privy Purse.
Pitt, with some emotion, declined this offer also. Finally,
he condescended to take a loan of some £12,000 from a
few personal friends. This discharged the most clamant
and petty creditors. But it left a heavy balance, and
the loan was never paid off ; for nearly all the con-
tributors refused to include it in the debts paid by
Parliament at Pitt's death. And to the last day of his
life executions were threatened and even levied in his
house.

This is not altogether a pleasant picture. He had
enjoyed fully £10,000 a year for many years from

his various offices ;[1] although it is only fair to remember that at his death his salary as First Lord of the Treasury was no less than seven quarters in arrear. He had no expenses except those of homely hospitality. But his ideas of public and private finance differed widely. We are told that, when he could not pay his coachmaker, he would order a new carriage, as an emollient measure. And so with the other tradesmen. His household was a den of thieves. While he watched over the Treasury like Sully, he conducted his own affairs like Charles Surface.

In other respects, this year redounded greatly to his credit. He not merely gave an ardent support to Addington, but conducted the negotiations for a peace. By this he pledged himself to the preparation and defence of a treaty, any honour from which would entirely benefit his successor, and of which the blame only could devolve on himself : an episode surely rare in the annals of ex-ministers.

The preliminary articles were signed on the 1st of October 1801. We restored all the colonies that we had taken, except Trinidad and Ceylon. We agreed to give up Malta to the Knights of St. John. The fisheries in Newfoundland and in the Gulf of St. Lawrence were to be replaced on the same footing as before the war. Egypt, from which an expedition, despatched by Pitt, had driven the French just after his resignation, was given back to Turkey. In return, the French did little more than withdraw from Southern Italy. It was a treaty which could only be justified on the plea of imperious necessity. Much was conceded, for it was necessary to concede

[1] See Appendix C.

much. A prolonged armistice,—for with Napoleon it could be little more,—was absolutely needed. At any rate, it was hailed by the public with rapture, and it greatly strengthened Addington's Administration.

Grenville and Windham were, however, furious. They were joined by Spencer. Pitt's following was rapidly breaking up. Already Auckland, who was under every conceivable obligation to Pitt, and whose daughter Pitt had nearly married, had snapped and yelped at the heels of the departing minister. The new Government had succeeded to Pitt's majority, which they maintained at a general election in 1802 ; he had, indeed, pressed all those whom he could influence to join or support the Administration. Consequently, his personal following consisted only of those adherents, such as Rose and Canning, who would not take his advice.

The years of Pitt's retirement were mainly spent at Walmer, with occasional excursions to London and Bath. From April 1802 to May 1803 he does not appear to have entered the House of Commons. In May 1802, he received the greatest compliment that has ever been paid to an English statesman. Sir Francis Burdett had moved an indirect, and Nicholls, the author of some paltry *Recollections*, a direct vote of censure on the late Government. Both were rejected by immense majorities. But such rejection did not satisfy the House ; a mere negative was insufficient. By an overwhelming majority, against a minority of 52, it was carried : "That the Right Hon. William Pitt has rendered great and important services to his country, and especially deserved the gratitude of this House." And immediately afterwards, there took place that spontaneous celebration of his birthday, which was repeated for a full generation afterwards. It was for that first banquet that Canning composed the exquisite verses, "The Pilot that weathered the Storm."

Under honours so unparalleled, Pitt could well remain in contented quiet at Walmer. That repose was greatly needed for his health, which, as has been seen, gave way in 1798, and now continued slowly declining to the end. He who had been at work by nine had become a late riser, he had ceased to answer letters; and the visits to Bath, commenced in October 1802, became a frequent and periodical necessity. In September 1802 he was again seriously ill. But his enjoyment of Walmer was intense. No "disencumbered Atlas of the State" ever returned to country life with a keener relish. Shooting, and laying out his grounds, and the society of a very few old friends were his main amusements, and perhaps he was equal to no more. But, in the summer of 1803, the apprehensions of a French invasion gave a novel employment to his active mind; for he construed his office of Lord Warden in its ancient and most literal sense. In August of that year he raised and drilled a volunteer corps of 3000 men. Amid the derision of his enemies and the apprehensions of his friends, he spent his days in feverish activity, riding and reviewing and manœuvring along the coast committed officially to his charge. He would not even go to London, unless the wind was in a quarter that prohibited a hostile landing.

Meanwhile, Addington and his colleagues drew their salaries with regularity, and, so long as peace lasted, there was no objection to the process. Pitt, indeed, pricked his ears at Addington's budgets; but he had

promised support as long as possible, and remained
silent rather than disapprove. It was not, however, in
the nature of things that these relations could continue.
Both men were surrounded by friends, whose interest
it was to set them against each other. Addington's
followers saw that they could only keep their places,
under his Administration, and by the exclusion of Pitt.
Pitt's followers were indignant that his post should be
so inadequately filled. There were, moreover, little
causes of irritation; want of zeal in defence, inspired
pamphlets, the petty political smarts so easily inflamed into blisters by the timely assistance of toadies.
The Whigs of course stimulated Addington with extravagant eulogy to prevent his thinking of making way for
Pitt; and the minister purred under the process.

When, however, it became clear that there was no
possibility of preserving peace with Napoleon, all eyes,
even Addington's, instinctively turned to Pitt. Men,
so different as the Russian Ambassador and Wilberforce,
spoke of ministers with undisguised contempt. "Their
weakness is lamentable," wrote the philanthropist. "Si
ce ministère dure, la Grande Bretagne ne durera pas,"
remarked the more caustic Woronzow. In March 1803,
Addington sent Dundas (become Lord Melville) to Pitt,
to propose that he should enter the ministry. Lord
Chatham was to be Prime Minister,—a recognition of
primogeniture which may fairly be called extravagant;
Addington and Pitt joint Secretaries of State. Pitt,
however, never learned the post destined for himself,
for Melville never got so far. Already, no doubt,
sufficiently conscious of the absurdity of the proposition,
he broke down at the beginning. "Really," said Pitt

with good-natured irony, "I had not the curiosity to ask what I was to be."

It was profoundly galling to Addington to admit that Pitt could be more than his equal, and might possibly be his superior. But under stress of circumstance he went that length. In the ensuing month (April 1803) he renewed the negotiations in person. He offered the Premiership to Pitt; who in exchange requested Addington, with cruel ignorance or heedlessness of the Prime Minister's opinion of his own qualifications, to return to the Speakership, the duties of which he had so admirably discharged; but, as the Speakership of the House of Commons was filled, he proposed to create a similar position for him in the House of Lords. Addington concealed his mortification; but begged that Grenville, Spencer, and Windham should not be included in the new Cabinet, as they had spoken disrespectfully of himself. Pitt declined all exclusions. On this the negotiation broke off, and with it all friendly relations between the principals.

In the succeeding month, war was declared against France, and a few days later Pitt resumed his attendance in the House of Commons to defend that measure. His reappearance created a unique sensation. There were some 200 new members in the House of Commons who had never heard him; many of whom had never seen him. As he walked up to his seat, the feeling was irrepressible, and there was a cry of "Pitt, Pitt," as if proceeding from the very helplessness of showing emotion in any other way. Whitbread and Erskine were heard with impatience, and then he rose, greeted with a renewed storm of acclamation.

He spoke for two hours and a half, and the termination of his speech was received with round upon round of enthusiastic applause. But keen observers noted with pain his altered appearance and the sensible signs of his weakened health. The House immediately adjourned. On the succeeding night, Fox delivered a speech of three hours in reply, of which he says simply, "The truth is, it was my best." There is little doubt that Pitt was at his best also, and that the fortunate members who sat in the House of Commons on the 23d and 24th of May 1803 heard the highest expression of English eloquence. During Pitt's speech, however, the reporters were unluckily excluded, and we have only a jejune abstract of Fox's. Our regret must be for ourselves and not for the orators : as few speeches which have produced an electrical effect on an audience can bear the colourless photography of a printed record.

Some days afterwards, a vote of censure was moved on the ministry. Pitt interposed, and proposed that the House should proceed to the Orders of the Day, for he would not censure and could not defend. He found himself in a mortifying minority of 34 against 275, a curious contrast to his triumph less than a fortnight before. The same motion was defeated in the House of Lords by 106 to 18. Such was the influence of the King; for, in truth, Addington represented nothing else. The strange contrast was between the moral and the voting power. A few days before this last division, Fox had proposed to accept the mediation of Russia. Hawkesbury, the Foreign Secretary, followed him and warmly opposed the proposition. Then Pitt rose and supported it. On which Hawkesbury at once assured

the House that the Government would readily agree to
it. A month later, Addington brought forward a
plan for a renewal of the income tax, which he had
abolished on the conclusion of peace. On this Pitt
moved an instruction, aimed at a distinction that Addington had drawn between landed and funded property
on the one hand, and all other forms of property on the
other. Addington resisted this instruction with vigour;
sharp words passed between the minister and his prede-
cessor; Pitt was beaten on a division by three to one. But
the next day Addington came down to the House and
accepted Pitt's suggestion. "His influence and authority
in the House of Commons," writes Romilly, a strong
opponent, "exceed all belief. The Ministry seems in
the House of Commons, in comparison with him, to be
persons of no account."

In the session which began in November 1803, the
predominance of Pitt was equally apparent. On the
question of the Volunteers he made some drastic proposals; and, the next evening, the Secretary at War
brought in a Bill embodying them. But his relations
to the Government were becoming more and more tense.
He declined, however, to ally himself with others in
opposition; for he felt that his position was unique and
must be maintained free from unnecessary complications.
Grenville, always more extreme in hostility, and anxious,
some thought, to be independent of his late leader,
entered into a definite alliance with Fox, and pressed
Pitt to do the same. Pitt steadily refused. This was in
January 1804, and was in fact the last confidential communication that passed between them; for the inter-
change of letters in May was of a very different character.

In February 1804 the King's mind once more gave way. Meanwhile, Addington's Ministry was drawing steadily to an unlamented end. He became peevish and irritable ; his majority began to waver ; the Whigs, formerly so friendly, openly ridiculed him ; and his Chancellor, with the prescience then inherent in the woolsack, prepared for a change. In March, Eldon sent a communication to Pitt, and they met. In the ensuing month Addington himself sent a message to Pitt, begging him to state through a common friend what could be done. Pitt haughtily replied that to the King alone, or to any person deputed by the King, would he make such a communication. This was Addington's last signal of distress ; it occurred on the 17th or 18th of April (1804). He now agreed to advise the Sovereign to commission Eldon to see Pitt. On the 21st of April Pitt sent a long letter to the King, which was put into the royal hands on the 27th. By that time the division had taken place, which was to end the Ministry. On the 25th of April their majority had shrunk to 37 — a majority, which many administrations would hail with pious rapture, but which betrayed so great a shrinkage as to convince Addington that his position was untenable. On the 26th of April he communicated this decision to the King, and on the 29th to his colleagues. They concurred ; and on the 30th Eldon called on Pitt, by the King's orders, to furnish a written scheme for a new Government.

In reply, Pitt urged the claims of Fox. He had drawn up the scheme of a cabinet on a broad basis, which still exists in his autograph. He was to hold the Treasury ; but two out of the three Secretaryships of

State were to be made over to Fox and Fitzwilliam, and
Grey was to become Secretary at War, while for Grenville he reserved the significant sinecure of Lord President.
But he had also formally stated in a letter to Melville,
dated on the 29th of March 1804, that he could not force
the King, recovering from an almost mortal malady,
mental and bodily, to take as ministers persons he had so
long proscribed. "From various considerations, however," he wrote, "and still more from this last illness, I
feel that a proposal to take into a share of his councils
persons against whom he has long entertained such
strong and natural objections ought never to be made
to him, but in such a manner as to leave him a free
option, and to convince him that if he cannot be sincerely
convinced of its expediency there is not a wish to force
it on him. I should therefore at the same time, let His
Majesty understand distinctly, that if after considering
the subject, he resolved to exclude the friends both
of Mr. Fox and Lord Grenville, but wished to call upon
me to form a government without them, I should be
ready to do so, as well as I could, from among my
own immediate friends, united with the most capable
and unexceptionable persons of the present Government ;
but of course excluding many of them, and above all,
Addington himself, and Lord St. Vincent."

This passage has been given at length ; because it
succinctly defines Pitt's position in Pitt's own words.
Once more his kindness for the aged King, slowly sinking
into permanent darkening of sight and mind, was to
prove a cruel obstacle in his path. The monarch himself received Pitt's letter with cold displeasure ; he
answered it in a letter, which betrayed the lingering

influence of mental disease, in its violence and want of courtesy. He at once saw the weak joint in Pitt's armour—the tenderness for himself ; and loudly refused to have anything to do with Fox or Grenville ; the mere proposal of their names was an insult. He even ignored Pitt's request for a personal interview. He could not get over the separation from Addington ; poignant indeed must have been the parting between those congenial mediocrities.

At last, by the intervention of Eldon, a meeting with the King was arranged. The Sovereign, who had passed his former minister without notice the year before, now received him with astute cordiality. But, when they came to discuss the formation of the new Government, they were both put on their mettle. The contest raged for three hours. Never was Pitt more urgent ; he seems to have forgotten in the heat of argument the limitations which he had set himself in his letter to Dundas. But never was the King more stubborn. The contest ended in a compromise, which was in reality a victory for the sovereign. Grenville was admitted, but Fox excluded, though it was conceded that Fox might receive a foreign embassy. The monarch afterwards went so far as to say that he should prefer civil war to Mr. Fox. But the exclusion of the one confederate entailed the exclusion of the other, and so the King carried both points.

The new Minister at once communicated the result to Fox and Grenville. Their answers were characteristic. The lifelong enemy said that he did not care for office, but that he hoped his friends would join Pitt. The lifelong friend, colleague, and kinsman, persuaded Fox's

R

friends to stand aloof, and stood aloof himself. It was the finest moment of Fox's life, and not the most auspicious of Grenville's.

It is fair to say that Grenville might well be sensitive to the charge that would have been brought against him of having used Fox as a ladder to return to power. But from this imputation he was released by Fox himself. The very objection urged against Addington's Administration was that the crisis required the strongest possible Administration. Grenville's action rendered the new one deplorably weak. Had he entered it with Fox's friends, it would have been exceptionally powerful,—a ministry of all the talents save one;—and the admission of Fox himself must soon have followed. These considerations would make Grenville's action difficult to explain; but there is another circumstance which makes it wholly inexplicable. Exactly a year before, he had urged upon Pitt precisely the course which he now resented, and which Pitt now proposed to adopt. At the end of March, or the beginning of April, 1803, he went down to see his former chief at Walmer; and had a conversation or negotiation so elaborate that he himself wrote out and preserved an account of it. "After this," he says, "I suggested to Mr. Pitt the great advantage which, in my view of the state of the country, he would derive from endeavouring to form a government on a still more extensive foundation than that of which he had spoken, and from trying the experiment of uniting in the public service, under circumstances of extreme public danger as the present, the leading members, not of the three parties who had been in his view, but of all the four into which public men were now divided. I stated the reasons I had for believing that, with regard to the old Opposition, this might be done by including in his arrangement only Lord Moira and Grey, and perhaps Tierney (the latter in some office subordinate to the Cabinet), *and that Fox would be contented not to take any personal share in the government so formed*; and on a subsequent day . . . I took occasion from that circumstance to renew this suggestion." It is clear, then, that the plan of forming a Cabinet of all parties, excluding Fox, was so far from being repugnant to Grenville that it was his own proposal. It was supported by Fox's own wishes; it was at the moment the only practicable method of forming an efficient Administration. Grenville, however, threw over his own plan, and put every possible obstacle in the path of his old chief, who the year before had refused the Premiership at the price of Grenville's exclusion. In this gloomy crisis of the fortunes of his country, he thought that the proper course was to hunt down the new Ministry with inveterate hostility, so that he might succeed it at the head of a mongrel, dubious assortment of all the extremes of politics, and with the public men whom he had most bitterly denounced. But Pitt was not to be cowed. "I will teach that proud man," he said, "that in the service and with the confidence of the King I can do without him, though I think my health such that it may cost me my life." As indeed it did.

It must also be borne in mind as one of Pitt's greatest difficulties that the inclusion of Fox would have been profoundly repugnant to his own followers both in Parliament and in the country. It would have been a coalition enough to try any faith. In Scotland this feeling was strangely strong. Nothing less than Pitt's authority could have restrained it. Nevertheless, he persevered again and again in attempting to persuade the King to receive Fox.

To all such efforts, however, if politics be indeed an affair of principle and not a game to be played, there is an obvious limit. There is, moreover, a point of honour involved. A minister may find it necessary to yield to political forces beyond his control, and to change his policy. In doing so, he may ask for the admission to office of the representatives of that policy. It is a very different matter, however, for a minister pursuing consistently the policy which he has carried out for years, to demand, as an administrative necessity, the inclusion of his principal opponent in a Cabinet of which that opponent has been the inveterate enemy during its entire duration; who has criticised and resisted its every measure, tooth and nail, in letter and substance, in sum and in detail. Such a proceeding is lacking in common dignity and common sense; it is a surrender in the present and a reproach to the past; no hostile vote can carry a deeper condemnation than so self-inflicted a blow. In an acute crisis, and for the pressing purpose of some supreme juncture, such a sacrifice may be made. But Pitt, who had administered Government for eighteen years, not merely without Fox, but under the unrelenting fire of Fox's opposition, could hardly say in the nineteenth that he could not and would not enter office without him. Such a declaration, carried to extremes, would have been a confession of previous error and present impotence that would have gone far to prove he was not fit to be a minister at all.

CHAPTER XIV

THE END

So began Pitt's Hundred Days; for his second Administration can only be compared to that second impotent reign of Napoleon's, after their triumphant dictatorships. His new Cabinet was deplorable. So null was it that it was called "the new Administration composed of William and Pitt"; for, though some of its members afterwards attained eminence under the shade of Pitt, they displayed no such promise. There was Melville indeed, but Melville was in the House of Lords; and his intimacy with Pitt was much less close than in the former Cabinet, presumably since he had accepted a peerage from Addington and undertaken to be his emissary to Walmer. He was, moreover, to be the means of inflicting on his chief a mortal wound. There was Harrowby, who twice afterwards refused the Premiership; and Hawkesbury, who held it for fifteen years as Lord Liverpool; but the first soon retired from illness, while the other had so far displayed little promise, and was indeed something of a butt. Castlereagh was Pitt's only Cabinet colleague

in the House of Commons, and he in debate was
disastrous. And there was of course the ordinary
domestic furniture of Pitt's cabinets; the Portlands
and Montroses and Westmorlands, the Camdens and
the Mulgraves.

There was also Pitt's brother, Chatham, an underrated
figure. He was, no doubt, indolent and extravagant; as
a general, he was a conspicuous failure; he was useless
as the head of a department; he had no trace of the
oratorical abilities of his father or his brother; but,
as a minister in Cabinet, he was of singular value.
Eldon, who was shrewd, and in such a matter neither
paradoxical nor biassed, gave it as his deliberate opinion
that "the ablest man I ever knew in the Cabinet was
Lord Chatham. He sat apparently inattentive to what
was going on, but when his turn came to deliver his
opinion, he *toppled* over all the others." As a wretched
general, a wretched administrator, a mute senator, and
yet a Cabinet minister, Chatham represented to the
world a glaring example of Pitt's partiality. They
could not know those qualities of counsel that preserved
him, as they have many indifferent orators, in the
Cabinet. Men forget that judgment is at least as much
wanted in a government as agile fence; that the possession of eloquence by no means implies the possession
of the other requisites of government; and that, for
instance, any minister would prefer as a Cabinet colleague Godolphin to St. John, or Althorp to Brougham.
There have been orators like Pulteney, who have
shrivelled at the first contact with power. There have
been statesmen like Cromwell, who could not frame
an intelligible sentence. Pitt's second Government

was endowed with neither a Cromwell nor a Pulteney; but, curiously enough, although so universally derided, it contained no less than four future Prime Ministers—Portland, Perceval, Liverpool, and Canning —while Harrowby might, had he chosen, have made a fifth.

Pitt took his seat in the House of Commons as Prime Minister on the 18th of May 1804. That same day his supreme foe, the First Consul, was proclaimed Emperor of the French. Shortly afterwards Livingston, the American minister in Paris, escorted by Fox and Grey, brought Pitt a vague and dubious overture for peace, which came to nothing. This was the last of the rare occasions on which Pitt and Fox met in the same room. The Minister's military and financial measures (the latter including, as usual, another of the shocking demands of £500,000 to pay off debt on the civil list) he carried by majorities, varying from forty to fifty, in the same House which had furnished him in the previous session with the modest contingent of thirty-three followers. The session closed without incident on the 31st of July. In the recess he continued to discharge his military duties; and, in view of the army that Napoleon had assembled at Boulogne for the invasion of England, no precaution could be superfluous.

His political preoccupations were scarcely less urgent. He resolved to gratify the King and increase his parliamentary support by the admission of Addington. Their mutual feelings were softened, and they returned to something of their early intimacy. Addington became Viscount Sidmouth and President of the Council. A place was also found in the Cabinet for his principal

adherent, that Earl of Buckinghamshire who had married
Eleanor Eden, Pitt's only love. Another domestic
incident occurred, which was curious if not important.
The Archbishop of Canterbury had long been dying,
and Pitt was determined that his tutor, secretary, and
friend, Bishop Tomline of Lincoln, should be the next
Primate. The King was equally determined that the
succession should not fall to that too acquisitive prelate.
Having received early news of the Archbishop's death,
George III. hurried across to the Deanery at Windsor, the
residence of Bishop Manners Sutton. The Bishop was at
dinner; and was informed that there was a person outside,
who wished to see him and would not take a denial. He
went out and found the King, who had come to offer him
the Primacy. The business was settled in a moment,
and at the front door; the Sovereign went off chuckling
at having outwitted Pitt. It is said, however, that,
when they met, language of unprecedented strength
passed between King and Minister. It cannot, though,
be doubted that the King was right.

The royal speech, at the opening of the session in
January 1805, announced that we were at war with
Spain : one of those measures, founded rather on secret
knowledge than on open rupture, which were then not
uncommon, and which were rendered necessary by the
multiplicity of occult policies and subterranean agreements then prevalent in Europe. The British Ministry
were aware that a secret alliance had been concluded
between Spain and France, and determined to strike the
first blow. Fox, who had been silent for the last four
years, and was to be silent ever afterwards on the
question, thought fit now to urge complete Catholic Eman·

cipation as pressing and indispensable ; but was easily
defeated. The Budget provided for enormous expenses.
It became necessary to find forty-four millions for the
current year. The army figured for eighteen millions
and a half, the navy for fourteen millions and a half,
the Ordnance for close on five millions ; and five millions
were taken for probable subsidies, though little or
none of this last sum was spent. To meet these war
estimates, Pitt proposed a new loan of twenty millions.
Besides, therefore, continuing the existing war taxes,
he had to find another million for interest. For this
he principally relied, in the spirit of modern finance,
on an increase in the death duties.

The supreme event of the session was the successful attack upon Lord Melville. That statesman was
now first Lord of the Admiralty, where he displayed
his wonted vigour and ability. But he had previously
held for many years the office of Treasurer to the Navy,
to which, it was afterwards remarked, he had always
clung with strange persistence. A commission of naval
inquiry had been sitting for three years, and now presented a report on Lord Melville's conduct as Treasurer.
It showed that his paymaster had used the public
balances for his private purposes. Although the public
had not thereby sustained any loss, the Commissioners
rightly visited this proceeding with the severest censure.
It was also admitted by Lord Melville that he had
sometimes, as a confidential minister of the Crown,
advanced monies from these balances for the purposes
of secret service. The Opposition alleged that he had
used these sums to his own profit ; but of this charge
there was never the slightest proof, nor indeed any

probability. Still, he had shown blamable laxity in a matter which requires the nicest precision of scruple. Whitbread brought forward in the House a series of resolutions condemning Melville's conduct. Pitt would have wished to meet them with a negative. But Addington hated Melville, and would consent to no stronger amendment than a reference to a Select Committee. Even that motion was not carried. It was a case in which the House of Commons vindicated its independence. It passed beyond party leaders and party considerations, and sought unbiassed guidance. The speech of Wilberforce was, therefore, eagerly looked for; he was one of Pitt's dearest friends, but one also whom, in a matter of public morals, friendship could not sway. As he rose, Pitt bent forward and fixed an eagle glance of inquiry upon him. Wilberforce felt all that that mute appeal implied, but did not waver. He declared that he must vote for Whitbread. Not in his Slave Trade triumph did he hold a prouder position.

The numbers were equal. The Speaker, as he announced them, turned white as ashes, for the responsibility of decision devolved upon him. After a painful silence of many minutes, he gave the casting vote against the Government. Then arose a shout and turbulence of victory such as this generation has once at least witnessed, when senators behaved like schoolboys, and passion ran uncontrolled. There were viewhalloas. "We have killed the fox," shouted one sturdy sportsman with some confusion of idea. Pitt pressed his hat on his head, and it was seen that this was to conceal the tears trickling down his cheeks. Some

unmannerly Whigs pressed up to see how he bore his
friend's political death. But a little band of his younger
followers rallied round him, and thus unconsciously
encompassed he moved out of the House. It was the
greatest blow that he had ever received. Some have
ascribed his death to Ulm, and some to Austerlitz; but,
if the mortal wound was triple, the first stab was the
fall of Dundas. "We can get over Austerlitz," he said
to Huskisson at Bath, "but we can never get over the
Tenth Report."

Melville of course resigned at once. He was succeeded by an octogenarian member of his board, Sir
Charles Middleton. Addington, who wanted the place
for one of his followers, retired in dudgeon; and, though
this difference was patched up, his secession was only
deferred. After the Easter recess, the attack was renewed. The report was referred to a Select Committee.
Whitbread moved an address to the Crown, praying that
Melville should be removed from the Privy Council. Pitt
at first resisted; but at the request of Melville himself
erased his name before the motion could be put. As
he made this announcement to the House he almost
broke down. Traces of this emotion, hitherto so rare in
him, were not, indeed, uncommon during the short remainder of his life. The report of the Committee was unfavourable, and, after Melville had addressed the House
of Commons from the bar, an impeachment was resolved
upon. He was ultimately acquitted, but the divisions
on the question of impeachment, in which Addington's
friends voted strenuously against Pitt, produced Sidmouth's final resignation. An ex-premier is usually
found, by any Cabinet in which he may serve as an

ordinary member, to be a fleeting and dangerous luxury. Addington was no exception to the rule.

The fall of Melville was chiefly felt in Scotland. There he had long reigned supreme, with general popularity and good-nature, by the exercise of a double patronage. While he had Scotticised India, he had orientalised Scotland. He had imported into India a splendid staff of Scottish administrators; he had imported into Scotland the absolutism of a Guicowar or a Nizam. When he fell, the air was cleared, and men, who had sat in darkness under his shadow, saw the light once more.

The Prime Minister's arrangements to supply the places of Sidmouth, Buckinghamshire, and Melville were only temporary. He still clung to the hope of inducing the King to consent to the admission of Fox and Grenville and their friends. With that object he set out for Weymouth, where for hours he urged upon his sovereign every plea and argument for such an arrangement. But the King was obstinate. It was not necessary, he said; Pitt could do well enough without them. He knew, in fact, that in the last resort he could always rely on Pitt's pride; that Pitt would never resign on account of gathering difficulties or hostile coalitions. But, had he yielded now, he might have saved Pitt's life. With a melancholy foreboding, the Minister said, a fortnight before his death : "I wish the King may not live to repent, and sooner than he thinks, the rejection of the advice which I pressed on him at Weymouth." For the burden fell now solely on the enfeebled shoulders of the dying Premier : the brilliant chiefs of opposition might have relieved him of much. As it was, "if Pitt has the

gout for a fortnight," said Rose, "there is an end of us."
And so it proved.

The Minister was thus at bay, but never had he
shown a richer conception or a greater energy of resource.
He had determined to oppose to Napoleon the solid
barrier of the European concert. For that purpose he
had been maturing a gigantic alliance, which should employ the fleets and treasure of England, and the vastest
armies that Russia, Prussia, and Austria could put into
the field. He commenced with Russia. On the 11th
of April 1804, a treaty was concluded at St. Petersburg.
Five hundred thousand men were to be arrayed against
France. Great Britain was to contribute ships and men
and money. On the 9th of August, Austria signified her
adherence. This was the Third Coalition. Prussia, ruled
by covetous incapacities, wavered; and was wavering
when the Coalition was crushed. So she escaped that
fall; but a worse fate awaited her.

At this moment (August 1805), Napoleon was still
bent on striking a mortal blow at England. He only
awaited the fleet which was to give him command
of the Channel for the fatal twelve hours. Daily he
gazed intensely at the horizon, till the tidings came
that his admiral had retreated into Cadiz. There
was no time to be lost, for he was well aware of the
new league. He instantly moved his collected legions
to Germany. The Empire which possessed the Archduke Charles preferred to oppose to him General Mack;
a strategist of unalloyed incompetency, and unvaried
failure. In a few marches Napoleon cut off Mack from
Austria, and surrounded him at Ulm; and the first
event in the history of the Third Coalition was the

absolute surrender of thirty thousand of their choicest troops.

This was on the 19th of October. At the end of October, and in the first days of November, there were rumours of it in London. Pitt almost peevishly contradicted them. But on Sunday, the 3d of November, came a Dutch paper, which Pitt brought to Malmesbury to translate, and which told the worst. He went away with a look in his face which never again left it. But his spirit did not quail. On the 5th of November a despatch was on its way to Vienna, in which Pitt made a supreme appeal to Austria not to flinch. He had already, he said, sent Lord Harrowby to Berlin "to urge the early activity of the Prussian armies. There seems at present every reason to hope that this mission will be effectual. . . . Great as have been the pecuniary efforts which His Majesty has made for the common cause, he is ready still to extend them to such a farther amount as may enable those Powers to bring an active force of from two hundred to two hundred and fifty thousand men; and His Majesty has no doubt of being enabled himself to augment his own active force . . . to not less than sixty thousand men." With objects so paramount in view, with such vast means in reserve, these efforts could not fail. And in a glowing sentence, so like one of Pitt's perorations that one can almost hear his voice in it, he says that, even should the enemy plant his standards on the walls of Vienna, he is sure "that the antient spirit of Austria would still remain unshaken and undismayed"; and that Napoleon would still "have to encounter the concentrated energy of a great and loyal nation and the united efforts of powerful allies."

A few days afterwards, the news was eclipsed by the tidings of Trafalgar. Nelson had attacked with an inferior force the combined French and Spanish fleets, consisting of thirty-three ships of the line and seven frigates. Of these no less than twenty struck their flag. But even this consummate achievement was over-bought by the death of England's greatest warrior. It is for this reason, perhaps, that Trafalgar is inscribed as a victory in the Museum of Arms at Madrid unto this day.

The nation was profoundly moved by the double intelligence, but triumph predominated. The minister himself, once so equable, when roused at night to read the despatches so full of joy and sorrow, could not resume his rest. The day afterwards, he was present at the annual dinner of the Lord Mayor. The populace had forgotten Ulm, and could think only of Trafalgar. Once more, and for the last time, they received him with acclamations, and drew his chariot in triumph to the Guildhall. There his health was drunk as the saviour of Europe. Pitt replied in the noblest, the tersest, and the last of all of his speeches. It can here be given in its entirety. "I return you many thanks for the honour you have done me. But Europe is not to be saved by any single man. England has saved herself by her exertions, and will, as I trust, save Europe by her example." That pageant was in some sort a State funeral, for he was never seen in public again.

A month afterwards (December 7) he set out for Bath. Austerlitz, the battle of the Emperors, had been fought on the 2d. One Emperor was in flight, the other sullenly sustained defeat; their armies were scattered; a peace was being negotiated; amid the shattered ruins of the Coalition, Pitt alone remained. But even in the wreck of his life, his intrepid foresight survived. Nothing, he said, but a war of patriotism, a national war, could now save Europe, and that war should begin in Spain. Melville and Ulm had borne heavily on Pitt; Austerlitz killed him.

He was at Bath when he received the news. Tradition says that he was looking at a picture gallery when he heard the furious gallop of a horse. "That must be a courier," he exclaimed, "with news for me." When he had opened the packet he said, "Heavy news indeed," and asked for brandy. He hurriedly swallowed one or two drams; had he not, says an eye-witness, he must have fainted. He then asked for a map, and desired to be left alone.

He had gout flying about; the shock of the tidings threw it back on some vital organ. From this day he shrank visibly. His weakness and emaciation were painful to witness. Still, he did not abate his high hopes, or his unconquerable spirit. He wrote cheerfully to his friends. He was better, but wanted strength: Bath was of no further use; he would return to the house which he had hired at Putney—a mansion still existing, and locally known as "Bowling Green House." There, in a spacious and sunny room, from which one may still look out on Pitt's green lawns and avenue of limes, he was destined to die. On the 9th of January he set out home. So feeble was he, that it took three days to compass the journey. He arrived at his villa on the 12th. As he entered it, his eye rested on the map of Europe. "Roll up that map," he said; "it will not be wanted these ten years."

On the 14th Wellesley, just returned from his great
proconsulate, had a long interview : the last, for no one
again saw Pitt but his immediate family, among whom
Rose and Tomline may be included, and his physicians.
He fainted indeed, while Wellesley was in the room.
That old friend felt it his duty on leaving Putney to go
to Lord Grenville, and warn him that Pitt was at the
point of death. Wellesley found him drafting resolutions of censure, and concerting the fiercest opposition
to the Minister. On learning the news Grenville broke
into a passion of grief. It is difficult to test the temperature of tears, but it is easy to believe that these were
both bitter and sincere.

Party hostilities were at once suspended. There
was, indeed, nothing left to fight against. Fox displayed a generous emotion : "Mentem mortalia tangunt,"
he said. The address to the Crown was agreed to, and
the House adjourned. As the Speaker and members
were proceeding with this address to the palace on the
23d (January 1806), they learned that Pitt had died early
that morning.

From the time that he saw Wellesley, he had
gradually declined. He could take little or no nourishment. Early on the morning of Wednesday the 22d,
Tomline had thought it his duty to warn his old
pupil that death was imminent, and to offer the last
sacrament. Pitt declined, as he had not strength ; but
he joined earnestly in prayer. He threw himself, he
said, on the mercy of God, and trusted that the innocence
of his life might plead for him : the same thought which
had solaced the last moments of the Emperor Julian.

S

He then bade a solemn farewell to Hester Stanhope, the niece who had kept house for him, and who was to develop so fierce an eccentricity. To her he gave his blessing; "Dear soul," he said, "I know she loves me." All Wednesday night he was delirious. His wandering mind revolved round the mission of Harrowby, whom he had sent, as has been said, to fix the fickle energies of the Court of Berlin, the last hope of Europe. He constantly asked the direction of the wind. "East, that will do, that will bring him quick," he murmured. At midnight the end was near; at half-past four it came. A short time previously, with that strange recovery which so often precedes death, he said with a clear voice, "O my country! how I leave my country!" [1] After that last note of anguish he neither spoke nor moved again.

A motion was at once brought forward to provide a State funeral, and a public monument in Westminster Abbey; it was agreed to by 258 to 89 votes. Fox, in spite of a personal appeal from Grenville, deemed it his duty to oppose it. Such an opposition was in the highest degree distasteful to a nature eminently generous. But, after a parliamentary opposition of twenty years, he could not stultify himself by paying honour to Pitt as an "excellent statesman." No one can blame such a course, though abstention had been perhaps less painful and more dignified.

He had, however, an opportunity of showing the purity of the principle on which he proceeded. It was proposed to vote £40,000 to pay Pitt's debts, to award

[1] See Appendix D.

life pensions of twelve hundred a year to Lady Hester
Stanhope, and of six hundred a year to each of her two
sisters. "Never in my life," said Fox, "did I give a
vote with more satisfaction than I shall do this night
in support of this motion." No wonder such a man
had such friends.

A month after his death Pitt was laid in the Abbey
by his father's side, amid a splendid pomp of public
grief. "The statue of the father," said Wilberforce with
fine feeling, "seemed to look with consternation at the
vault that was opening to receive his favourite son."
"What sepulchre," exclaimed Wellesley, who was also
present, "embosoms the remains of so much excellence
and so much glory?"

The Ministry, as Rose had predicted, crumbled
instantly to pieces. Hawkesbury was content with the
Cinque Ports as his share of the great inheritance. Portland was not thought of. Castlereagh had the courage,
but neither weight, nor standing, nor speaking power.
The Sovereign appealed to them in vain; they were
unanimously of opinion that their headless body contained no principle of vitality. The King, without
hope or resource, succumbed helplessly to fate. So
was formed the ministry of "all the Talents," and, it
may be added, all the incongruities. Fox and Addington,
Grenville and the Lord Chief Justice of England, were
the strange chiefs of this dubious fellowship. It is
not now possible to discover the burning principles
which had impelled these eminent men to fight Pitt
to the death; for they at once abandoned the Catholics,
and proceeded with the war. In any case, their

Administration, after an inglorious year, came to a guileless end. Then succeeded a long government of which Portland was the first nominal head; and twenty years of much glory without, and utter darkness within.

CHAPTER XV

CHARACTER AND POSITION OF PITT

So passed Pitt. Cromwell and Napoleon yielded their breath amidst storms and tempests; but no natural convulsion could equal the political cyclone that raged round that lonely bed at Putney. All Europe lay at the feet of the enemy. The monarchs whom Pitt had leagued together in a supreme alliance were engaged either in negotiation or in retreat. The Prussian minister, ready for either event, had also hurried to the conqueror's tent to secure his friendship and a share of the spoil. There was not the vestige of a barrier to oppose the universal domination of Napoleon, but the snows of Russia and the British Channel. Well might Pitt, in a moment of despair, roll up the map of Europe.

At home his prospects were no brighter. He had to meet Parliament, with Trafalgar indeed to his credit, but with Nelson dead; with Ulm and Austerlitz as the result of his continental combinations; with a scanty and disheartened following. Arrayed against him, and thirsting for his overthrow, were the legions of Fox and Grenville, and the domestic circle of Addington. His friends had no conception of any resource that could save him. Rose and Long competed in dismay. Pitt, however, did not seem greatly to trouble himself. He had defeated a more formidable coalition before, and he believed in himself. His calculation was probably right. With health he would have maintained himself. His last reception in the city showed that he had preserved or regained his popularity with the people at large. He had a working majority in Parliament. And though his colleagues of the Cabinet were flaccid and null, he had a boundless resource in Canning, his political son and political heir. Fox was not to live long; and, after his death, even had Pitt once more failed to induce the King to receive him as a minister, the long desired Administration of all the capacities must have been formed.

Of the private life of Pitt there is not much to be said. There are constant attestations of his personal fascination in that intimate and familiar intercourse which was the only kind of society that he enjoyed. He seems to have liked that country house life, which is the special grace of England; we find him visiting at Longleat and Stowe, at Wycombe and Dropmore, at Cirencester and Wilderness, at Buckden and Short Grove, at the villas of Hawkesbury, and Rose, and Long, and Dundas, and Addington. Here we find him indulging—*proh pudor*—in a game of cards; the once fashionable Speculation or Commerce, now relegated to children. In all these societies he seems to have left but one unfavourable impression. A high-born spinster, who met him at Dropmore, says: "I was disappointed in that turned-up nose, and in that countenance in which it was impossible to find any indication of the mind, and in

that person which was so deficient in dignity that he
had hardly the air of a gentleman. If not tropes, I fully
expected the dictums of wisdom each time that he
opened his mouth. From what I then heard and saw I
should say that mouth was made for eating." This is a
harsh judgment. On the other hand, one of the choicest
ladies of the French aristocracy, who met him during the
Revolution, expressed her delight in his grave and lofty
courtesy, and long recalled the patient pleasure with
which he heard French books read aloud. To the purity of
his French she also paid a tribute. Butler records that
his talk was fascinating, full of animation and playfulness.
Pitt said of Buckingham that he possessed the condescension of pride. It was said of his own manners in society
that he possessed the talent of condescension ; than
which, if it means that he made condescension tolerable,
there is perhaps none more rare.

Curiously enough, he seems to have preserved his
boyish spirits to the end. Miss Wynn when she met
him at Dropmore, and drew the crude portrait just quoted,
records the competition of unearthly howls raised by Pitt
and the other assembled statesmen chasing a bird out of
the drawing-room, which disturbed her rest and possibly
gave her an unfavourable bias. And Sir William
Napier, who as a young ensign first knew Pitt in 1804,
has recorded the romp when he and the young Stanhopes and Lady Hester succeeded in blacking the Prime
Minister's face with a burned cork. The struggle was
interrupted by the arrival of Hawkesbury and Castlereagh ; and Napier graphically records the change that
came over their playfellow as he received them ; how
the "tall, ungainly, bony figure seemed to grow to the

ceiling," while the Secretaries of State bent like willows before him. Few, without these testimonies, would have suspected Pitt of being addicted to those sports known to the present generation as "bear-fights." But it is certain that nothing could be more easy and familiar than the footing of that little set of people with whom he habitually lived, and who seem to have been known among themselves as "the firm" or "the gang."

His friendship, although, like all worthy friendship, not lavishly given, was singularly warm and was enthusiastically returned. Nothing in history is more creditable and interesting than his affectionate and lifelong intimacy with Wilberforce, so widely differing from him in his views of life. Hardened politicians such as Rose and Farnborough were softened by their intercourse with him, and cherished his memory to the end of their lives with something of religious adoration. This indeed was the posthumous feeling which he seems to have inspired more than any other person in history. Even Sidmouth, who had loved him little during the last lustre of his life, shared this, and boasted that he had destroyed every letter of Pitt's which could cause the slightest detriment to Pitt's reputation. Canning, Pitt loved as a son. There is nothing more human in Pitt's life than the account of his affectionate solicitude and absorption at Canning's marriage. Canning's love for Pitt was something combined of the sentiments of a son, a friend, and a disciple.

The usual epithet applied to him is "haughty." A truer light is thrown by the conversation which is recorded to have taken place as to the quality most required in a Prime Minister. While one said Elo-

quence, another Knowledge, and another Toil, Pitt
said Patience. Rose in a close intimacy, private and
official, of twenty years, never once saw him out of temper.

His family affections were warm and constant. His
letters to his mother are pleasant to read ; he was indeed
the most dutiful of sons. His grief at the death of his
favourite sister, Lady Harriet, and her husband, Mr. Eliot,
was beyond description. His kindness to his oppressed
nephews and nieces, the Stanhopes, was constant and extreme; the father who harassed them had long quarrelled
with him. It was truly remarked that he unselfishly
made a great sacrifice and cheerfully ran a great risk, when,
after a life of bachelorhood, he took his niece Hester to
keep house for him. She led him an uneasy life with her
terrible frankness of speech ; but he bore all with com-
posure, and she repaid him with the rare devotion of
that vain, petulant nature, which fretted off into something like insanity.

Once, and once only, he formed an attachment
which might have led to marriage; though he liked
women's society, and is even said to have drunk a
toast out of the shoe of a famous Devonshire beauty.
But in 1796 his feeling for Eleanor Eden, the eldest
daughter of Lord Auckland, went so far that he wrote
to her father to declare his affection, but to avow that
his debts made it impossible for him to contemplate
marriage. Auckland was obliged to take the same view ;
Pitt discontinued his visits ; and the lady married Lord
Hobart, afterwards Lord Buckinghamshire. Lady Hester
said that this nearly broke Pitt's heart; but Lady Hester's
statements do not impress one with conviction. Lord
Holland, also an indifferent authority on this subject,

says that Pitt paid attentions to Miss Duncan, who was afterwards Lady Dalrymple Hamilton. But there seems no further confirmation of this statement. However, though we cannot imagine a married Pitt more than a married Pope, it is clear that he did seriously contemplate the married state; and cynics may remark with a smile that he afterwards showed a certain dislike of Lord Buckinghamshire, and a reluctance to admit him to the Cabinet; though other reasons might well account for that.

His life was pure; in an age of eager scandal it was beyond reproach. There was, indeed, within living recollection a doorkeeper of the House of Commons who from some chance resemblance was said to be his son; but Pitt's features, without the intellect and majesty which gave them life, lend themselves easily to chance resemblance and ignoble comparison. Wraxall hints at a licentious amour; but even Wraxall expresses his scepticism. The austerity of his morals inspired many indecorous epigrams, but also a real reverence.

His one weakness, it is said, was for port wine. We have seen that he was reared on port from his childhood; and, when he arrived at man's estate, he was accustomed to consume a quantity surprising in those days, and incredible in these. The habits of that time were convivial; but it is not till Pitt's health was broken that the wine which he took seems to have had more effect on him than a like measure of lemonade. Bishop Tomline has left a memorandum stating that never before 1798 did he see Pitt the least affected by wine. Addington, when questioned on this point, declared that Mr. Pitt liked a glass of port very well, and a

bottle better.   Sometimes, indeed, the Speaker, who
himself was decorously convivial, had to stop the supplies and say, " Now, Pitt, you shall not have another
drop ; " though Pitt's eloquence would usually extract
another bottle.   Addington, however, averred that
never had he seen Pitt take too much when he had anything to do, except once when he was called from table
to answer an unexpected attack in the House of Commons.   It was then so clear that he was under the
influence of wine as to distress his friends.   One of
the clerks of the House was, indeed, made ill by it ; he
had a violent headache.   " An excellent arrangement,"
remarked Pitt ; " I have the wine, and he has the
headache."

We read of hard drinking at the Duchess of Gordon's ;
of Thurlow, Pitt, and Dundas galloping home, after a
dinner at old Jenkinson's, through a turnpike, the keeper
of which, in default of payment, discharged his blunder-
buss at them ; and of Stothard, the painter, being told
by an innkeeper, as Pitt and Dundas rode off, " I don't
care who they are, but one of those gentlemen drank four,
and the other three bottles of port last night."   But all
this must be judged by the habits of that time and not of
ours ;— when Scottish judges sat on the bench with their
stoup beside them ; when at least one Viceroy of Ireland
could die of drink ; when Fox and Norfolk would after a
debate get through a *great deal* of wine, (and what this
last meant by a *great deal* it is scarcely possible to compute) ; when the English clergy are said to have considered
their cellars more than their churches ; when a great
Scottish patron only stipulated that the ministers whom
he chose should be " good-natured in their drink " ; when

a university common room could only be faced by a
seasoned toper ; when Lord Eldon and his brother could
drink any *given* quantity of port. It is hardly conceivable, if Pitt had been guilty of habitual excess,
that Wilberforce should have been his constant host or
guest at dinner. There is, however, little doubt that,
if he dined with a party now, it would be thought that
he drank a good deal; and, while the Tories said that he
died of a patriot's broken heart, the Whigs averred
that he died of port. But in this, as in so much else,
it must be constantly reiterated that he must be
judged by the temper of his own times and not of ours.

He was tall and slender in appearance. The early
portraits by Gainsborough represent a face of singular
sweetness and charm; the last portrait by Lawrence,
who only saw him a few weeks or months before his
death, represents a figure of rare majesty, with gray if
not white hair. Of this picture a replica was painted
for the King, and hangs in the great Gallery at Windsor.
One who had sat with him in Parliament, and who
survived until this generation, said that "he had a
port-wine complexion, but the most brilliant eye ever
seen in a human face"; much the same description
as is given of Sheridan's appearance. Hoppner, who
painted Pitt from the life for his colleague Mulgrave in
1805, gives him tints of this kind; as Wilberforce said, on
seeing Hoppner's portrait, "His face anxious, diseased,
reddened with wine, and soured and irritated by dis-
appointments. Poor fellow, how unlike my youthful
Pitt!" Fox said that he could see no indications even
of sense in Pitt's face—"did you not know what
he is you would not discover any." Grey thought

otherwise; but Wraxall agrees with Fox. "It was not till Pitt's eye lent animation to his other features, which were in themselves tame," says Wraxall, "that they lighted up and became strongly intelligent. . . . In his manners, Pitt, if not repulsive, was cold, stiff, and without sincerity and amenity. He never seemed to invite approach, or to encourage acquaintance. . . . From the instant that Pitt entered the doorway of the House of Commons he advanced up the floor with a quick and firm step, his head erect and thrown back, looking neither to the right nor to the left; nor favouring with a nod or a glance any of the individuals seated on either side, among whom many who possessed five thousand pounds a year would have been gratified even by so slight a mark of attention. It was not thus that Lord North or Fox treated Parliament." His nose, said Romney, was turned up at all mankind. How many a vote he and Peel and Lord John Russell may have lost by this shy self-concentration of demeanour, or how many have been gained by the sunny manner of Palmerston, or the genial face-memory of Henry Clay, must remain a permanent problem for the student of politics and man.

His action as a speaker, that might have been supposed to resemble the majestic stateliness which a later generation admired in Lord Grey, was vehement and ungraceful, sawing the air with windmill arms, sometimes almost touching the ground. Unfriendly critics said that his voice sounded as if he had worsted in his mouth; but the general testimony is that it was rich and sonorous. Fox never used notes, and Pitt rarely; a specimen of these is given by Lord Stanhope.

His eloquence must have greatly resembled that with which Mr. Gladstone has fascinated two generations, not merely in pellucid and sparkling statement, but in those rolling and interminable sentences, which come thundering in mighty succession like the Atlantic waves on the Biscayan coast,—sentences, which other men have "neither the understanding to form nor the vigour to utter." It seems, however, to have lacked the variety and the melody; the modulation of mood, expression, and tone, which lend such enchantment to the longest efforts on the least attractive subjects of his great successor.

"To Pitt's speeches," says a contemporary by no means prejudiced in his favour, "nothing seemed wanting, yet there was no redundancy. He seemed as by intuition to hit the precise point, where, having attained his object as far as eloquence could effect it, he sat down." This is high praise, indeed; but it can hardly be believed that Pitt was never open to the charge of diffuseness. In those days the leader stood forth as the champion of his party, and stated every argument in a speech of exhaustive length; private members had little to do but to cheer. It was, however, calculated as an almost certain matter of proportion that, if Fox were three hours on his legs, the reply of Pitt would not exceed two. Butler says, not untruly, that, as Fox was verbose by his repetitions, so was Pitt by his amplifications. Neither had before him the terror of the verbatim report, and the coming spectre of that daily paper in which the evening's speaking bears so ill the morning's reading. Had it been otherwise, they must have condescended to compression; and probably to those notes which guide and restrain argument. Sheridan, indeed, said of Pitt that his brain only worked when his tongue was set agoing, like some machines that are set in motion by a pendulum or some such thing; but this opinion bears the stamp of a certain envy of Pitt's ready and spontaneous flow of speech, felt by one to whom laborious and even verbal preparation was necessary.

Lord Aberdeen, who was Pitt's ward and had heard all three, preferred the oratory of Canning to that of either Pitt or Fox. Sheridan made a more famous speech than either. But no criticism can now affect Pitt's place as an orator. Wilberforce, himself no mean orator, writing in 1825 spoke of the brilliancy of the speaking at that time, when Brougham and Canning and Plunket were at their best, but said also that it was on a distinctly lower level than that of Pitt and Fox. The stupefaction produced by Pitt's Slave Trade speech on the greatest minds of the Opposition has already been recorded; Dudley, the most fastidious of judges, breaks into enthusiasm in speaking of him. Fox did not seek to disguise his admiration. He said that, although he himself was never in want of words, Pitt was never without the best words possible. His diction, indeed, was his strongest point. His power of clear logical statement, so built up as to be an argument in itself, was another. And as a constant weapon, too often used, he had an endless command of freezing, bitter, scornful sarcasm, " which tortured to madness." This gave him a curious ascendancy over the warm and brilliant natures of Erskine and Sheridan, over whom he seemed to exercise a sort of fascination of terror. We

can scarcely conceive an assembly in which there were
greater orators than Erskine, Windham, Sheridan, Grey,
and even Burke. But all contemporaries placed Pitt and
Fox on a level apart. This alone enables us to compute
their genius. And when we consider their generation and
those that preceded, we cannot but arrive at the belief
that eloquence and stenography are not of congenial
growth; and that in an inverse ratio, as the art of reporting improves, the art of oratory declines.

It is said that Pitt did not read much or care to talk
about books. It is probable that he had no time to
keep abreast of modern literature, though we know that
he delighted in Scott. But we possess a graphic account
of the little sitting-dining-room at Hollwood, with the
long easy chair on which the weary minister would
throw himself, below the hanging shelf of volumes,
among which a thumbed and dog-eared Virgil was
specially paramount. His rooms at Hollwood and
Walmer, says one of his friends, were strewn with
Latin and Greek classics. Lord Grenville, a consummate judge, declared that Pitt was the best Greek scholar
he ever conversed with. He was, adds Wellesley,
as complete a master of all English literature as he
undoubtedly was of the English language. He especially loved Shakespeare and Milton, and recited
with exquisite feeling the finer passages of *Paradise
Lost*. It is unnecessary to multiply testimony of this
kind. But it is also, somewhat unexpectedly, recorded
that he relished the *Adventures of Telemachus*, and
especially enjoyed the speeches of the dreary Mentor
in that too didactic tale. His well-known anxiety to
possess a speech of Bolingbroke's seems to have arisen,

rather from curiosity as to an orator so renowned, than from any peculiar admiration of his style. He considered, we are told, *Gil Blas* the best of all novels.

All this does not amount to much. Few Prime Ministers are able to give much time to literature, when in office ; especially at a period when an interminable dinner took up all the leisure that could be snatched from work. As an author he did little ; his collected works would scarcely fill a pamphlet. During his last stay at Bath two of his colleagues committed a crime worthy of the lowest circle of the *Inferno* by sending him their poems to correct. What, perhaps, was venial in Canning was unpardonable in Mulgrave ; but it shows that he was considered as great an authority in literature as in politics. Of his own poetic faculty nothing remains but the dubious reputation of having contributed a verse to the "University of Gottingen"; two couplets which he bestowed on Mulgrave, and of which it suffices to say that they are not to be distinguished from Mulgrave's own ; a translation of an ode of Horace ; and some lines not less insignificant. They are on the same level as the stanzas which we unluckily possess of Chatham's. In prose we have only the political articles which he wrote for the *Anti-Jacobin*, of which those on Finance in Numbers II., III., XII., XXV., as well as the Review of the Session in XXXV., are by him. At least Canning has so ascribed them, in his own handwriting, in his own copy.

He has been loudly blamed for his insensibility to literary merit ; so far, at least, as such sensibility is shown by distribution of the funds and patronage of the Crown. We do not know what were his principles

T

as to such matters, for during his twenty years of government he was, though assailed by Mathias and Montagu, never taken to task in Parliament on that subject. This fact, while it deprives us of his explanation, throws so remarkable a light on contemporary opinion as possibly to illustrate his own. If he was convinced that literature, like war, thrived best upon subsidy, he was culpable indeed. But it is conceivably possible that he may have thought differently. He may have believed that money does not brace but relax the energies of literature; that more Miltons have remained mute and inglorious under the suffocation of wealth, than under the frosts of penury; that, in a word, half the best literature of the world has been produced by duns. Pensionless poetry may at least bear comparison with that which has flourished upon bounties. Under the chill rays of Pitt, we had Burns, Wordsworth, Cowper, Southey, Scott, Coleridge, Canning, Crabbe, Joanna Baillie, Rogers; and even under the tropical effusion of twelve hundred a year, dispensed in heat-drops of fifty or a hundred pounds apiece, we have had nothing conspicuously superior. It is not easy at any rate to cite the names of many eminent men of letters, who have received material assistance from the State since the time of Pitt. Hook and Moore had reason even to curse the ill-judged bounty of their country, and yet they were provided with lucrative offices. Nothing, Pitt may have thought, is so difficult as for a Parliamentary Government to encourage literature. It may begin by encouraging a Shakespeare, but it is far more likely to discover a Pye. You start with a genius and end with a job. Apart from these arguments, a

more practical and pressing plea can be urged for Pitt.
Government then rested largely on patronage—he lived
in that respect from hand to mouth; and, when he had
but half satisfied the demands of politics, there was no
surplus for literature.

His exercise of patronage has been attacked on
another point. He is said to have advised the creation
of too many peers. He did, indeed, ennoble with
unsparing hands. During the first five years of his
ministry, he bestowed forty-eight peerages; in two subsequent years (1796 and 1797) he created and promoted
thirty-five; and when he resigned in 1801 he had created
or promoted a hundred and forty. He nearly, in fact,
doubled the peerage as it stood at the accession of
George III. This profusion had the strange result that
the Reform Bill of 1831 was, it is said, rejected by Mr.
Pitt's peerages against those of older creation.

Pitt had a triple reason for this excessive bounty.
In the first place, the economic measure of reform in
the civil list, which had been passed in 1782, had so
crippled and confined the patronage of ministers, that a
profuse creation of peerages was almost the only resource
of government, as carried on in those days. But his
own reductions of this kind were enormous, and with
this special distinction. Burke had reduced the patronage of the Crown and of ministers. Pitt as Prime
Minister laboured faithfully and indefatigably to reduce
his own. Between 1784 and 1799 he abolished eighty-
five absolute sinecures in the Customs with salaries of
from £2000 a year downwards. He collected a revenue
of twelve millions with 747 fewer officials than it had
taken under previous governments to collect a revenue

of six. All this was done in the service of the public
to make enemies for himself, and diminish the opportunities of rewarding his followers and strengthening
his government. Conduct of this kind was unique in
those days, and has not been too common since.

He desired, secondly, to recruit and refresh the House
by large additions from various classes—from the old
landed gentry and the commercial, banking aristocracy.
And, thirdly, it was necessary for the security of his own
and any future governments to render impossible combinations of great peers to overset the Government.
He had to destroy the Whig oligarchy, which had so long
wielded a perilous and selfish power. It was on this
ground that he secured the cordial co-operation of
the Crown in the creation of peers; though to the end
of life he called himself a Whig; a term which it must
be remembered was then the only one to describe every
shade of what we call Liberalism—the Radicalism of
Chatham, or the selfish oligarchy of the Revolution
families.

One thing more must be said on this head, which is
essential to a right understanding of the subject. The
main reason which prevailed, consciously or unconsciously, with Pitt in his creation of peers was his disdain
of the aristocracy. His sympathies, his views, his policy
were all with those middle classes, which then represented
the idea of the people. By a strange accident, he became
the leader of the nobility; but they supported him on
their necks, for his foot was there. They were the
puppets through which he conducted the administration
of the country; but he scorned them, and snubbed them,
and flooded their blue blood with a plentiful adulteration

of an inferior element. Read, for example, the anguish
of the Duke of Leeds under his treatment; read his
letters to the brother of Cornwallis and the son of
Chichester, both noble bishops, discreetly ready for
the enlargement of their spiritual opportunities. Pitt
and the aristocracy had not an idea or a sentiment in
common; his attitude to them resembled the earlier
relations of the late Lord Beaconsfield to the magnates
of the party. He was willing to give a peerage to any
decent possessor of ten thousand a year; as for his
baronets, their name was legion, and his knights were
as the sand of the sea. But he had no sympathy
with their sympathies, and regarded their aspirations
with a sort of puzzled scorn. His mission to appease
Buckingham, when that potentate was raging over a
distribution of Garters from which he was excluded,
must have been one of the most solemn farces on record,
for he could not understand the feelings that he had to
soothe. He considered the peers as his election agents;
therefore the more the better. And as regards their
further objects of promotion or decoration he would, had
he had the power, have satisfied them all. A minister
of this temper may gratify, but he is not likely to
strengthen, an aristocracy.

To estimate Pitt as a statesman, to sum up his career,
to strike his account with history, one must take adequate
means and scales. Jauntily to dismiss him as a super-
annuated prodigy, with an account of the reforms he
projected and abandoned, with a summary record of his
loans and gagging acts, with a severe gaze at the corruption of the Union and the horrors of the Irish Rebellion,
with an oblique glance at port wine; to consider him as

a trained liberal who became one of the King's tools, and then held power by prerogative in some form or another; to regard him as a man infirm of purpose and tenacious only of office; is to take a view, justified by passages and aspects and incidents of his career, but one neither adequate nor comprehensive.

Men will long canvass his claims and merits as a minister, for the subject matter is so unparalleled. Lord Beaconsfield, for example, who delighted in political paradox, wrote a letter in 1873 to Sir William Harcourt, (whose kindness affords me the opportunity of printing it), which contains his view of Pitt:

"I do not at all agree with you in your estimate of Pitt's career. It is the first half of it which I select as his title deed to be looked upon as a Tory Minister. Hostility to boroughmongering, economy, French Alliance, and commercial treaties, borrowed from the admirable negotiations of Utrecht — the latter half is pure Whiggism, close parliaments, war with France, national debt and commercial restriction—all prompted and inspired by the Arch-Whig Trumpeter, Mr. Burke."

These sentences express perhaps rather the light scoff of a bantering spirit than the cold results of historical research. But they represent an opinion always worth reading, even when given partly in jest; and one which derives colour from the confusion caused by the necessary change between Whiggism and Toryism before and after the sure establishment of the Protestant Succession.

The various classes of opinion have crystallised, roughly speaking, into two schools of thought. The first—the most common and the least informed—is that which honours Pitt as one who became Prime Minister at the age of an ensign, who achieved the Union with Ireland, and who was the great antagonist of the French Revolution. The other—the more recent and scientific school—is that which severely divides the life of Pitt into two parts; the first embracing his Administration up to 1793, which was entirely praiseworthy, and which might from its character deserve the commendation of Peel or Cobden; the second the remainder, which was entirely and conspicuously blameworthy.

It may be permitted to hold aloof from both parties; the one does not go sufficiently into detail, the other draws a distinction which is not natural. If you take two portraits of a man, one at the age of three, and the other at threescore and ten, you will trace no resemblance whatever between the faces depicted. And yet the change from the one to the other is so gradual, that there is no one day of his life at which you could say that a man was unlike what he was the day before. As with the natural, so it is with the political man. A politician may make a sudden and complete retractation, and so abruptly change his historical aspect; just as an individual may meet with an accident that entirely changes his personal appearance. But, putting such catastrophes on one side, it is not possible to draw a line across the life of a statesman with the declaration that all is white on one side and all is black on the other. With Pitt, at any rate, it was the circumstances that changed, and not the man. And the circumstances resolve themselves mainly into one—the French Revolution.

No man can understand Pitt without saturating

himself with the French Revolution, and endeavouring to consider it as it must have seemed at its first
appearance. In the first five years he had not to deal
with it, and they were fruitful years for England.
He found our average imports in 1784 £11,690,000;
in 1793 they had risen by seven millions. In the
same period our exports of British merchandise had
risen from ten to eighteen millions, and of foreign
merchandise from £4,330,000 to £6,560,000. In
December 1783 the Three per Cents stood at 74; in
1792 they stood at over 96. But the new element
clouded the whole firmament. It is safe to say that
there was not a sane human being then living in Europe
so exalted or so obscure or so dull as not to be affected
by the French Revolution; except perhaps that traditional Marquis de l'Aigle, who snapped his fingers at it,
and went on hunting at Compiegne without interruption.
Was it possible that Pitt, and Pitt alone, should remain
heedless and insensible ? Was it desirable ?

We are now able to fix epochs in the French
Revolution, to fancy that we can measure its forces, to
point out exactly what, in our philosophical opinions,
might have modified, or turned, or arrested it; just
as we calculate what would have happened if Hannibal
had captured Rome; or as men of powerful imagination have composed eloquent dialogues showing what
eminent personages would have said to each other, had
they happened to meet. It is all cut and dried; a
delicate speculation of infinite science and interest,
though critical minds may differ as to its value. But
Pitt could only perceive the heavens darkened, and the
sound of a rushing mighty wind that filled all Europe.

Seeing and hearing that, he formed perhaps a juster
judgment than those who discussed the matter as an
elegant question of political balance. He saw that uncontrolled it was overwhelming, and he did not pause to
reason as to what might be its eventual effect when
another century had passed. An earthquake, or the
movement of snows surcharged, or the overflow of some
swollen river, may cause absolute ruin for the moment,
and great subsequent benefit. But the philosopher who
is speculating on the fifth act will disappear in the first.
Pitt faced the cataclysm, and made everything subservient to the task of averting it. All reforms were put
on one side, till the barometer should rise to a more
promising level. It is impossible, said Windham, to
repair one's house in the hurricane season. It is impossible, it may be added, to put Pitt's French Revolution
policy in a form more terse and more true. Many may
profess to regret that we did not allow full play to the
agitation, that we did not sit still to receive what
should be prescribed from Paris. They may be right.
But those may also be right who, without dogmatising
one way or the other, feel unable to estimate the result
of the sudden flow of so fermenting a vintage into the
venerable vessel of the British constitution.

It is probable that most people will think that Pitt
was right in his forecast of the Revolution, and in his
inability to accept it as a boon for a country of such
different conditions. For there was no middle course;
the Revolution had to be accepted or repelled. But
if his view be right, a large latitude must be given
for his acts of repression, and suspensions of *Habeas
Corpus*; for the enemy he had to fight was as much

subterranean as external. The French fought not less
by emissaries than by armies; and so, Pitt would say,
if the thing had to be done at all, it had to be done with
all possible might and main; there could be no refine-
ment as to means, any more than in a storm with much
mutiny on board. His case for his repressive acts
depends on the reality and extent of the alleged conspiracy. It is common now to think that it was exaggerated. That is always the case with regard to such efforts
when they have been baffled. It was so said in the case
of Catiline, and so in the case of Thistlewood. What
has been rendered abortive it is common to think would
never have possessed vitality. But it must be remembered that what Pitt did was not a vain imagination
of his own, but founded on the solemn, anxious inquisition and report of Parliament itself. It was Parliament
that instructed the Executive : it was Parliament that
ordered repressive measures. It is impossible to carry
the matter further than this, and there it must be
left.

Had he lived now, his career would of course have
been different. Instead of being a majestic and secluded
figure, supreme in the House of Commons and supported
by the direct, incalculable influence of the Crown, he must
have looked outside to great democratic constituencies
with his finger on their pulse. He would have addressed mass meetings all over the country ; he must have
lived not so much in Parliament, as with a nation outside,
and a nation vastly larger than that with which he
had to deal. That, however, was not his position, or the
position of any minister then, or for long afterwards.
He had to deal with powers which we neither know

nor understand; on the throne, an active and ardent
politician, buying boroughs by the dozen, and con-
tributing £12,000 at each dissolution to the election
fund of every minister whom he approved, besides what
he might spend at bye elections ; whose personal party in
the House of Commons numbered perhaps a third of
that assembly, and whose party in the House of Lords
controlled that body.   Secondly, he had to deal with
the boroughmongers, who required to be fed as regularly as the lions at the Tower.

These are the vanished factors of Government.   But
because he was supported by them, it is not to be supposed
that he was not supported by the people.   The people
were then, politically speaking, the middle classes, and he
was the man of the middle classes.   When he took office
he did so by the act of the King, but the King was clearly
the interpreter of the national will.   The petitions, the
municipal resolutions, the general election clearly proved
this.   And the nation seem, so far as wo can judge by
the limited but sole expressions of their will, by elections and by acclamations, to have followed Pitt to the
end of his long administration.   Wilkes, who was himself no bad test of popular feeling, followed him from
the beginning.   He had, it is true, the King and the
aristocracy with him ; but he truckled to neither the one
nor the other.   Indeed, it is one of his singular merits
that he managed to combine into a solid array of support king, lords, and people.   But it is no real charge
against him that he utilised as an aid the King and the
aristocracy, for there was no possible Government without them.   Nor, when the Whigs succeeded him, did
they dream of introducing any other system.   They

only complained that the King withheld his election contribution from them.

It is perhaps unnecessary to say more of the circumstances and surroundings of Pitt. But it is impossible to complete any sketch of his career, or indeed to form an adequate estimate of his character, without setting him, if only for a moment, by the side of Chatham. Not merely are they father and son; not merely are they the most conspicuous English Ministers of the eighteenth century; but their characters illustrate each other. And yet it is impossible for men to be more different. Pitt was endowed with mental powers of the first order; his readiness, his apprehension, his resource were extraordinary; the daily parliamentary demand on his brain and nerve power he met with serene and inexhaustible affluence; his industry, administrative activity, and public spirit were unrivalled; it was perhaps impossible to carry the force of sheer ability further; he was a portent. Chatham in most of these respects was inferior to his son. He was a political mystic; sometimes sublime, sometimes impossible, and sometimes insane. But he had genius. It was that fitful and undefinable inspiration that gave to his eloquence a piercing and terrible note which no other English eloquence has touched; that made him the idol of his countrymen, though they could scarcely be said to have seen his face or heard his voice or read his speeches; that made him a watchword among those distant insurgents whose wish for independence he yet ardently opposed; that made each remotest soldier and bluejacket feel that when he was in office there was a man in Downing Street, and a man whose eye penetrated everywhere ; that made his name at once an inspiration and a dread ; that cowed the tumultuous Commons at his frown. Each Pitt possessed in an eminent degree the qualities which the other most lacked : one was formed by nature for peace, the other for war. Chatham could not have filled Pitt's place in the ten years which followed 1783 : but, from the time that war was declared, the guidance of Chatham would have been worth an army. No country could have too many Pitts : the more she has the greater will she be. But no country could afford the costly and splendid luxury of many Chathams.

To sum up : it is not claimed that Pitt was a perfect character or a perfect statesman. Such monsters do not exist. But it may be confidently asserted that few statesmen and few characters could bear so close a scrutiny. He erred, of course ; but it is difficult to find any act of his career which cannot be justified by solid and in most cases by convincing reasons. It may be said that his party acted more on him than he on them ; but the relations of a successful leader with his party are so subtle that it is difficult to distinguish how much he gives and how much he receives. It is, no doubt, true that the changed conditions of the world compelled him to give up his first task of educating his followers, and to appeal rather to their natural instincts or prejudices. It may be alleged that he clung to office. This is said of every minister who remains long in power. Office is, indeed, an acquired taste, though by habit persons may learn to relish it ; just as men learn to love absinthe or opium or cod-liver oil. But the three years which Pitt spent out of place and almost out of Parliament seem to have been the happiest of his life; and his resignation was generally condemned as groundless and wanton. It may, however, be conceded that unconsciously he may have become inured to office, and as leaving it implies at any rate a momentary defeat, he may have been unwilling to face this. Men who pine for unofficial repose dread the painful process of leaving office—the triumph of enemies and the discomfiture of friends and the wrench of habit—as men weary of life fear the actual process of death. It may also be said that, though he generally saw what was right, he did not always ensue it. What minister has or can? He has to deal not with angels but with men; with passions, prejudices, and interests, often sordid or misguided. He must, therefore, compromise the ideal, and do, not the best, but the nearest practicable to the best. But let us remember what is indisputable. No one suspected his honesty; no one doubted his capacity; no one impeached his aims. He had, as Canning said, qualities rare in their separate excellence, and wonderful in their combination. And these qualities were inspired by a single purpose. "I am no worshipper of Mr. Pitt," said Wilberforce in the House of Commons, long after Pitt's death, "but, if I know anything of that great man, I am sure of this, that every other consideration was absorbed in one great ruling passion—the love of his country." It was this that sustained him through all. For he ruled during the convulsion of a new birth at the greatest epoch in history since the coming of Christ, and was on the whole not unequal to it. There let us leave him; let others quarrel over the details. From the dead

eighteenth century his figure still faces us with a
majesty of loneliness and courage.   There may have
been men both abler and greater than he, though it is
not easy to cite them; but in all history there is no
more patriotic spirit, none more intrepid, and none
more pure.

APPENDIX A

Year.	Foreign State or Potentate.	Amount of Subsidy.		
1793	Hanover	£492,650	17	11
	Hesse Cassel	190,622	16	5
	Sardinia	150,000	0	0
1794	Prussia	1,226,495	0	0
	Sardinia	200,000	0	0
	Hesse Cassel	437,105	1	9
	Hesse Darmstadt	102,073	0	0
	Baden	25,196	5	7
	Hanover	559,375	11	3
1795	Baden	1,793	15	3
	Brunswick	97,721	13	9
	Hesse Cassel	317,492	11	2
	Hesse Darmstadt	79,605	5	6
	Hanover	478,347	17	6
	Sardinia	150,000	0	0
1796	Hesse Darmstadt	20,075	13	8
	Brunswick	12,794	9	5
1797	Hesse Darmstadt	57,015	3	4
	Brunswick	7,570	11	6
1798	Brunswick	7,000	0	0
	Portugal	120,013	13	0
1799	Prince of Orange	20,000	0	0
	Hesse Darmstadt	4,812	10	0
	Russia	825,000	0	0
1800	Germany	1,066,666	13	4
	German Princes	500,000	0	0
	Bavaria	501,017	6	0
	Russia	545,494	0	0
1801	Portugal	200,113	15	4
	Sardinia	40,000	0	0
	Hesse Cassel	100,000	0	0
	Germany	150,000	0	0
	German Princes	200,000	0	0
1804	Sweden	20,119	4	11
	Hesse Cassel	83,303	19	5
1805	Hanover	35,340	14	6
	Total .	£9,024,817	10	6

APPENDIX B

I.—ACCOUNT showing the amount of stock created in respect of loans raised and Bills funded from the commencement of the French Revolution war till the end of Mr. Pitt's first administration in March 1801 ; and also the amount of stock purchased by the Sinking Fund during that period:—

FINANCIAL YEAR.*	LOANS OF WHICH THE CHARGE WAS BORNE BY GREAT BRITAIN.			LOANS OF WHICH THE CHARGE WAS BORNE BY IRELAND.*		SINKING FUNDS.	
	Raised for Supply Purposes.	Raised for assistance of Foreign Powers.	Raised in respect of Bills funded.	Funded in Great Britain.	Funded in Ireland (but expressed in British currency).	Great Britain.	Ireland.
1793-4	£6,250,000	...	...	...	£323,077	£2,174,405	...
1794-5	†13,750,000	...	£1,926,526	...	†950,446	2,804,945	...
1795-6	†50,095,800	§£3,833,333	1,609,898	...	†1,469,231	3,083,455	...
1796-7	†30,918,669	...	26,026,900	...	†890,769	4,390,670	...
1797-8	†25,350,000	3,669,300	...	† £2,925,000	†1,047,692	6,716,153	£73,870
1798-9	†35,624,250	...	...	†4,000,000	1,886,723	7,858,109	244,766
1799-1800	21,875,000	...	...	5,250,000	1,846,154	7,221,338	269,169
1800-1	29,045,000	...	...	3,140,000	2,307,692	7,315,002	363,950
1st Feb. 1801 to 17th March 1801	44,816,250	...	...	4,393,750	...	...	...
Totals . .	£257,724,969	£7,502,633	£29,563,324	£19,708,750	£10,721,784	£41,564,077	£951,755

£325,221,460

£42,515,832

II.—ACCOUNT showing the amount of stock created in respect of loans raised and Bills funded during Mr. Pitt's second administration; and also the amount of stock purchased by the Sinking Fund in that period :—

FINANCIAL YEAR.	LOANS ON WHICH THE CHARGE WAS BORNE BY GREAT BRITAIN.			LOANS ON WHICH THE CHARGE WAS BORNE BY IRELAND.		SINKING FUNDS.	
	Raised for Supply Purposes.	Raised for assistance of Foreign Powers.	Raised in respect of Bills funded.	Funded in Great Britain.	Funded in Ireland (but expressed in British currency).	Great Britain.	Ireland.
1804–5 . .	£18,200,000	...	...	£8,190,000	...	£9,137,515	£107,980
1805–6 . .	34,400,000	...	...	{ 4,300,000 / †360,000 }	£2,566,154	12,972,913	255,352
Totals . .	£52,600,000	...	...	£12,850,000	£2,566,154	£22,110,428	£363,332

£68,016,154

£22,473,760

U 2

* The financial year (for debt purposes) of Great Britain ended on the 1st February, and the financial year of Ireland ended up to and inclusive of 1800 on the 25th March, and subsequently on the 5th January. § With an annuity for 25 years.
† With long terminable annuities expiring in 1860.
‡ With short terminable annuities of various currencies.

III.—ACCOUNT showing the Estimated Capital Value of

(NOTE.—*Rate of Interest*

GREAT

FINANCIAL YEAR.	ANNUITY										
	£62,791 13 4			£85,500			£58,500			£20,582 7 6		
	£	s.	d.	£	s.	d.	£	s.	d.	£	s.	d.
1794–5	1,205,663	18	5	......			......			......		
1795–6	1,203,155	7	10	1,638,271	9	8	......			......		
1796–7	1,200,521	5	8	1,634,684	15	2	1,118,468	10	5	392,610	9	0
1797–8	1,197,755	18	9	1,630,919	6	10	1,115,892	3	7	391,658	10	3
1798–9	1,194,851	16	6	1,626,964	19	4	1,113,186	11	1	390,659	0	8
1799–1800	1,191,802	13	2	1,622,813	1	8	1,110,345	15	11	389,609	14	11
1800–1	1,188,601	10	10	1,618,454	5	8	1,107,363	9	4	388,507	15	4
1801–2	1,185,239	13	6	1,613,876	12	6	1,104,231	7	6	387,350	16	7
1802–3	1,181,710	3	2	1,609,070	13	5	1,100,943	1	10	386,136	1	2
1803–4	1,178,004	3	10	1,604,024	9	2	1,097,490	8	5	384,860	7	3
1804–5	1,174,112	7	4	1,598,725	3	5	1,093,864	11	10	383,521	1	4
1805–6	1,170,026	10	3	1,593,161	13	8	1,090,057	19	11	382,114	13	6

IRELAND

FINANCIAL YEAR.	ANNUITY										
	£4500			£4916 13 4			£9504			£16,670		
	£	s.	d.	£	s.	d.	£	s.	d.	£	s.	d.
1794–5	......			......			98,648	5	9	......		
1795–6	......			......			94,076	13	8	173,028	18	8
1796–7	......			......			89,276	10	4	165,010	6	11
1797–8	85,837	17	2	......			84,236	6	11	156,590	17	3
1798–9	85,629	14	8	93,558	5	9	78,944	3	2	147,750	8	2
1799–1800	85,411	4	4	93,319	10	8	73,387	7	5	138,467	18	5
1800–1	85,181	16	1	93,068	17	8	67,552	14	5	128,721	6	5
1801–2	84,940	17	6	92,805	12	11	61,426	7	6	118,487	7	10
1802–3	84,687	18	7	92,529	5	7	54,993	13	9	107,741	15	2
1803–4	84,422	6	7	92,239	2	0	48,239	7	6	96,458	16	9
1804–5	84,143	8	7	91,934	7	3	41,147	7	0	84,611	15	8
1805–6	83,850	12	4	91,614	8	9	33,700	14	4	72,172	7	7

B—*continued*

Terminable Annuities created during Mr. Pitt's Administrations

taken at 5 per cent.)

BRITAIN

OF

£39,000			£36,875			£75,000			£230,000			TOTAL ESTIMATED CAPITAL VALUE OF ANNUITIES SET UP IN GREAT BRITAIN, AT THE END OF EACH YEAR.		
£	s.	d.	£	s.	d.	£	s.	d.	£	s.	d.	£	s.	d.
......			......			...			......			1,205,663	18	5
......			......			...			3,241,606	4	0	6,083,033	1	6
......			......			...			3,173,687	4	0	7,519,972	4	3
743,928	2	5	......			..			3,102,371	2	0	8,182,525	3	10
742,124	7	5	701,688	2	1	...			3,027,490	0	0	8,796,964	17	1
740,230	10	7	699,897	9	1	...			2,948,864	10	0	8,703,563	15	4
738,242	6	2	698,017	11	4	...			2,866,308	6	0	8,605,495	4	8
736,154	5	0	696,043	5	7	...			2,779,623	12	0	8,502,519	12	8
733,962	1	2	693,970	10	9	...			2,688,605	14	0	8,394,398	5	6
731,660	5	7	691,794	3	6	...			2,593,036	2	0	8,280,869	19	9
729,243	1	2	689,508	13	3	.			2,492,687	2	0	8,161,662	0	4
726,705	6	7	687,109	4	2	1,397,510	0	0	2,387,321	16	0	9,434,007	4	1

OF

£7905			£14,250			£16,731			TOTAL ESTIMATED CAPITAL VALUE OF ANNUITIES SET UP IN IRELAND, AT THE END OF EACH YEAR.			TOTAL ESTIMATED CAPITAL VALUE OF ANNUITIES SET UP IN GREAT BRITAIN AND IRELAND, AT THE END OF EACH YEAR.		
£	s.	d.	£	s.	d.	£	s.	d.	£	s.	d.	£	s.	d.
......			......			......			98,648	5	9	1,304,312	4	2
......			......			......			267,105	12	4	6,350,138	13	10
76,653	15	9	133,858	8	4	......			464,799	1	4	7,984,771	5	7
73,101	9	3	126,301	6	10	202,199	9	9	728,267	7	2	8,910,792	11	0
69,371	10	9	118,366	8	0	195,578	10	7	789,199	1	1	9,586,163	18	2
65,455	2	4	110,034	14	6	188,626	9	4	754,702	7	0	9,458,266	2	4
61,342	17	4	101,286	9	3	181,326	14	7	718,480	15	9	9,323,976	0	5
57,025	0	3	92,100	15	8	173,662	1	10	680,448	3	6	9,182,967	16	2
52,491	5	4	82,455	16	4	165,614	3	3	640,513	18	0	9,034,912	3	6
47,730	16	7	72,328	12	3	157,163	17	5	598,582	19	1	8,879,452	18	10
42,732	7	3	61,695	0	11	148,291	1	5	554,555	8	1	8,716,217	8	5
37,483	19	8	50,529	1	7	138,974	12	3	508,325	16	6	9,942,333	0	7

APPENDIX B—*continued*

IV.—SUMMARY of preceding Accounts.

	Total Amount of Stock created in Mr. Pitt's Administrations.	Estimated Capital Value of Terminable Annuities at close of Mr. Pitt's Administrations.	Total Capital Liability.	Amount of Stock purchased by Sinking Fund during Mr. Pitt's Administrations.	Total Net Capital Liability.
Additions to debt in Mr. Pitt's first administration	£325,221,460	£9,323,976	£334,545,436	£42,515,832	£292,029,604
Additions to debt in Mr. Pitt's second administration	£68,016,154	£9,942,333	£77,958,487	£22,473,760	£55,484,727
Total additions to debt for which Mr. Pitt was responsible	£393,237,614	£9,942,333	£403,179,947	£64,989,592	£338,190,355

APPENDIX C

For this Appendix, and much besides, I am indebted to my friend Mr. E. W. Hamilton of the Treasury.

Mr. Pitt's income derived from official sources is generally stated to have been about £10,000 a year. It may be interesting to show how these emoluments, somewhat understated, can be arrived at :—

1. *First Lord of the Treasury.*

(1) Salary as a Lord of the Treasury, charged on Civil
List £1600*
Less deductions on account of Land
Tax and other duties . . 380

Making net salary . £1220
(2) Salary as First Lord, likewise charged
on Civil List . . . . 4022†
Less deductions amounting to . 242

Making net salary . 3780

So as to bring total receipts of First Lord to £5000

---

* Cf. Fifteenth Report from Select Committee on Finance, ordered to be printed 19th July 1797 ; and other House of Commons Papers, No. 147 of 1803, No. 309 of 1806, No. 17 of 1830, and No. 366 of 1869 (pp. 586-90).

† Cf. Fifteenth Report from Select Committee on Finance, ordered to be printed 19th July 1797, etc.

2. *Chancellor of the Exchequer for Great Britain.*

(1) Salary as Chancellor of the Ex-
　　　chequer charged on Civil List　.　£1800‡
　　　Less deductions on account of duties　　148
　　　　　　　　　　　　　　　　　　　　　　　————
　　　　　　　　　　　　　　　　　　　　　　　£1652
(2) Exchequer fees, amounting to about　　　　800‡
　　　　　　　　　　　　　　　　　　　　　————

　　　Total receipts of Chancellor of the Exchequer　£2452

3. *Warden of the Cinque Ports (or Constable of Dover Castle).*

(1) Salary as Warden, charged on Civil
　　　List　.　　.　　.　　.　　.　£4100
　　　Less deductions on account of duties
　　　and salaries to subordinate officers,
　　　amounting to (about)　　.　　.　　1300
　　　　　　　　　　　　　　　　　　　　————
　　　　　　　Making net salary　.　　　£2800§
(2) Further salary, charged on Army
　　　Votes, amounting to (about)　.　　　280§
　　　　　　　　　　　　　　　　　　　　————

　　　Total receipts as Warden of the Cinque Ports　£3080

4. *Summary of Mr. Pitt's Emoluments.*

(1) First Lord of the Treasury　.　　.　　.　　.　£5000
(2) Chancellor of the Exchequer for Great Britain　2452
(3) Warden of the Cinque Ports　　.　　.　　.　3080
　　　　　　　　　　　　　　　　　　　————
　　　　　Total emoluments　　.　　.　　.　£10,532

Note.—Prior to 1797, the First Lord and Chancellor of
the Exchequer had a share in (what was called) " New Year's
Gifts," of varying but trifling amounts, which may be put at

---

　‡ House of Commons Paper, No. 322 of 1831.
　§ Cf. Appendix to Report on Select Committee of Finance, ordered
to be printed 19th July 1797.

about £40 and £80 a year respectively.* These casual receipts were abolished that year by Mr. Pitt himself, on the recommendation of a Select Committee.

While Mr. Pitt held the Wardenship of the Cinque Ports there were also occasional receipts, which, arising from lost anchors, cables, and other droits, were attached to the office, but which must have been of insignificant as well as uncertain amount.

APPENDIX D

Mr. Disraeli, in the more genial and less majestic days before 1874, used to tell a sardonic story of this time. When he first entered Parliament, he used often to dine at the House of Commons, where he was generally served by a grim old waiter of prehistoric reputation, who was supposed to possess a secret treasure of political tradition. The young member sought by every gracious art to win his confidence and partake of these stores. One day the venerable domestic relented. "You hear many lies told as history, sir," he said; "do you know what Mr. Pitt's last words were?"—"Of course," said Mr. Disraeli, "they are well known. . . . 'O my country! how I love my country!'" for that was then the authorised version. "Nonsense," said the old man. "I'll tell you how it was. Late one night I was called out of bed by a messenger in a postchaise, shouting to me outside the window. 'What is it?' I said. 'You're to get up and dress and bring some of your pork pies down to Mr. Pitt at Putney.' So I went; and as we drove along he told me that Mr. Pitt had not been able to take any food, but had suddenly said,

---

* Cf. Report from Select Committee on Finance, ordered to be printed 19th July 1797; and House of Commons Paper, No. 309 of 1806.

'I think I could eat one of Bellamy's pork pies.' And so I was sent for post-haste. When we arrived Mr. Pitt was dead. Them was his last words: 'I think I could eat one of Bellamy's pork pies.'"

THE END

Printed by R. & R. CLARK, *Edinburgh*.